ALEXANDER POPE
Catholic Poet

ALEXANDER POPE: *Catholic Poet*

BY FRANCIS BEAUCHESNE THORNTON

PELLEGRINI & CUDAHY · New York

Library of Congress Catalog Card Number: 51-12760

Copyright, 1952, by Francis Beauchesne Thornton

Published simultaneously in Canada by George J. Mc-
Leod, Ltd., Toronto. Manufactured in the United States
of America by the Belgrave Press, Brattleboro, Vermont.

Contents

Preface

THIS study of Pope's life and works was begun in 1931 at Columbia University. It was further advanced during three years at Oxford and one year at the British Museum. A large part of the basic research was completed in 1937 but other duties of more immediate importance made it impossible for me to finish my task at that time.

The first draft of my completed study was started at the Huntington Library in 1947, and was finished in the Library of Rare Books at the University of Texas in 1948.

The aim of the work is a simple one. Pope's life seems mysterious to many scholars and students because the facts of it indicate one direction and interpretation, while the official teaching regarding the *Essay on Man* would appear to nullify everything the facts would seem to prove. It has been my purpose to show that the *Essay on Man* does not depend on Bolingbroke in the way in which many have thought it does. Once this is established, it is possible to demonstrate the logic and consistency of Pope's life—in so far as any man's career can be called logical or consistent.

The salient facts of Pope's life have already been exposed in many splendid studies and biographies. My task, except for the new research on the *Essay of Man* and Pope's religion, has been one of integration and interpretation.

PREFACE

In a work of this size no man can hope to complete his task without being indebted to many scholars. I am grateful to L. Rice-Oxley, of Keble College, for his even-tempered guidance through the mazes of my thesis on the *Essay of Man*, and I am also grateful to C. S. Lewis for hints which prevented me from going astray on several philosophical points. My friends Shane Leslie, Wilfred Meynell, and Hilary Pepler all helped me in many ways and George Sherburn was generous in giving me some insights into the vexing problems connected with Pope's letters.

In the final work of preparing this study, I am deeply indebted to Professor R. H. Griffith, of the University of Texas, who opened both his heart and library in the best tradition of Charles Lamb. His generosity took further luster from the kindness of Miss F. Ratchford, Curator of the Rare Book Collections at the University. Miss Ratchford and her assistant, Paul Tracey, were kind and very efficient.

I also owe particular gratitude to Allen Tate, John Pick and Victor Hamm, who gave my manuscript a critical scrutiny which was of inestimable value to me.

The librarians and their staffs at the Bodleian, the British Museum, the Huntington Library and the University of Texas Library were all most helpful and courteous.

For the work on the many revisions of my manuscript I owe a cordial vote of thanks to Sister M. Florian, C.S.C., Mrs. M. M. Miller, and Timothy Murphy Rowe.

It is my hope that this study of Pope's life and works may play some part in the revival of Pope's poetry. Our age needs Pope; his satires contain powerful antidotes for the follies of our time.

Francis Beauchesne Thornton

To His Excellency

Most Reverend John Gregory Murray, S.T.D.

Archbishop of St. Paul

ALEXANDER POPE

After two centuries, he whom fair Fame wed
Might find her rather fickle—hardly trust her
Now to renew the brilliant bay-leaves' cluster
Round the once fondled, once Fame-fingered head—
Hope that, at most, she'd flick a casual duster,
Strike a stray match to read what once was read
By no-more-needed light than the bright lustre
Themselves upon his pristine pages shed.

But she's done right by you. No seed of poppy
Encrusts the brow she decked with bay and laurel;
Your star-play seems no pyrotechnic copy,
Your war's not dwindled to a conies' quarrel;
Nor—here's her miracle—have the myriad motes
Of noted pedants dulled you by their notes.

GEOFFREY TAYLOR

1

Alas, Poor Yorick

Know well each proper character. . . .
Religion, country, genius of his age—
Without all these at once before your eyes,
Cavil you may, but never criticise.

Essay on Criticism

ALEXANDER POPE is still an enigma. He has never had
a satisfactory interpreter. The amiable Dilke seemed on the
verge of producing a dispassionate study; he had the heart for
the job and the scholar's detachment, but the pointers he set
out in the field of Pope studies were never followed by himself
or by any other student. Pope studies, today, are still a straining
at gnats and a swallowing of camels.

There are many reasons for the existing confusion and mystery. The romanticists continue to pity Pope. They see into
his psychology of composition and techniques of verse with
Sitwellian verve and X-ray clarity. They are too ready to ignore the religious power which peers through the many-win-
dowed perfection of Pope's numbers. The baroque in Pope's
couplets calls to an echo in their own hearts and they mistake
the tendril for the vine.

The fact-turners are in a still worse fix. Year after year
they continue to unearth new scraps of paper. They have
conned the gazettes. They have fingerprinted the letters. They

have deciphered old words with a new "Eureka." Their chase remains in effect a paper chase. The "fox" of Twickenham eludes them. As for the religion of the man, Spence and Warton and other Anglican divines have given us the dates and the evidence for that! It may seem odd to a logical man to be expected to take for Catholic gospel the utterance of men—whatever their amiable qualities—who stood poles removed from Catholic consciousness, and, more to the point, Catholic secretiveness. How could men of alien faith do more than report what they were told, like Spence? Their blood, bones, and cerebral cortex, their prejudices, desires, and hopes conditioned their very reporting. It needn't have been conscious, but it was inevitable. It is scant wonder that Pope the skeptic emerges from their sketches of him.

Such initial misapprehensions or half-statements provided a rich compost for the growth of the tares Bolingbroke and Mallet sowed. Lord Bolingbroke put his mark on the theories concerning the *Essay on Man,* and his coterie of gossips whispered his proofs of his slanders or conjectures. "Liar, miser, cheat, lecher, deist": the music went round and round, until the mystery of Pope was walled up in a forest of surmise.

Biographers have failed to understand Pope because no one has cared to understand his religion; and Pope was a religious man. His early education was pious. His first poems are saturated with piety. Piety flashes out of his letters. Pope moralized, not because he was a Puritan or a hypocrite, but because it was native to him to do so. The Douay Version of the Bible, the unction of à Kempis, the fiery draughts of Pascal, the suavity of Fénelon, may not have formed Pope's style, but they molded his heart and outlook. From first to last Pope reasoned like a cleric, and a strong verbiage of piety obtrudes in his final satires as it does in *Eloisa to Abelard.*

Naturally, if Pope's religious bases were to be ignored, or

scanted, or not seen into, biographers were bound to begin their studies with certain gratuitous assumptions. The first of these was that Pope suffered little or no actual inconvenience from the penal laws which existed to dragoon English Catholics into religious conformity.

It is usual to deprecate the force of the penal laws; to infer that Pope, because of his fine connections and noble friends, was able to secure himself against any danger of molestation. Any honest and complete investigation will prove that, on the contrary, the penal laws straitened Pope his whole life long, both in mind and substance. It was stark terror of them which reduced the poet to a state of nervous idiocy when it was necessary for him to appear before the Lords as a character witness in the trial of Bishop Atterbury. It was obedience to them which kept him from the convenient attention of London doctors in his last illness; only the law held more terror for him than death.

The penal laws of Henry VIII, Edward VI, Elizabeth, and James I, so scathingly condemned by the great Laud, were scientifically designed to root Catholicism out of the land. The clergy were to be hunted down and hanged. Catholicism was not to be taught. The Mass and the Sacraments were forbidden. Wearing an Agnus Dei was a capital offense. All Catholic books and publications were banned. This was the top beam of the rack. Catholics were compelled to pay double taxes; they were fined £20 a month for absenting themselves from the services of the Established Church, and £100 for failing to take the Sacrament once a year. Inability to pay these fines resulted in the seizure of the recusant's estates and personal possessions. Of course only the greatest fortunes could stand the perpetual strain. Many noble Catholic families emigrated to the Continent, and of those that remained to face the naked fury of the laws, many of the most faithful and uncunning families were reduced to penury and perpetual imprisonment in squalid debtor's jails. It is true that many non-Catholics, perhaps even a large number of officials, were well disposed toward the Catholics. But there was a brake to their charity in the fat rewards which were offered to the officious and the bigots, who much, much too often earned them.

The brief relaxation of the penal laws under James II brought about the "Glorious Revolution" of 1688. Though William III, it is said, was averse to persecution, the character of the times and the close marriage of politics and religion led to the enactment of still more stringent laws. They were added to the brutal code of Elizabeth and her successors, *which was still in force.* All the visible ratholes were meticulously stopped. A new test act was designed for more exact detection of recusancy, with the usual staggering fines. Informers, if accompanied by a constable, were empowered to search the houses of papists at any hour, day or night, for the purpose of seeking out arms and weapons of offense. Catholics refusing the test oaths were forbidden to remain within ten miles of London and were not allowed to own a horse worth more than £5; they could not acquire new lands (in their own name) and were excluded from the practice of law; they could not be executors or guardians or receive gifts or legacies, and could not be elected to Parliament.

It would appear, from an examination of remaining records, that the Stuarts—perhaps it was also true of the Georges and William III as well—persecuted their Catholic subjects less from conviction than from motives of political expediency. The relaxing and tightening of the penal laws during the period of the proposed Spanish marriage of Charles I (then Prince of Wales) opens a window onto this circumstance. In a gesture of amity toward the Spanish King, the prisons were thrown open by royal command. Four thousand Catholic priests and laymen were set free. Their freedom was of short duration. They were hurried back to their cells when the marriage negotiations fell through.

Wily James I and Charles next turned their attention to a French marriage. A horde of Catholic prisoners were freed once again as a sign of good faith. This time there was no failure: Charles married Henrietta Maria of France with royal pomp and circumstance. The marriage had scarcely been consummated when the well-known recusants were rounded up and returned to their jails. The honeymoon, for them at least, was over.

Of themselves, the kings seemed inclined to grant some degree of religious toleration to their subjects, but Parliament stubbornly adhered to a policy of persecution and repression, sponsored by the Whigs. Any tendency of the kings toward mildness led to conjured plots and the marching of "no popery" mobs. This persecuting spirit persisted, in general, until the end of the eighteenth century.

During the reign of William and Mary, further acts increased the severity of existing penal laws. A reward of £100 was offered to any informer apprehending a popish bishop, priest, or Jesuit saying Mass or exercising clerical functions. By another clause a penalty of £100 was inflicted on any person sending a child overseas without a license (obviously for the purpose of Catholic education) and the whole fine was allotted to the informer. Still another clause stated that "all Catholics over eighteen years of age, not taking the prescribed oaths and declarations are disqualified to inherit any landed property or tenements in England: but all such property is to be enjoyed during the recusant's life by the next Protestant heir: and all papists are further disabled to purchase or possess any manors, lands, profits and out-land, or tenements within the Kingdom of England."

[7]

It will be and has been alleged that these things were more an annoyance than a threat to Pope's security—a curiously unrealistic point of view not borne out by facts. Pope felt the drain of the constant fines for recusancy; he was forced to conceal his assets, to vest the title of his property in alien, hands, to live out of London at inconvenient intervals, to deprive himself of the use of horses. He also suffered endless unsavory insinuations from Grub Street because of his religion. To be blind to these things is to miss the facts. It is to ignore any reasonable conclusions which might be drawn from the unhappy situation.

Men in authority, favorable to Pope at the moment, might change on the morrow; and, like his friend John Caryll, twice imprisoned for recusancy, Pope might easily have found himself exposed to the unfenced fury of the laws. As a child he had seen one of his Catholic tutors, Thomas Deane, imprisoned falsely once or twice for being a priest, and at least once exposed in the pillory, accused of concealing a pamphlet against the government. This was the same Thomas Deane, M.A., of University College, who upon becoming a Catholic with his master, Obediah Walker, was forced to flee from Oxford to escape the fury of the mob at the time of the Revolution of 1688. Deane, beggared by the laws against recusancy, spent most of his later days confined for debt behind the scrofulous walls of the Fleet.

There were other sharp reminders of brooding mischance. Pope had seen something of the fury of "no popery" mobs at times of political change or stress. He must have heard often the story of Nicholas Potgate, put to death at York, August 7, 1679, for saying Mass. The case of Sir Henry Fletcher of Hutton Hall, who had legacies of £850 seized by the commissioner of forfeited estates, must have been frequently discussed by papists. In all, with costs, £960 were realized in the Fletcher seizure, and the huge sum of £225 was paid to the informer on this occasion. These are but two instances of a vast and omnipresent terror.

It may be said without exaggeration that the penal laws awakened in Catholics of the eighteenth century much the same "pogrom mentality" which characterized the Jews under the benign rule of Adolf Hitler. There is every reason to believe that Pope lived in constant dread of poverty and, at the very least, the possibility of imprisonment for debt. Under the circumstances, he could not be sure of either his property or his fortune. In an adverse turn of the wheel he might lose his money and his life.

All these things bred in Pope an attitude of caution and concealment. He was forced to vest his property in the hands of his Anglican cousins, the Mawoods; he wrote satires on people in such a way that he could disown his work—and did disown it, if pressed too closely; he plotted to be *forced* to publish his letters in order that he might escape the law, which was not as kind as kings.

Even the *profession* of Pope's faith had to be hedged with concealment. He constantly acknowledged his religion in public, but nearly always in a jocose manner. When Atterbury and Warburton urged Pope to go over to the Establishment, he drew a hundred red herrings across the trail.

By weighing the effects of the penal laws and the real fear they must have begotten in Pope and all his coreligionists, it is possible to understand why Pope can sometimes be accused of dishonesty in his dealings with others; why plots and counterplots became almost second nature to him. For, as Francis Bacon says with wisdom, "They are the most dangerous discontents where the fear is greater than the feeling; grief has bounds but fear has none."

Persecution and terror give us some clues to the understanding of Pope's religion and life. There are other circumstances more important still. It is generally assumed that brutal repression imposes complete unity on the persecuted. Such an impression is an inhuman simplification. In cases of direct danger and extremest need the persecuted are drawn together. But the moment the immediate danger is past and the constable has retreated over the hill, dislikes, differences of opinion, various ideas of tactics to be pursued, and all the individual urges to power and pride, reassert themselves. Unity becomes a word which waits on the next crisis.

So it was in Pope's England—even as it had been in Henry VIII's England. Had Catholics really been united, the English Reformation would not have happened. Dissident and disaffected Catholics made it possible. They were the instrument ready to the hand of clever and unscrupulous men. For one Thomas More there were a thousand Cecils. "Paris was worth a mass," as Henry IV said in a cynical phrase. The Cecils and their ilk were of the same mind. They rattled their beads in public during Mary's reign, but they brooded on their plans to alter the old religion and carried them out when Mary was a bloody memory. They carried them to triumph because they knew the extent of the disaffections in the body Catholic.

The furious rivalries, discontents, and differences of Catholics persisted even among those who adhered to the old religion in spite of the penal laws. Like the devotee of Cynara, they were faithful in their fashion. If Pope's degree of Catholicity is to be judged, if Pope's orthodoxy is to be questioned, it is imperative that English Catholicism in Pope's time be understood in its complexity. Then perhaps we shall understand what kind of Catholic Pope was.

The penal laws made it difficult for Catholics to know and practice their religion. The missionaries' best-laid plans to be here or there could be shattered at a whisper of danger or pursuit. Catholics were the minority now in England. A thousand malicious eyes examined their comings in and goings out. Native English curiosity and respect for law put extra teeth in the statutes and increased beyond measure the efficiency of the pursuivants. Village gossip magnified the slightest pretext of disaffection. Officiousness, too, could make the lordly Pope complain that he "stood in some fear of a country justice."

For the sake of convenience, priests "on the mission" lived in the houses of the powerful nobles or influential gentry: they killed two birds with one stone in thus acquiring both a home and a hall in which the Mass could be offered.

Chapels were usually erected in large rooms on the second floors of great houses. This arrangement served to protect the secretly assembled congregation from curious servants, casual visitors, or prying neighbors. The relative inaccessibility of the Mass room was convenient in times of danger. Before the constable could ascend the staircase and penetrate the various doors between him and his prey, the congregation could be scattered and all evidence of "massing" or priests could be hurriedly concealed.

Necessity of concealment and perpetual uncertainty were not the chief engineers of Catholic ignorance of the faith or of Catholic diversity of doctrine. The true cause lay deeper. It was at the heart of the matter. Comprehension of it calls for a glance at the past.

Toward the end of Elizabeth's reign, Rome decided to reestablish some sort of secret church government in England. There had been petitions for and against the move from various groups of Catholics. Reluctantly, it appears, Clement VIII appointed George Blackwell Archpriest of England. As a measure of safety, twelve priests were selected to be his assistants. Their function was to advise and assist the Arch-priest. It seemed an excellent plan.

The Archpriest arrived in England and was well received. In a short time, however, he alienated many of the missionaries because of his rigid attitude toward those Catholics who believed the test oaths might be accepted with reservations. The ensuing bad feeling engendered a schism, the effects of which were to plague English Catholics for almost a hundred years.

While Elizabeth lived, Blackwell conducted himself with prudence, in spite of the sharp quarrel he had touched off. By one of those curious shifts of opinion, the accession of James I suddenly changed the whole pattern of the Archpriest's conduct. Now he came out in favor of any form of co-operation; he assumed a more lax and liberal attitude than that of the party of Appellants, which he had once opposed. Neither the advice or warning of twelve or twenty could move him or change him.

In consequence of Blackwell's persistence, the Pope deprived the Archpriest of his authority and suspended his faculties. Blackwell died penitent in an English prison from which all his liberalism had failed to save him.

The problems of the oaths were complicated and vexing. Could they be accepted with reservations? Was it possible to interpret them in two ways? Was limited co-operation possible with the King and the Establishment? Was the acceptance of the oaths a denial of the faith? These questions, a dozen shades between them, and the answers they provoked, did more than unseat Blackwell. They gave rise to the parties and schism in the Catholic Church. The bitter differences were not confined to the laity; within the ranks of the clergy opinions and divergences were far more intemperate. The question of the oaths actually gave place in importance to the burning problem of the proper procedure to be adopted in re-establishing papal authority in England. Who were to be the instruments of that authority—regulars or seculars? How were the privileges of each group to be protected? The violent quarrel over the control of Douay College and other missionary training centers on the Continent was a pale reflection of the struggle which went on behind the scenes in England itself.

Undaunted by the failure of the first attempt to establish a hierarchy and competent church government in England, Rome tried once again. In 1625, Pope Urban VIII, after almost painful deliberation, chose Richard Smith to be the new Vicar of England. He was consecrated in Paris by Cardinal Spada. Both the seculars and the regular clergy received Bishop Smith with apparent applause when he arrived in England early in January, 1626. Placing himself under the powerful protection of Viscount Montagu, the new Bishop carried out the offices of the Liturgy with splendor in the chapel of his patron. He held frequent confirmations and ratified the acts of his predecessor concerning the establishment of the Dean and Chapter of England, which was to be his *curia*.

The weather looked like spring, but it was English weather. Within two years of his consecration a question of jurisdiction arose which shattered the brief semblance of unity. Could regulars validly hear confessions in England without the consent and permission of the Ordinary of England? That was the burning question. The regulars, who had often been granted their faculties direct from Rome, thought, of course, that they were able to do so; the diocesan clergy denied the right. A flurry of pamphlets appeared on both sides. Such was the fierceness of the controversy that it came to the attention of the government, which found it hard to wink at the presence of the Vicar in the midst of so much sound and fury.

[13]

Goaded into action, the government decreed the banishment of Bishop Smith. He was forced into hiding in the houses of his friends. He was actually in double hiding: first from the law, and second from his coreligionists who wanted him out of England. To this end, a movement was initiated in Rome for his recall; and a further decree of banishment was passed in 1629, with a reward of £100 for his capture. This decree was never executed.

Bishop Smith had been accused by his Catholic enemies of being a member of the French party. There appears to be some truth in this assertion, for he found final refuge in the house of the French ambassador, the Marquis de Chateauneuf, and his successor, the Marquis de Fontenoy. He was obviously there with the full knowledge of Charles I, because the King on occasion communicated with the Bishop. Bishop Smith also continued to issue pastoral letters to his flock, and in the ambassadorship of the Marquis de Fontenoy the Bishop pontificated and preached to the public in the embassy chapel.

Those Catholics who disliked the Bishop or his politics prepared a strong declaration urging Bishop Smith's recall. It was placed in the hands of the Spanish Ambassador to be forwarded to the Pope. The moment the Bishop's friends had word of this move, a contrary petition was rushed to Rome in support of the Vicar.

Rome was not swayed by either party. The Pope sent Panzani to England. He was commissioned to report on conditions there so that the Pope might decide in favor either of those who wished the bishop to remain, or those who burned to speed his departure. What Panzani found in England showed without the shadow of a doubt the necessity of unity and authority. The report was, at least, a biting testimony to the lack of these qualities among English Catholics. Panzani's comments and observations give us a complete contemporary portrait of Catholicism in England. The picture is priceless in offering us an insight into Pope's religion and what might reasonably be expected of him in regard to it:

In England [said Panzani] are 150,000 Catholics of whom some are titled persons, many of the middle rank and many are without rank. But there are great differences to be noted among them in another respect. Some are Catholics in private only, and for their selfish ends, living outwardly in such a manner as not to be known for Catholics, and thus doing little benefit to their brethren in the faith. Among such persons are several of high rank who have all the greater fear on account of their position, lest they should lose the Royal favor. Consequently, even if they keep a priest in their houses, they keep him so secretly that not even their own sons, much less their servants, are aware of it, and so the poor Catholics in their neighborhood have no opportunity of resorting to their houses to hear Mass and receive Sacraments. On the other hand, many of the chief, and almost all the middle rank of Catholic nobles, and many wealthy Catholics of private station, either being more fervent or by some other cause, are bolder and make *almost** open profession of their religion. They give facilities to their poor Catholic neighbors to hear mass in their houses and to receive Sacraments, thus conferring a notable privilege on the poor, who, oppressed by various miseries and in terror of the laws, are reduced to extremities, there not being a single priest in England who is under obligation to administer the Sacraments. . . .

Besides the above-mentioned Catholics, there are Christians of another sort, who although they detest in their hearts heresy and schism, yet through fear of losing their properties, offices and benefices, and through desire of advancing themselves at Court, live outwardly as heretics; frequenting Protestant churches, taking the oaths of supremacy and allegiance, and speaking openly, when it serves

* Italics are the author's.

their purpose, against Catholics but inwardly they believe and live as Catholics, some of them even keeping a priest in their houses in order that in case of need they may be reconciled to the Church. Consequently they are often called schismatics by other good Catholics. Of this kind are some of the first rank *ecclesiastical* as well as *secular*, and many of every other condition of life.[1]

Here is no idealization of the Catholicism Alexander Pope knew and believed, but a realistic description sent by an impartial observer to his master who desired to know frankly the condition of the Church in England. If in our eyes Pope sometimes seems a shade liberal, must we not in fairness admit that the poet had a wide choice in electing shades of belief, and solid clerical backing for any shade he might choose?

In the body of Panzani's report are to be found many digressions which are of extreme interest to the historian and psychologist—little vignettes and strokes of brightness which provide some relief from their somber background.

Among these, Panzani notes the growing animosity between Puritans and the moderate Protestants, which had led to a *rapprochement* between anti-Puritans and Catholics. Like Marx and Lenin, the Puritans hated the moderates much more than they despised the Catholics. The situation at least bade fair to improve the position of Catholics.

The improvement in their situation is borne out in Panzani's cheerful picture of the throngs of people attending Mass in the chapel of Henrietta Maria and at the palace of George Conn, who was "in great favour" with the Queen. Charles I himself was said to be "clement and averse to bloodshed and albeit in want of money does not enforce fines against Catholics." Charles also moderated the fines for recusancy and with some liberality granted exemptions from Protestant worship under the great seal.[2]

These false portents of brightening weather for Catholics made Panzani optimistic. Obeserving at close range the leniency of King and court and the unabating zeal of the pursuivants in searching out papists, Panzani was betrayed into a naïve act. He made a vigorous attempt to halt the work of the pursuivants. Though he protested to both George Conn and the King, nothing was done. Persecution was established by law: the King could moderate its effects, but he dared not flout the statutes.

Panzani did his best to make the Pope understand the King's personal outlook on the test oaths which had caused so much dissension and heartburning among Catholics:

> There are two oaths. One is that of the supremacy, namely that the King is the supreme head of the Anglican church. The King is sensible that Catholics cannot take this oath. The other oath is that of allegiance, put forth on the occasion of the Gunpowder Plot, and asserting that the Pope can in no case absolve from their oaths of allegiance the subjects of princes, and that the contrary opinion is heretical. The King cannot allow Catholics to refuse this oath, which if tendered and refused is worse than excommunication and entails pecuniary loss. . . .[3]

The situation, in general, looked hopeful to Panzani. Though he was an incorrigible optimist at heart, there is evidence of singular balance in his judgments. He was far too much of a realist to shut his eyes to the darker tones in the picture he was drawing. Panzani found Catholics who were willing to suffer and die for their beliefs, but he found a larger number still who thought neither death nor suffering attractive. Many were Catholics in name only. They neglected to hear Mass on Sunday, passed the time in cards and frivolity, made no attempt to do penance in Lent, and treated their servants badly. Some of them led immoral lives, and there were occasional irregularities of the same kind among the missionaries themselves.

These were not the worst scandals Panzani noted. Lack of unified authority in enforcing Canon Law was the cause of innumerable abuses. The missionaries often arrived in England with "varied and unequal faculties." Some priests were able to grant the faithful special dispensations in marriage cases; others were not. Yet in many instances the missionaries acted like popes in their own right. Some Irish priests heard confessions without obtaining faculties from either Rome or the Vicar, and Panzani tells of one French Oratorian who did not scruple to administer the Sacrament of Penance although he had never been ordained.

Because there was no centralized authority, priests were not assigned to the districts where the need of the faithful was greatest. They went to houses and districts in which they could hope for support, protection, and concealment. Once established, they lived as laymen and spent their money in any way they desired.

Naturally, in the midst of such a confusion of authorities, the Mass and the sacraments were treated in a fashion contrary to all law and discipline. Some priests immersed their candidates for baptism, others sprinkled them. Some clerics failed to catechize candidates and left the "devil and his pomps" to the *ex opere operato* action of the sacrament. Heretical godparents were permitted; other than saint's names were given; infant baptism was not insisted upon, and no attempt was made to keep records of baptisms.

Confirmation "was thought by many to be unnecessary." So strong was this conviction among some of the clergy that pamphlets were boldly circulated among the faithful to prove the point at issue.

The administration of the Sacrament of Penance was accompanied by grave abuses. Penitents, if their sins were great, shopped about among the more liberal priests in order to obtain absolution. Many priests gave absolution without proper jurisdiction, "knowledge, or experience."

The Eucharist itself was exposed to danger of profanation. Communion was sometimes administered to those who had no knowledge of the Catechism, or who were notoriously immoral in their public life. There were even "forward-looking" priests who administered this sacrament "with words in the English tongue."

> Matrimony [Panzani continued] is full of abuses, as many of the priests who celebrate marriage have little knowledge of the contracting parties or their inequalities of condition and difference of religion. Clandestine marriages are often performed on the plea that the Council of Trent is not received here. Some employ the Roman, others the Sarum rite. Divorces and separations are frequently granted on trivial grounds, every priest pretending to be a competent judge and able to annul marriages. Many get married in London, although they have wives elsewhere. No records of these marriages are kept, although they ought and might be preserved. . . .

More astonishing than the abuses tolerated in administering the sacraments, Panzani found, was the strategy adopted by Catholics in attempting to bury their dead in the hallowed churchyards of pre-Reformation times which lay in the shadow of beloved churches. In this act, so open to the censure of public opinion, Catholics went to astonishing lengths to secure honorable sepulchers for their dead. Of course, such conduct is largely excusable for many reasons. For generations many Catholic families were accustomed to bury their dead in cemeteries eventually controlled by Protestants, and very often people desired or asked to be buried by the side of those they had loved so well. In addition to this, a burial is one of the few acts of life where, except in gangster circles, secrecy is practically impossible. In most cases, no Catholic priest of the time would have dared to conduct such a service. Yet, to inter a loved one without some pomp and circumstance is to earn from the public the reputation of penuriousness. It is also against all the personal drama in our race, which reveals itself never so strongly than at times of private sorrow—and provides an occasion for the discharge of accumulated ego.

For the sake of satisfying both their consciences and the laws, Catholics, according to Panzani, were accustomed to bless a little earth; and, having put this into the coffin with the corpse, they carried the body to the Protestant minister for burial. His co-operation was secured by paying up their tithes. By so doing they technically became members of good standing in the parish. Even "tender-minded" Catholics did not hesitate to do this, although it was tantamount to the denial of their religion.

Having completed this picture of English Catholicism in a troubled and confused era, Panzani proceeded to give massive reasons for the appointment of English Bishops, who, he proposed, should be clothed with complete authority to correct the abuses he had set down in the body of his report. Panzani's recommendations were eventually adopted in 1688, with the creation of four Vicariates: London, Midland, Northern, and Western. The London Vicariate, in theory, was to exercise jurisdiction over the other Vicariates.

This established, on paper, a framework of authority and control. In fact, because of the penal laws, the authority of

the Apostolic Vicars was more fictional than real. In times of
stress or danger the Bishops were forced to go into complete
hiding. Communication between them and their subjects was
often difficult, if not impossible. The missionaries proceeded
much as they had in the past, making their own decisions and
interpreting Canon Law and rubrics as necessity or caprice
dictated.

The impediments to the work of the Apostolic Vicars
were, it is clear, not the mild annoyances which can be
summed up in the word "inconvenience," as some authorities
have suggested. The first task of the new Bishops was to try
to curb the stubborn eagerness of James II, who, without a
semblance of tact, was attempting to force his ideas regarding freedom of worship on a reluctant people and their
alarmed leaders. It should be said in passing that James was
monstrously in advance of the time. Had he proceeded
toward his end of religious tolerance with more caution and
decorum, it is just possible that he might have preserved
England from a century of religious ill feeling and savage
cruelty.

The moderating advice of Bishop Leyburne of the London District and Bishop Gifford of the Midlands was scorned
by the stubborn King. They had to stand by idly while the
tragedy of James's downfall developed. With the outbreak of
the Revolution of 1688, Bishops Leyburne and Gifford were
seized on their way to Dover and were under arrest when
James was brought into the same town. The two prelates
were committed to prison, Bishop Leyburne being sent to
the security of the Tower. After two years he was released
to live in penury and squalor.

Dr. Gifford, who succeeded him after being released from
prison, wrote as late as 1714:

I have had no quiet, have been forced to change lodgings fourteen times and but once have lain in my own lodgings. . . . Besides the severe proclamation which came out on the fourth day of May, three private persons have been, and still are, the occasions of my troubles. The first, some fallen Catholics, who in hope of the great rewards of 100 pounds, informed and procured warrants for me. Mr. Joseph Levenson and some others. The second is *Mottram*, who being expelled from the University of Cambridge for his immoralities, got into Spain; there was entertained by the good Fathers at Seville, and in a very short time made a convert and a priest, but no sooner in England than he became as loose and immoral as ever; and now to gain money for his evil courses, is turned *priest-catcher*, has got a warrant for me and others. The third one is *Barker*, turned out of Douay, for his ill-behaviour; received at Rome, made a priest and sent hither; but always of so scandalous a life that no persuasions or endeavours could reclaim him; nay with much expense, we sent him to our good community in France, where he was so infamous, especially for frequently being drunk that they had him turned out; and now being returned follows Mottram's tread. A few days ago he took up Mr. Brears and has been in search of me and others; so that I am forced to lye hidde, as well as I can. I may truly say what was said of St. Athanasius, *nullibi mihi tutus ad latendum locus.* Whence I am obliged often to change my habitation. I have endeavoured to procure a little lodging in the house of some public minister, where I could be secure from the attempts of those wretches, but could not affect it. My poor brother* though much indisposed, was forced by Mottram, to retire into the country, which so increased his fever that in seven days he died. An inexpressible loss to me, to the whole clergy, and many more.

My service to Mgr. Bianchini and Marcolini. They saw my

* Andrew Gifford

[22]

little habitation, poor and mean; yet I should think myself happy if I could be permitted to lodge there. However *gloriamur in tribulationibus*, I may say with the Apostle, in *carceribus abundantius*. In one I lay on the floor for a considerable time; in Newgate almost two years; afterwards in Hertford jail; and now expect a fourth prison to end my life. I have always envied the glory of martyrs: happy! if God in his mercy will let me have that of a confessor. . . . Mottram took up Mr. Saltmarsh; but by a good providence, he got from him. The continual fears and alarms we are under . . . is something worse than Newgate. It is also some mortification for an old man, now 72, to be so often hurried from place to place. God grant me eternal rest. I am yours, B.G.[4]

Bishops Gifford and Leyburne were not alone in their sufferings. Most Church officials were harried and hampered in the same way. Under such circumstances the authority of the Apostolic Vicars was seriously lessened if not nullified. The quarrels between seculars and religious still persisted, and the political maneuvering of the various parties among the seculars lost little of its acrimony until the nineteenth century and the complete restoration of the hierarchy in England.

The background of confusion in Catholic authority, theory, and practice compels us to interpret Pope's words and actions in the widest and most charitable sense. He must not be judged by present Catholic standards, but by those of his own day. One is forced to concede that the unedifying example given Pope allowed him considerable scope.

Pope's statements regarding his religion are often said to be vague or loose. His defective religious training and the confused state of the Church will help to explain much of his vagueness. But it was the menace of the penal laws, above all, which forced Pope to modify and dilute his public professions

[23]

of faith. In much the same way, the priests of the mission flouted Canon Law and refused to keep records, in order that they might protect themselves and the people they served.

Perhaps it will be asked, Why recall past bitterness? Why resurrect past mistakes of Catholics which should be forgotten? The answer is, of course, that without such procedures Pope will never be seen against his own proper background and in the proper frames of atmosphere. His *disabilities* and his *possibilities* are both placed in correct focus by an accurate understanding of the religious temper and complexion of his times. Then, and then only, will the genuine Pope emerge and the logic in his life and character declare itself without equivocation.

In the mid-nineteenth century Dilke issued a challenge and a warning to Pope scholars. It was blunt and unequivocal:

> ... we have only to turn to a century of Pope's biographers, to find proof that what ought to have been developed has been obscured or passed over; and that what has been preserved in amber is but too frequently the current nonsense of the hour—the babble of ignorance—the falsehood of enemies—the misconstruction of friends.

So far as Johnson's Memoir is concerned this is of little consequence. Johnson did not care for facts:—too indolent for research, it was enough if what he said of Pope were true of human nature,—true as to the motives and feelings that influence men,—and the comment was of universal application. Johnson's speculation on the incidents or assumed incidents in the *Life of Pope* is philosophy teaching by example; and would be instructive had no such man as Pope ever lived,—had the work been a romance, like the *Life of Robinson Crusoe, Tom Jones*, or *The Vicar of Wakefield*.

But the abstract and imperishable value of Johnson's Memoir is no apology for another and for every other writer. In the works of common biographers if we have not facts,

we have waste paper—worse, rubbish that troubles and per-
plexes. It is the duty, the especial duty of such persons to
test tradition; to weigh opposing and contradictory authorities; to feel that their respectability grows out of their responsibility. If this be not felt—if this be not done, and with
great care and sound discretion—the very treasures which
time opens up to us only encumber our progress.

Dilke's words are a warning to his age and ours. The enlightened criticism of Edith Sitwell and G. Wilson Knight has
enlarged the appreciation of Pope's value and his eminence in
letters far, far beyond the point where the squeamish Warton
was content to place him. There still remains the task of
understanding Pope's character and evaluating his actions
with a greater degree of logic and sympathy. Then, at very
least and long last, Pope will have adequate justice done him.
Then most of the present mysteries in his life will be shown to
be the stuff of illusion or preconception.[5]

2

The Phoenix from the Ashes

They live, they speak, they breathe what love inspires,
Warm from the soul, and faithful to its fires.

Eloisa to Abelard

LONDON at the close of the seventeenth century was at once beautiful and foul. That lovely bubble, the dome of St. Paul's, dominated the sky line; and the soaring temples of Wren, St. Bride's and St. Mary-le-Bow, caught the soft light on their lucid points. Whitehall was a glimmering pearl against the crowded greenery of trees; the gentle curve of the river glittered like lapis between the ruffled bands of foam trailing behind the flying barges. There was still an air of the country about London: birds sang in the thickets, and over beyond May Fair scythemen could be seen swinging their brown arms above the lush meadow grass.

The great fire had purged much that was crowded and cheap, but already new tenements were rising along the river, faster than the palaces and town houses of the great nobles. The streets were dirty; there was no adequate system for the disposal of sewage. Horses, carts, and sedan chairs crowded the streets. The footpaths went underneath a forest of eaves and painted signs, and even in "fair Pall Mall" the way was muddy and precarious.

In Lombard Street, London, at the bottom of Plough Court, so tradition says, Alexander Pope was born, on May 21 in 1688, the exciting year of the revolution which put James II to flight and seated William and Mary on the throne of England. Both Pope's father and mother were Catholics, though it seems that both sides of the family were fairly well divided between those who kept the old faith and those who preferred the new.

Pope's father was a merchant of linen. He seems to have done well in trade with the thriving colonies, which had set up a new clamor for luxury goods from the mother country and the Continent. Mr. Pope had been twice married: his first wife, Magdalen, buried August 12, 1668, had one daughter, Magdalen, who was married to Charles Rackett.

Editha Turner, the second Mrs. Pope and the poet's mother, was of solid Yorkshire lineage. Many of her family were Protestants and of these, the Mawoods, in particular, were of later service to the poet in his transfers of property, which because of the penal laws could not be listed in Pope's name.

Probably because of the increased stringency of the penal laws growing out of the revolution of 1688, Pope's father retired from business the year Pope was born. The peril and confusion of the times in which the poet first saw the light of day, as "no popery" mobs marched up and down the countryside and Catholics came under the closest surveillance of both the authorities and their neighbors, would seem to account for the paucity of records regarding Pope's family in the years between 1688 and the period in which the youthful poet emerged from obscurity at Binfield.

The marriage of Pope's father and mother, undoubtedly before a priest and unregistered, is one of the many indications of the secrecy with which Catholics clothed all their actions in order to protect themselves and the priests who

[27]

served them. Pope recognized the danger of keeping records of any kind, and the peril which arose from speaking of religion and the Mass, however casually. The habit persisted to the very end of his days when Spence was compiling his pedestrian record of Pope's life. In telling anything which concerns his religion Pope was calculatingly vague; he modified his expressions of facts in ways which would permit him to retract such statements if it should be necessary. It was not until the middle of the eighteenth century that Catholics dared keep records of any kind in their secret chapels or missions. In those records, which after Catholic Emancipation were turned into the Public Records Office, it is noticeable that the names of priests were not set down until the end of the eighteenth century and, even then, were given with the utmost reluctance. This is a practical illustration of the ubiquitous terror in which Catholics of Pope's time lived. It helps us understand Pope's care in speaking of his faith or of the priests who had served him well, and who *still* lived in danger to the time of his death.

Pope, in his first years, was a healthy, rosy child. Whether his later deformity was a result of being gored by a cow, an incident communicated by his half-sister Magdalen with picturesque details, or whether he had inherited some tubercular infection from his father, is almost as much in doubt as the history of his early school years.

There is every indication that Pope's first education was pious. This was evinced in Pope's early manhood by his temporary revolt against the long prayers three times a day, and is also indicated by the stern atmosphere of the household, which frowned upon worldly pleasure at all seasons of ecclesiastical penance.

In sending the young boy to school, Pope's father attempted to secure him the advantages of a Catholic education. Pope was first sent to the school of Father Tavener at Twyford. This establishment was well known to Catholics of the time, and no doubt was under observation by the authorities as well. It is said that Pope was dismissed from Twyford for writing a lampoon on his master, but it is more than possible that the religious difficulties of the time and the penal laws played an active part in his removal from the spot. Catholics who dared keep their sons in schools which were known to be Catholic laid themselves open in a particular way to the threat of the penal laws and the bullying propensities of local magistrates.

There is a persistent tradition, also, that Pope was transferred from Twyford to John Bromley's school in Devonshire Street, London. Gillow says Pope left this school "in consequence of a thrashing and punishment that he received from writing a satire on his master." The reports made to Spence by Pope and his half-sister would seem to rule out the possibility of the poet's attendance at Bromley's school. However, Pope's ambiguity about his early Catholic training, which he must have remembered very well, seems designed to conceal and confuse; because of this, it is not unlikely that the twice-told tale of lampooning his master, which Gillow places at Devonshire Street school and not at Twyford, indicates at least a probability that Pope may have spent some time at Bromley's establishment.

Whatever the reasons advanced for Pope's quitting Twyford, he was, according to his own report, later placed under the tutelage of Mr. Thomas Deane of University College, Oxford. This is the man, considered a good tutor at Oxford, who was arrested and annoyed by one of the local magistrates of Hyde Park. If Pope learned little at Deane's school it is not astonishing under the circumstances. Though it is hard to forgive Edith Sitwell's snobbish picture of the persecuted Deane —she called him "an unhappy raggle-taggle creature"—it is possible to show some indulgence to Pope for the casual manner in which he made light of Deane's influence. In spite of his words, Pope did have warm gratitude to Deane, and sent him frequent gifts of money in the later years of his life.

Pope, it would seem, designed to make it appear that he had no formal education after leaving Deane's school. This may not be entirely correct. He may have had occasional training under Father William Mannock, who is said to have given further details of Pope's life to Spence. This priest, a younger son of Sir William Mannock, Leicestershire, England, was educated at Paris and Douay. He was sent to the mission in 1702 and according to Catholic records, such as there are remaining, he exercised his priestly functions in Northamptonshire. His older brother, John Anselm Mannock, O.S.B., came to the English mission in 1709 and was stationed for years at Foxcote, the seat of the Cannings in Warwickshire. Both brothers were intimates of Pope's family circle.

Pope's family assisted him in covering up all the trails which might lead to priestly tutors. Like Pope himself, they were unwilling to talk of Catholic training. Instead of doing so, they drew glib pictures in the following manner:

He set out to learning Latin and Greek by himself, about twelve; and when he was about fifteen he resolved that he would go up to London and learn French and Italian. We in the family looked upon it as a wildish sort of resolution; for as his health would not let him travel, we could not see any reason for it. He stuck to it: went thither; and mastered both those languages with a surprising dispatch. Almost every thing of this kind was of his own acquiring. He had had masters indeed, but they were very indifferent ones; and what he got was almost wholly owing to his own unassisted industry.[1]

[30]

The noticeable emphasis in this passage is upon Pope and not his Catholic training. Also mentioned in Pope's letters to the Dancastles is a Father Phillips, who is supposed to have had some hand in tutoring Pope. In all probability that would be Father Thomas Phillips. His career was extraordinary and had a flavor of literary interest which may have commended him to Pope in a particular way. Phillips was born July 5, 1708. His mother was a staunch Catholic, and young Phillips, sent against her will to a Protestant school, supplied his religious deficiencies by reading the *Imitation of Christ, Introduction to a Devout Life*, and *Telemachus*. Phillips was a brilliant student and desired to be a priest.

In pursuing his ideal he studied for some years with the Jesuits, but left the Society and proceeded toward his goal under the patronage of the Cardinal Protector. Soon after his ordination, Phillips was dispatched to England. He became chaplain to the Earl of Shrewsbury at Heythrop Park, Oxford. He remained there until 1753. His excellent life of *Cardinal Pole* caused a great stir among the divines of the Established Church, who rushed into print with heavy volumes of refutation.

Being much younger than Pope and coming late to the "missions," there is scant chance that Phillips played any part in Pope's early education. Pope must, however, have been well acquainted with Father Richard Caryll, S.J., who in 1718 was stationed at Ladyholt, the Caryll estate, under the assumed name of Paul Kelly. If he was there earlier, he may very well be one of the clerics who had some part in molding Pope's ideas. With the death of his younger brother John, Father Caryll took up his task of keeping the family diary, and except for a brief stay at Lulworth Castle in 1722, was certainly in and out of Ladyholt between 1718 and 1724.

Pope told Spence vaguely that "four priests" played a part

in his education. With one or both of the Mannocks or Father Caryll added to the name of Tavener, we can be fairly sure that all the possibilities have been surveyed, though the Abbé Southcote must also be considered. Pope's indefiniteness in retailing this part of his life is comprehensible: Father Mannock and Richard Caryll were still alive in 1744, the year of Pope's death. He would be bound in honor to protect them. If they had tutored him or taught him his religion, and he readily admitted it, the admission alone provided sufficient grounds for the law to proceed against them.

All Pope's statements regarding his religion had a delightful flavor of ambiguity. Let men take his words with a pinch of salt, or without savor—it was all one to Pope. Secure his purposes! Lock the truth away in the dark vaults of the mind! His own age might stare and raise an eyebrow, the ages following throw up their hands—he at least, in spite of present threats or future sneers, would tether his chariot in the stabbing spotlight of fame. The face might wither but the laurel would glitter immortal and green.

It is certain, however, that Pope's wide education was largely the result of his own voracious reading at home. His use of aids in preparing his editions of Homer is a well-known fact, and the presence of a number of both Greek and Latin translations in the remains of Pope's library at Hartlebury Castle may indicate a lack of precision in translating both languages. Yet the men of Pope's time who knew their classics well, men like Swift, George Berkeley, and Spence, who was no fool in such matters, were impressed by the breadth and depth of the poet's culture. Pope's wide reading, though it may have lacked the discipline of such work done under the guidance of a wise college tutor, gave the poet an easy acquaintance with classical authors which more than satisfied the scrutiny of Spence, Swift, and Berkeley.

[32]

Pope's schooling, whatever its width and depth, was at the mercy of the laws and mischance of the times. In 1696, a conspiracy against the life of King William was "discovered" by Prendergast, an Irish Catholic. The conspiracy, if it existed, was abortive, but it led to an outcry of "no popery," and Parliament put into effect brutal measures for curbing the Catholic "menace."

The Commons, in 1697, petitioned the King for the removal of papists and nonjurors from London and for the merciless execution of the penal laws. As a result of this petition, it became necessary for the Pope family to remove from London. Looking about him for a place of refuge, Pope's father purchased, in 1698, a house at Binfield. The property was purchased from Charles Rackett, who, then or later, married Mr. Pope's daughter by his first wife. In 1700, the house and grounds were conveyed to Mr. Pope's Protestant nephews, Samuel and Charles Mawood. They held the estate in trust because of the recent penal legislation which made it impossible for Catholics to purchase property.

By 1701 the Popes were in residence at Binfield. In the low, timbered house set in its bowering trees the little poet began "to lisp in numbers for the numbers came." He had very early in his life—just how early is a matter of conjecture— begun to write "verses." Looking back into the warm dawn of memory, Pope honestly believed his literary destiny had revealed itself to him early in divers ways. While at Deane's school Pope produced a play in verse which is said to have been acted out by the young scholars with the aid of Deane's gardener. Pope, according to his own story, had also prevailed upon some acquaintance to take him to Will's coffeehouse. There, in a daze of wonder, he observed the great Dryden at a distance. Pope pretended to describe the old poet's ruddy countenance and small conversation in public. Whether Pope embroidered on his desire to see Dryden, or did in fact see him, is not of special significance. It is more *portent* than important. Once Pope had become famous, the incident took on depth of dramatic meaning. By implication of gesture and look Pope had in that brief moment received the mantle of Elias.

At the period when the poet's father purchased the house at Binfield he is reputed to have retired with a fortune of £10,000. Gossip, or the mental arithmetic of scholars, has changed the sum with each new scrap of evidence or convenient assertion. It was probably not a great fortune, because Pope later complained he had little money to buy books at the time when he first projected his translation of the *Iliad*. In the initial years at Binfield there was no complaint of lack of funds: on the contrary, Pope found it easy to go back and forth to London in pursuit of French and Italian masters. Pope's frequent visits with his fashionable London and provincial friends must have cost a great deal. Since Pope's father was in retirement for twenty-nine years, it is not surprising that the fall of interest on the French *rentes* in which a great part of his capital was invested, the fines for recusancy, and family expenses should have lowered the *income* from the modest fortune.

At Binfield two things engrossed Pope: his studies—reading and observation—and the circle of new and influential friends who were beginning to be caught in the silken net of his charm. He pored over his Greek and Latin authors, with at least some help from translations; devoured the best in English and Continental literature; studied French and Italian; wrote verses incessantly.

It is not to be presumed, however, that Pope spent all his waking hours indoors. His early poems—*The Rape of the Lock* and *Windsor Forest*, in particular—show his minute observation of and love of nature. For that study Pope had an almost romantic passion, whose intensity, at its best, was matched but not surpassed by the poets of the nineteenth century. In Pope's early poems there is glowing evidence that he rambled solitary in the forest, charmed by its beauty.

According to Pope's own dramatic story, he applied himself to learning and study with violent enthusiasm. Within four years he had induced a complete nervous breakdown. So threatening was his actual or fancied *malaise* that Pope wrote dramatic notes to all his dearest friends bidding them farewell and acquainting them with his approaching dissolution. It was all very adolescent and Ciceronian. Among those who received a preview-of-death message was the Abbé Southcote —a man of action. Taking the poet at his word, Southcote went to Dr. Radcliffe, exposed the nature of Pope's illness and, setting down the good doctor's prescription, carried the directions at once to Binfield. Pope was ordered to "apply less and ride every day." Following this advice, the young student was soon restored to health.

Pope was fortunate in having the good Abbé for a friend. He was equally fortunate in all those who surrounded him at Binfield. Within his home he was ringed with the adoring interest of his family. Pope's father was an excellent gardener; the fame of his melons and artichokes brought him into cordial relationship with the neighbors, particularly those who were Catholic. Among these were the Carylls of Ladyholt; the Dancastle brothers, John and Thomas, squires of Binfield Manor; the Englefields, nine miles away at Whiteknights; and their granddaughters Teresa and Martha Blount at Mapledurham.

Pope was attracted to these two sisters. They stimulated him to a sense of gallantry. This was too often lacking in his crippled life, which was made still more difficult by the piercing pain of "meagrim" headaches. Yet he had a romantic heart; his early poems are ablaze with romanticism. Had Pope been merely a little man—he was only four and a half feet tall —he might have strutted into deeds of romantic daring. But with the added handicaps of spindle legs and a hunched back, Pope was incapacitated for anything more than verbal adventure and gallant declaration. His face, however, was intelligent, quicksilver in its changes of expression. Under the plume of the periwig his fine eyes looked out with discerning amusement, and his voice was remarkably sweet in timbre and variety of inflection. These things made his company charming and lent further delight to his witty insights and comments upon life.

Teresa and Martha Blount responded to his charm. They corresponded with Pope at regular intervals, and spent with the poet drifting, idle hours under the sun-drenched trees of the forest, and in the lovely gardens surrounding Mapledurham manor. They saw Pope, too, in the larger atmosphere of Whiteknights, their grandfather's home: no ordinary grandfather this, but a man who sparkled at the center of every joke, and whose companionship was one of the delights of Pope's youth.

The two sisters, in addition to their youthful charm and sharp contrasts of person, were not without social and mental graces. Their family was one of the oldest in England. They had the poise of breeding, and in addition to this were educated at Hammersmith convent, which was under the direction of Mrs. Cornwallis, a woman of remarkable attainments. At the conclusion of their schooling in England, Teresa and Martha went abroad to France for further study.

It was the most natural thing in the world that Pope and the two charming girls should have at once formed the bonds of a friendship, which, in the case of Martha, was to last beyond the grave. Why shouldn't they have loved one another? They were all bursting with youth. They enjoyed life and idle wit; they belonged to the hated Catholic minority which the crushing force of the penal laws had molded into a hard core of secrecy and deceit toward the world and all who stood outside the charmed circle of the faith.

With youth's penetrating intuitions Teresa and Martha must have warmed to Pope's myriad talents and brilliance; his high spirits and vulgar sense of fun added a further luster to the attraction. Pope is often birched by nineteenth- and twentieth-century critics for the frequency with which he indulged his talent for low comedy. Perhaps his pranks and wit had a tinge of coarseness at times. But was the eighteenth century without coarseness? It darkens the plays and manners of the times everywhere. In their conception of the eighteenth century, most critics, like the nineteenth-century prudes, mince about perpetually between the shades of priggish Addison and schoolmaster Johnson. They leave no place for Swift or Prior, and all the dramatists who thought of life in terms of broad farce or high tragedy.

History, in spite of her mannered scribes—Thackeray pointed out—will at times take off her mask: the great Queen Anne will appear a coarse, red-faced woman driving her chariot like Jehu as she hunts stags in the forest, or George I will be seen as Pope observed him, under the garden wall giving audience to the birds, with no more trappings of state than the light of the moon. Being the most noted poet of a magnificent age—one which had evolved a complicated ritual of public manners at Versailles—Pope was somewhat indiscreet in sending copies of his coarsest jokes to many of his friends. The indiscretion was accentuated by the hovering presence of a vulture publisher, the disgusting Curll, who scrupled at no vileness that he might secure scraps and scourings of the works of great men. Pope's offense was a commonplace in his age, but his prominence on the public stage lent a tinge of rouge to his embarrassment at seeing his barnyard witticisms of the moment held up for comparison with his published verse, which went grandly in plum velvet and taffeta.

Remembering both the age and Curll, it is not too much to assert that Pope has been unjustly swinged for every momentary deviation from the varied blandness of his heroic couplets. It is evident that many critics will allow him neither the snigger of Sterne nor the belly-laugh of Rabelais.

This queasy criticism smacks of the rankest injustice, and of a determination to blacken Pope's character or impeach it at any cost of logic or knowledge of the manners of his day —an age which loved farce and the broadest practical jokes. No, Pope was not nice; but as Oscar Wilde said with wit, "Nice is a nasty word."

In addition to his wide circle of Catholic friends, Pope had found many others at Binfield who, being on the "right side of politics and religion," were able to help him to the career he coveted. Chief of these was Sir William Trumbull, of East Hampstead Park. Sir William was much traveled; he loved the classics and classical lore sententiously and consciously in the eighteenth-century manner. Pope got on well with older men because he was a good listener and appeared to take their advice to his heart. In Pope's friendship with Trumbull, then, we may suppose that Pope listened and followed.

The two men, no doubt, often read and discussed classic authors, and Pope must have been eager to take advantage of such occasions. They stretched his education; they lent wings to his poetic ambitions.

In addition to their sedentary discussions over tea and scones, or port and nuts, Pope and Trumbull often rode in the forest all the long, fragrant afternoon. The exercise became a daily pleasure after Pope put Dr. Radcliffe's advice into execution.

Among Pope's other friends of Binfield days were Walsh, the critic, who lived at Abberly; Wycherley, poet and last of the Restoration rakes; Congreve, the playright; Henry Cromwell, Rowe, and Parnell; lovable John Gay; and the "Beau Chevalier," Wogan. From Wogan, Pope learned the art of dress and deportment so admired by the men of his age; Walsh, Wycherley, Congreve, and Cromwell taught Pope something of polite criticism, and gave him an introduction to the fashionable coffeehouse society of his time; Rowe and Parnell schooled him in the brutal wit of the period; and John Gay taught him fun without bitterness, and the perpetual delight of dependable friends. Pope was an apt pupil, we may suppose, for even before the *Essay on Criticism*, which made his reputation, the fashionable world of magnificent nobles, Latin-steeped dons, and plum-cheeked bishops had begun to cultivate his acquaintance.

The first Binfield years overflowed with tutors. The best theories and practices of education are to be found there in prodigal abundance; in books, persons, and the honeyed delights of contemplation. But Pope's education cannot be estimated without understanding the core of the man. That core was religious. The years in the forest which saw his growth in knowledge, powerful friends, and poetic brilliance had behind their fluctuating patterns of light and conduct something which did not vary or admit of fluctuation—Pope's religion.

Just what sort of a Catholic was Pope? He showed a calculating silence about his childhood faith, but it is possible to reconstruct a comprehensive picture of his religion. We know from Pope's letters and poems that his father insisted on prayer three times a day. We know, also, that Pope revolted against this stern and pious atmosphere for a time in his young manhood. Because of these facts, it is possible to say that Pope was a pious and practical Catholic. He was required to know his Catechism, was made to read the Bible—he quotes it from his earliest letters—and *The Following of Christ*. Then, of course, he went to Mass in the homes of the Dancastles, Blounts, or Englefields when that was possible, and was well schooled in the lives of the saints, devotion and prayer, and a small amount of meditation. There is no indication whatever that Pope knew the intellectual splendors of the Church. On the contrary, the early display of his satirical attitude toward the schools and schoolmen and his poor opinion of monkish learning connotes his lack of training in both Catholic philosophy and history.

Pope's allegiance to the Roman Church was founded on sentimental and devotional bases. He was a traditional Catholic. Pope's life and actions corroborate this assertion. There is little to show he understood, except in a confused way, the philosophical ideas which made his position tenable. To Alexander Pope, the example of his father and mother was worth a library of books on the subject of religion. This attitude is a splendid example of filial love but it also exposed Pope to the subtle blandishments of clever men who knew how to be both plausible and reasonable about skepticism or unbelief. Pope's lack of philosophical training made him trust his own opinion too much. Like the priests of his day, he was at times content to be a law to himself in matters of discipline. And, like all strong traditionalists, he also dismissed or dispensed with things which affected his peace of mind and his undisturbed intercourse with his fellow men.

Some Catholic scholars today call Pope a "liberal Catholic." Catholics of his own day, who took pride in his eminence and his public confession of the faith, would not have done so, for

Pope was respected and admired by the majority of Catholics in his age. The modern student is led to false conclusions on this subject because of Pope's freedom from bigotry, a freedom which was far in advance of his time. Because it was so advanced, it is easy to misinterpret it.

If modern scholars appear determined to misconstrue this virtue, Pope's intimates were not so easily led astray. His closest non-Catholic friends, Gay and Swift, made broad jokes about his faith. Pope retorted in kind. He found no malice in their badinage. With Swift, above all, Pope loved to make the coarsest jibes at pious pretentiousness, but such jokes should occasion no more alarm than Chaucer's bawdy tales or the innuendoes of Shakespeare. When a man is at home with holy things he uses them in a haphazard fashion which sometimes causes scandal to those of less faith and more propriety. It frequently happens, too, that close friends make broad jokes regarding religious divergences which they consider a detriment to their friendship. By treating such matters in a chaffing fashion all danger of difference is fancifully charmed away and made to appear innocuous.

With all their mutual jesting on the subject of religion, Swift knew to a fine point Pope's attitude toward his faith. As late as 1735, Swift, in writing to Pope upon hearing of his illness, paid a great tribute to his friend which is of some point in helping us understand how Pope's religious profession squared with the truth in the eyes of those who knew him best:

> It is some time since I dined at the Bishop of Derry's where Mr. Secretary Cary told me with great concern that you were taken very ill. I have heard nothing since, only I have continued in great pain of my mind, yet for my sake and the world's more than for yours; because I know how little you value life both as a philosopher and a christian,

particularly the latter, where hardly one of us *heretics* can equal you.

The tribute is a handsome one indeed, and the word *heretics* used by a divine of Swift's learning and shrewdness can mean but one thing, Pope's confirmed Catholicism. This is but a single example from the great body of evidence of the same kind which might be brought forward to prove Pope's *eighteenth-century* orthodoxy. Gay's constant references to Pope's religion and the affectionate solicitude of Caryll and Martha Blount, the very slanders of Grub Street, and the official records of confirmed recusants make the story plain to those who can or will read it.

The evidence of Pope's pietism does not in any sense depend upon his friends: it tumbles out of his letters, his habits of mind, and the golden march of his verse.

Pope's complete and easy familiarity with the saints, angels, Heaven, Hell, Purgatory, the Mass, Sacraments and Sacramentals, all are declared in his letters with monotonous regularity.

Familiarity with such terms and their employment is more than a casual revelation of Pope's piety. The evidence at hand in the letters is far deeper and more complex. There is a certain texture in works of piety which marks them with an atmosphere of their own. The *Introduction to a Devout Life* of St. Francis de Sales has an ambience rather than a logic. Pope's voluminous letters to Caryll, as Dilke turned them up—undoctored and unrefined for formal publication—have an atmosphere similar to that found in the *Introduction to a Devout Life*. The wisdom of God declares itself in things, persons, or events: they may seem, to those who see not, mere occasions of sadness or pain; but to the understanding soul insight breathes out of them. They are "intimations of immortality."

This is the real atmosphere of the letters Pope wrote to Caryll. Most Pope scholars have misinterpreted the Caryll letters because they have not understood how a layman can talk like a cleric. Pope's employment of this style was neither "hypocritical moralizing" nor "a full-dress appearance for posterity," which some critics called it. Pope wrote like a spiritual writer because his prose style was formed by spiritual books in his childhood. They were the voice of his soul.

One example taken at random from the Caryll letters will serve to demonstrate Pope's accent of piety—the yeast which worked nearly always in his consciousness and determined his modes of thought and precise patterns of expression:

> This miserable age is so sunk between animosities of party and those of religion, that I begin to fear most men have politics enough to make the best scheme of government a bad one, through their extremity of violence, and faith enough to hinder their salvation. I hope, for my own part, never to have more of either than is consistent with common justice and charity, and always so much as becomes a Christian and honest man—that is, just as much as you. Though I find it an unfortunate thing to be bred a papist, where one is so obnoxious to four parts in five, as being so too much, and to the fifth part for being so too little; I shall yet be easy under both their mistakes, and be what I more than seem to be, for I suffer for it. God is my witness that I no more envy the protestants their places and possessions, than I do our priests their charity or learning. I am ambitious of nothing but the opinion of all good men of all sides, for I know that one virtue of a free spirit is worth all the virtues put together of all the narrow-souled people in the world.[2]

Pope thought well of this lay sermon and others like it. He had such an admiration for them that he used many in preparing his correspondence for publication in 1737. He was not content with the mere idea of including the letters in his volume of correspondence. They were more important to him than such an action would signify. In consequence, Pope lifted passages from the letters he had written to persons of little or no importance and redirected them to some of the greatest personages of his time. The foregoing letter, for example, was wrenched from the Caryll correspondence and directed to Addison. That great man was long since dead, and Pope may have seen no great harm to either Addison or Caryll in changing the direction at the top of the letter.

One can but wonder what the "little senate" thought as they read and pondered its directness and the lofty independence of Pope's tone in speaking to their great patron who had hardly a peer when he chose to speak sententiously.

Of much interest to the student of literature are the many passages in Pope's poems which reveal his early religious formation and the pious atmosphere in which he moved.

His first verses declared him a religious poet. One of his earliest childhood efforts—which he later destroyed—was a tragedy "founded on the legend of St. Genevieve." Even without this poem's naïve lights and pious musings, we are able to re-create a fairly comprehensive picture of the mind of its creator in this period.

The *Messiah* and the *Ode to St. Cecelia* have strong religious touches. They are in the grand tradition of *The Book of Emblems* and the metaphysical efflorescence of Crashaw. Another poem of Pope's taken from the same period illustrates the precise texture of his pietism. It is the *Dying Christian to his Soul*. This was an adaptation of a famous Roman poem which every schoolboy student of Latin has construed with some pleasure and pain.

Pope takes the whispering strophes and the sad agnosticism

of Hadrian and turns them into a poem of Christian triumph. This is no Roman skeptic looking into the endless flatland of the shades. The poem voices an *almost* mystical contemplation of death such as that pictured by St. Paul and spiritual writers:

> Vital spark of heavenly flame!
> Quit, oh quit, this mortal frame;
> Trembling, hoping, ling'ring, flying,
> Oh, the pain, the bliss of dying!
> Cease, fond Nature, cease thy strife,
> And let me languish into life!
>
> Hark! they whisper; Angels say,
> "Sister Spirit come away!"
> What is this absorbs me quite?
> Steals my senses, shuts my sight,
> Drowns my spirits, draws my breath?
> Tell me, my Soul! can this be death?
>
> The world recedes; it disappears;
> Heav'n opens on my eyes! my ears
> With sounds seraphic ring:
> Lend, lend your wings! I mount! I fly!
> Oh Grave! where is thy Victory?
> O Death! where is thy sting?

These lines are clearly the work of an eighteenth-century Catholic, but a Catholic who knew well his atmosphere of Christian piety. He "languishes into life"; the angels bear him up on gales of light and seraphic song to victory over death and the grave.

The background of this poem, all the force of suggestion in it, its quintessential atmosphere, are pious and Catholic, but this warmth is a pale drift of moonshine compared with the blazing pietism found in the texture of Pope's *Eloisa to Abelard*, which some critics consider the best poem Pope ever wrote.

It is perhaps the poem in which he achieved the closest union of sense and form, but, even more than that, it is a telling description of Pope's early Catholic training. The poet understands and feels the romantic plight of the two lovers, the fine nuances of the convent life, and the workings of the cloistered mind, but he goes far beyond this point. The whole atmosphere of the poem is drenched with sentimental, pious light which makes it seem enervated. The "relentless walks," the "rugged rocks," "shrines where their vigils pale-eyed virgins keep," and "pitying saints whose statues learn to weep"; all these, apart from their Miltonic echoes, reveal the mind of one whose education and training were pietistic, whose childhood was steeped in the chronicles of sanctity. The idealized picture of the vestal nun is the work of a painter who knew his subject and loved the poetry of Crashaw and Milton:

> How happy is the blameless Vestal's lot!
> The world forgetting, by the world forgot.
> Eternal sun-shine of the spotless mind!
> Each pray'r accepted, and each wish resign'd;
> Labour and rest, that equal periods keep;
> "Obedient slumbers that can wake and weep;"
> Desires compos'd, affections ever ev'n,
> Tears that delight, and sighs that waft to heav'n.
> Grace shines around her with serenest beams,
> And whisp'ring Angels prompt her golden dreams.
> For her th' unfading rose of *Eden* blooms,
> And wings of Seraphs shed divine perfumes;
> For her the Spouse prepares the bridal ring,
> For her white virgins Hymenæals sing;
> To sounds of heav'nly harps, she dies away,
> And melts in visions of eternal day.[3]

Nowhere else in the compass of English poetry has the mystical life of a cloistered nun been described with greater fidelity. The whole force of her dedication is set in frames of starry reference.

Eloisa is rich with the stored harvest of much spiritual reading and contemplation. Pope is not content to versify the simple liturgy of her tranquil days. The background of the life is drawn in: "serene grace," "virtue heavenly fair," "fresh blooming hope," and "faith our early immortality." Light flashes out; the whole scene is charged with deepest feeling. Heaven, Purgatory, the Mass, are lifted on waves of triumphant couplets to the scene describing the victorious consummation toward which the contemplative nun reaches through dark nights of the soul and seasons of intuitive union:

> In trance extatic may thy pangs be drown'd,
> Bright clouds descend, and Angels watch thee round,
> From opening skies may streaming glories shine,
> And Saints embrace thee with a love like mine.[4]

The usual picture of the frail poet wearing himself into a decline by excessive study in the low-ceilinged room while he pored over the tomes of antique learning and wrote his childish lines is incomplete. New tones and depths are communicated to that portrait by watching the tiny figure concentrated on books of spiritual import and the wonderful lives of the saints. They are so real to the bent boy in the flickering candlelight that something of a mystical glow seems to play about his large eyes and the nimbus of his cropped hair. If one still doubts the correctness of these strokes of the portrait, one has only to shake out the yellowed page of a manuscript of a poem which Pope wrote when he was a child of twelve, living in Windsor Forest:

A Paraphrase of Thomas Kempis; L.3, C.2.

Speak, Gracious Lord, oh speak; thy Servant hears:
For I'm thy Servant, and I'll still be so:
Speak words of Comfort in my willing Ears;
And since my Tongue is in thy praises slow,
And since that thine, all Rhetorick exceeds;
Speak thou in words, but let me speak in deeds!

Nor speak alone, but give me grace to hear
What thy cœlestial Sweetness does impart;
Let it not stop when entred at the Ear
But sink, and take deep rooting in my heart.
As the parch'd Earth drinks Rain (but grace afford)
With such a gust will I receive thy word.

Moses indeed may say the words, but Thou
Must give the Spirit, and the Life inspire;
Our Love to thee his feverent Breath may blow,
But 'tis thyself alone can give the fire:
Thou without them may'st speak and profit too;
But without thee, what could the Prophets do?

Nor with the Israelites shall I desire
Thy heav'nly word by Moses to receive,
Lest I should die: but Thou who did'st inspire
Moses himself, speak thou, that I may live.
Rather with Samuel I beseech with tears
Speak, gracious Lord, oh speak; thy Servant hears.

They preach the Doctrine, but thou mak'st us do't;
They teach the misteries thou dost open lay;
The trees they water, but Thou giv'st the fruit;
They to Salvation show the arduous way,
But none but you can give us Strength to walk;
You give the Practise, but they give the Talk.

Let them be Silent then; and Thou alone
(My God) speak comfort to my ravished ears;
Light of my eyes, my Consolation,
Speak when thou wilt, for still thy Servant hears.
What-ere thou speak'st, let this be understood:
Thy greater Glory, and my greater Good![5]

3

The Mouths of Babes

Ah! why did he write poetry,
That hereto was so civil;
And sell his soul for vanity
To Rhyming and the Devil?

Sandy's Ghost

POPE'S retirement at Binfield was more complete than we are sometimes willing to believe. During the period that the poet lived at Whitehill House, Binfield was an island of seclusion. The low timbered house occupied by the Pope family was built on the high ground of a ridge which offered delicious views in almost every direction. Gazing about him in his solitary rambles, Pope could look down at the heaths about Ascot, and lifting his glance, take in the wooded hills with the depth-deceptive hazes characteristic of the English countryside. In Pope's day the forests were almost intact: the great oaks and elms were massive foils for the occasional thrust of birches of feminine grace and delicacy of foliage. Deer roamed at ease in the thick woods. The hedges were the nesting places of grouse and pheasants.

In this complete seclusion Pope's father had bought a house and twenty acres of land, much of it pasture. He was happy pottering about his greenhouse, cultivating the pine-

apples, artichokes, and meaty melons which gave him great
kudos among his neighbors. The modest house snuggled in its
gardens and forest was described by Pope in a charming couplet:

> A little house with trees a row
> And like its master very low.

In the morning Pope applied himself to his studies: folios of
Stathius and Tully, Horace and Virgil. There were happy
excursions into Ogilby's translation of Homer, and tall volumes of Fontenelle, Vida, and Chaucer; Dryden, Milton, and
Waller. In Lent his diet would vary: The Bible in the Douay
Version, which he quoted often in his letters; "Thomas
Kempis"; perhaps Pascal's *Thoughts*, in Thomas Walker's
translation; the inevitable *Telemachus* of Fénelon, designed
for a king's son; the *Lives of the Saints;* and according to
Pope's own word, some extensive acquaintance with sermons
and the controversial religious literature which had sprung
up since the Reformation. Perhaps it was through Pope's
readings in these controversial books, too often more distinguished for fire than light, and through his early acquaintance with the works of Erasmus, that the poet conceived an adulation of the great Dutchman and a hatred of
religious intemperance, which he never failed to condemn,
even if it emanated from those of his own faith.

It has been pointed out that many Catholics and nonjurors
lived in the Forest, a circumstance which arose, no doubt,
from the quiet in which they were able to voice some shreds
of their opinions among themselves, and, in the case of Catholics, a seclusion which permitted priests to move undetected
in the offices of their ministry. From centers such as the great
houses of the Stonors, Petres, and Shrewsburys it was possible
for priests to go back and forth, with some security, to the

manor houses of the Blounts, Dancastles, and others of the minor gentry who tried to make up in their prayers, fasts, and liturgical faithfulness for the lack of unity and the diversity of religious opinion found among them. The severity and integrity of Pope's family in their religious profession was too rare an atmosphere for one of Pope's independent and opinionated frame of mind. This circumstance made Pope turn to Catholics outside his family circle. In his friendships with Martha Blount and the younger Caryll, Pope found the liberal atmosphere and good-natured tolerance toward all religion which much of his life reveals.

Pope did not give the whole day to studious pursuits as his fancies pretended in those days after he became a great poet. In the afternoon, followed by his dog, he meditated on the beauties in the forest about him and the glittering lines of verse which danced through his head. Accompanied by the red-faced Trumbull, with his somewhat prosy comments on life and literature, Pope rode under the great trees and paused to watch the huntsmen stalking their prey with bated breath:

> See! from the brake the whirring pheasant springs,
> And mounts exulting on triumphant wings:
> Short is his joy; he feels the fiery wound,
> Flutters in blood, and panting beats the ground.
> Ah! what avails his glossy, varying dyes,
> His purple crest, and scarlet-circled eyes,
> The vivid green his shining plumes unfold,
> His painted wings, and breast that flames with gold?

At other times, Pope went into London on horseback or by coach. Brushed and periwigged, he would drop in at Will's or Button's to participate in the interminable but witty discussions of literature, philosophy, and politics. At Button's he could barely manage to insinuate himself into the tight "little senate" over which Addison presided with a fine eye of rebuke for any deviation from propriety or Whiggish principle. At Will's the atmosphere was looser. The grave Mr. Cromwell, who dearly loved a spicy story if it was wittily told, would be there. Walsh, Wycherley, Congreve, Wogan, and their compeers would scintillate verbally under the tutelary eye of the divinity at the cash desk, while the light of the candles flickered on the beamed ceiling and the smell of fresh roasting coffee provided rumors of ambrosial draughts to come. The talk was strong like the coffee: polite and mannered in form, but hard-hitting and wittily coarse. Doubtless the young Catholic poet retired from these sessions, many a night, more disturbed than settled in his mind; or with the younger gallants sallied forth to the more vicious resorts of the city.

Always, or nearly always, Pope went to London well armed for the future he had in mind. Copies of his latest verses, written out in the beautiful script he copied so well, would circulate among his friends. They were quick to see the poetic excellence of this quaint little man. He was dwarfed and young, but full of wit and promise, as he walked among the giants like a character out of Lilliput.

In London, Pope yearned for the country; in the forest he hankered for the adequate stage at Will's with its atmosphere of importance and appreciation for genius; but he was shrewd enough to spend more time at home than he did in the feverish climate of that "damned distracting town." For, though he loved London, it tired him like the flasks of champagne drunk at the theater or his lodgings.

Pope may have preferred Binfield for another reason; it offered him complete quiet and security for the creation of poetry. Just how early he had begun to write is a matter of conjecture. Pope liked to pose as an infant prodigy. This often led him to antedate his earliest works by a year or two at least, making them seem in the light of his statements more extraordinary still in their varied music and smooth precision.

While still a child, Pope told Spence, he had written a tragedy of the life of Saint Genevieve, and between his thirteenth and fifteenth years, an epic poem of some four thousand lines, dealing with the life of Alcander, Prince of Rhodes. A letter of Atterbury's seems to bear testimony to the truth of Pope's statements to Spence. In any event, Pope destroyed these juvenile productions, and possibly his earliest poems remaining are his translations of à Kempis, the *Ode to Solitude*, his satires on Elkanah Settle, and the first book of Stathius' *Thebias*. The last three were not published until 1712, which would seem to indicate that Pope with his passion for perfection had not left them as he first wrote them, but had polished and disciplined them in the interval.

For several years before Pope had had an opportunity to publish anything he had circulated his handwritten manuscripts at Will's. Such was the impression his works created on the minds of Walsh, Wycherley and others, that Pope's work was brought to the attention of Tonson, the publisher. Tonson finally asked the young poet for poems which were to be included in his sixth *Miscellany*. Pope was more than willing to oblige: he sent his *Pastorals* to Tonson. One can imagine the eagerness with which Pope awaited the date of publication in the year 1709.

It must have galled him somewhat when he discovered, along with his own poems in the *Miscellany*, pastorals by Ambrose Philips, one of the literary men lurking in the fringes of Addison's select circle at Button's. Compared with the work of Philips, Pope's verse is far superior. Pope at first mentioned the pastorals of Philips with commendation, but in the year following their appearance, when he found his own superior efforts largely ignored and those of Philips often praised in the *Guardian*, Pope may have felt that neglect and bias required a definite purge.

Some of Pope's biographers have censured the poet for the revenge he planned and executed. They have called it "indecorous" and pushing. They seem to infer that such vices in Pope were unworthy of a great poet. One may differ with such judgments, for Pope was by his own admission and circumstances not likely to be "worth a groat as a papist and a poet" unless he forced his way to public notice against the warped partiality of the times. He was also possessed of a cool impudence and high spirits, which at twenty-one makes it possible to excuse his impetuosity on the grounds of youth and high temper.

In any event, Pope proceeded to concoct a clever, anonymous satire, in which he simulated to perfection the style and phrasing of the *Spectator* papers, and compared his own pastorals to those of Philips. He pointed out the superiority of Philips's work with a wealth of absurd examples, and concluded with the paragraph:

> After all that hath been said, I hope none can think it any injustice to Mr. Pope that I forbore to mention him as a Pastoral writer; since upon the whole, he is of the same class with Moschus and Bion, whom we have excluded that rank; and of whose Eclogues, as well as some of Virgil's, it may be said, that (according to the description we have given of this sort of poetry) they are by no means Pastorals, but something better.

The ironical twist of the piece may seem more than obvious today, since we are in on the secret, but Bickerton, Ayre, and Aphra Behn found it easy to believe that Steele had written the paper as an unfriendly gesture toward Pope.

Pope may have schemed to persuade Steele to publish this

satire. Addison may have rebuked Pope for his bustling endeavors. Whether these things are true or not is without more than passing importance. The paper did appear in *Guardian* (No. 40), and Pope's satire was soon detected by the town. Philips was furious with rage. It is said, on his own authority, that he hung up a switch at Button's for the purpose of chastising Pope, should he appear, but that the poet fled to the country to escape the wrath of his bulkier adversary. Addison's rebuke and the story of Pope's flight seem to be more or less apocryphal. Pope continued to contribute to the *Guardian* after this "horse-opera" episode, and there is every indication that he and Addison remained on at least glacial good terms until 1714.

In 1709, the same year in which the *Pastorals* appeared, Pope was already at work on a poem which was to be the first solid foundation of his fame, The *Essay on Criticism*. It was a subject which had long interested Pope. In working out his critical theories under the watchful eye of the critic Walsh, Pope selected and arranged his principles in a solid body of doctrine which he followed to the very end of his poetic career. Today we may admire no more in the work than the smooth precision in verse which made proverbs of seeming commonplaces, but to the men of Pope's day the *Essay on Criticism* summed up, in a superb manner, the theories of their own age and the past, and it looked to the future with an arrogant optimism which fitted the lordly times to perfection. To Pope himself, the *Essay* was to provide guidance and a program of poetic progress which made him, in spite of his obvious handicaps of birth, religion, and deformity, the first poet of his time.

> The critical defects of a work so designed [says Courthope] lie naturally on the surface. The Essay has many incorrect observations, and in spite of its own axioms, many

bad rhymes, many faulty grammatical constructions. But these cannot weigh against the substantial merit of the performance. They cannot obscure the truth that the poem is, what its title pretends, an "Essay on Criticism," an attempt made, for the first time in English literature, and in the midst of doubts, perplexities, and distractions, of which we, in our position of the idle heirs of that age, can only have a shadowy conception, to erect a standard of judgment founded in justice of thought and accuracy of expression. Nor will it be denied that, as a poem, the critical and philosophical nature of the subject is enlivened by bold, brilliant, and beautiful imagery. Lastly, when it is remembered that this extraordinary soundness of judgment and maturity of style are exhibited by a young man who was only twenty-three when the poem was published, and may have been under twenty-one when it was composed, the panegyric of Johnson, startling as it seems at first sight, will not be thought after all to be greatly exaggerated.[1]

If Courthope and Dr. Johnson found the *Essay on Criticism* of some importance and excellence, there was one person at least who was anything but pleased with its appearance. This was the critic John Dennis, one of the writers who frequented Button's. Dennis was a critic of the polysyllabic school of Rhymer. Though Dennis was blunt and honest according to his own convictions, he was dogmatic in the extreme, and pompous and choleric in the expressions of his opinions.

Near the beginning of the third epistle of the *Essay on Criticism*, in delineating rules for the conduct and correct manners of a critic, Pope had drawn a short but satirical picture of the man:

> Fear not the anger of the wise to raise;
> Those best can bear reproof who merit praise.
> 'Twere well might critics still this freedom take,

But Appius reddens at each word you speak,
And stares tremendous, with a threat'ning eye,
Like some fierce tyrant in old tapestry.

According to all reports the Appius picture was just, though personal. It summed up Dennis only too well. Dennis recognized the portrait with insane fury when he read it. Within six weeks Dennis replied to the slight in a vitriolic work entitled *Reflections Critical and Satrical, upon a late Rhapsody, Call'd An Essay upon Criticism.*

In thirty fierce pages Dennis castigated Pope's critical theories. He descended to the coarsest invective and innuendo regarding Pope's deformed body, calling him "a crippled toad" and other brutal things. According to the best gossip of the time, Pope pretended to be untouched at Dennis's blunderbuss of spleen, but, inwardly writhing, fled the town to escape the notoriety which Dennis's pamphlet had occasioned.

Many conjectures have been advanced which would attempt to explain Pope's selection of Dennis as an example of the bad-mannered critic. If any more reasons were necessary other than the furious bad manners Dennis displayed in answering Pope's somewhat playful satire, they may be found in the background of the man. Dennis was loud in calling himself the injured party, but his subsequent ferocious action points to the justice of the picture Pope drew. If more reasons are desired, they are not hard to find. Dennis, so often defended by those who have a distaste for Pope, was anti-Jacobite and anti-French. He was also anti-Catholic. In 1702 he had signalized his opinions by publishing a pamphlet entitled *The Dangers of Priestcraft to Religion and Government;* and he returned to the subject again, soon after the accession of George I, in his tract, *Priestcraft Distinguished from Christianity.* In satirizing Dennis, Pope without a shadow of doubt welcomed the opportunity to pay Dennis for many things in which the man himself had no consciousness of exceeding.

That Pope suffered very little from the "furious fret of Dennis" may be assumed. Pope was a genuine man of his age. His new poem was a glittering success. This alone must have shouted to his world, and to himself above all, his superiority to Dennis and Philips. Pope could afford to bide his time in meditating revenge on Dennis. It was sufficient for the moment, as the dazzling light of fame touched him, that friends like Gay, Steele, and Cromwell should rally to his defense. Pope himself was busied with many things. He was preparing his *Rape of the Lock* and *Sappho and Phaon* for early publication with Tonson. At the request of Steele, Pope was also hard at work on the *Messiah*, which appeared in the *Spectator*, May 14, 1712.

There was another matter arising from the *Essay on Criticism* which gave Pope far more concern than the Appius portrait; an accusation which touched him where he was most sensitive and vulnerable. Some strict Catholics, it is evident, had taken exception to passages in the *Essay* which they considered slights to the Church, and incompatible with Pope's professed Catholicism.

The first of these suspected excerpts was a long and complicated passage which Pope had used to point out the eclectic and progressive values of genuine criticism:

> Some foreign writers, some our own dispise;
> The ancients only, or the moderns prize:
> Thus Wit, like Faith, by each man is apply'd
> To one small sect, and all are damn'd beside.
> Meanly they seek the blessing to confine,
> And force the sun but on a part to shine,
> Which not alone the southern wit sublimes,
> But ripens spirits in cold northern climes;

Which from the first has shone on ages past,
Enlights the present, and shall warm the last;
Tho' each may feel increases and decays,
And see now clearer and now darker days.
Regard not then if wit be old or new,
But blame the False, and value still the True.

This offending passage and the scandal it had given some Catholics was probably first brought to the young poet's attention by his friend John Caryll. The letter may have been among those later destroyed by Pope, but Pope's answer to it remains. It is an angry answer, a young man's answer.

Pope's letter to Caryll is crammed with rage and verbal fencing. The lines in question he may have designed to justify the large-minded attitude of people like himself, who were tired of the quarrels of Reformation times and were willing to concede some honesty of intention and excellence of life to those men of good will outside the *body* of the Church. Pope, who no doubt fancied himself the champion of his Church in many things—his strictures on Settle and Dennis and the squinting satires in *Windsor Forest* concerning the spoilers of monasteries prove it—was deeply hurt to be so vigorously criticized by those he had somewhat quixotically attempted to defend. In trying to explain himself to Caryll, Pope's reasoning was confused and contradictory. He first claimed misapprehension of his meaning, through a failure to understand the grammatical construction of his lines, and he followed this claim with a false profession of humility and an expression of willingness to remove the offending lines. Next he descended to angry abuse of his critics, and as a final sop to Caryll dragged in the red herring of Erasmus. The letter concludes with a pious sermon on humility and charity.[2]

Pope was not without some backing in the stand he had taken. The saying, "Outside the Church there is no salvation," had sometimes been interpreted too rigidly by sterner Catholics, especially in the days of the Reformation and Counter Reformation. There are other principles in theology which mitigate and soften the seeming harshness of the saying: the admission of "baptism of water, blood and desire," the kindliness of theology to those of any religion who are what they are in good faith, prove that the Church tries to interpret the principle of exclusion with the widest charity.

The reasons Pope gave in his own defense failed to satisfy his correspondent, honest John Caryll. A week later Pope again wrote to Caryll on the same subject. He referred to a second passage in the *Essay* which had given further umbrage to Catholics. This passage on monkish learning:

> With tyranny then superstition join'd,
> And that the body, this enslaved the mind:
> Much was believ'd, but little understood,
> And to be dull was constru'd to be good;
> A second deluge learning thus o'er-run,
> And the monks finish'd what the Goths begun. . . .

had scandalized many learned Catholics to such an extent that a Catholic pamphlet appeared criticizing this passage and two other points in the *Essay*.

> You will see by this [Pope wrote in reply to Caryll] that whoever sets up for a wit these days ought to have the constancy of a primitive christian, and be prepared to suffer even martyrdom in the cause of it. But sure this is the first time that a wit was attacked for his religion, as you will find I am most zealously in this treatise. And you know, sir, what alarms I had from the opposite side on this very account. . . . Mr. Thomas Southcote is not of that number, who, with the utmost candour, and freedom of a friend, has modestly

[61]

told me what others thought, and shown himself one, as he expresses it very well, rather of a *number* than a *party*. . . . The only difference between us in relation to the monks is, that he thinks most sorts of learning *flourished* among them, and I am of opinion that only some sort of learning was barely *kept alive* by them. He believes the most natural and obvious sense of that line—'A second deluge learning overrun' will be thought meant of learning in general, and I fancy it will be understood only as it is meant, of polite learning, criticism, poetry, etc., which is the only learning concerned in the subject of the Essay.[3]

Southcote was indeed correct in fact, though Pope made it appear that Southcote's conviction was, like his own, a mere matter of opinion, not of fact. In this misapprehension, however, one should not judge Pope too harshly. The smart opinion of his time, held even by some Catholic scholars, was anything but flattering to the monks. Twentieth-century research has been forced to modify that opinion. That Pope should have believed such an unfair opinion of the monks and their learning is not in the least astonishing: as far as his superficial learning went, there was ample warrant for his belief.

Pope was not content to let the matter rest with the dispatch of his second letter. A half month later he returned to the old charge in a long rambling epistle. In this new explanation Pope was torn between anger and apology. In the first part of the letter, he came out from behind his screen of words and sophisms and stated his dislike of the narrow interpretation of the saying, "Outside the Church there is no salvation." In making clear his conviction that this principle must be interpreted in a charitable fashion, and by citing some of the divisions within the Church itself which made such charity necessary, Pope put up a spirited defense of his own position.

The grammatical subtleties he advanced were insufficient to bear out his original pretense of innocence.

In raising his points of grammar Pope also referred to a third passage in the *Essay* which had offended Catholics:

> So schismatics the dull believers quit,
> And some are damn'd for having too much wit.

His reasons given for including this passage are confused and illogical. The weakness of his position was well demonstrated by his appeal to the name of Erasmus.

The letter ends with a large *apologia* for Pope's charitable outlook. The poet expressed willingness to alter any lines which might possibly offend Catholic susceptibilities. In the case of the couplet on schismatics, Pope later altered *dull* believers to *plain* believers. Recalling Panzani's observations in regard to Catholics who called the liberals of their own persuasion "schismatics," it is interesting to speculate on the possibility that Pope, in the foregoing couplet, may have been referring to English Catholics of his day: the party of Appellants and others who were called schismatics becuse they used their good sense, and *outwardly* conformed to the laws. By doing so they demonstrated their wit, which "plain" or "dull" believers refused to do.

The inflamed criticism of his fellow Catholics troubled Pope in heart and mind. In August, 1711, he wrote again to Caryll, offering to give up his opinions if they were to deceive anyone.[4] He seemed very docile in his protestations of repentance, but another letter written to Caryll's son, while his father was in France settling the family estate, gives us some idea of the casual and angry way in which Pope attempted to dismiss the serious protests of those Catholics who had dared to criticize three passages in the *Essay*. "I have another storm, too, rising from the bigot, the most violent of animals, on the score of not having altered some true lines in the second edition of the Essay on Criticism. Yet, as to the first two quarrels, I can be satisfied in my conscience of having acted with honour; and as to the last, I dare stand to posterity in the character of an unbigoted Roman Catholic and impartial critic."[5]

The length of this correspondence, its tone of sensitive anger, and the confused reasoning displayed indicate that this incident *very much* concerned the poet. There is, however, no warrant for thinking, as many of Pope's biographers do—and some Catholics as well—that these passages in the *Essay* are the first indication of Pope's deism. They are the work of a charitable and ardent young man. They reveal the poet's defective training in Catholic history, philosophy, and logic, and his close association with skeptics and Whigs. In their company Pope leaned over backward in order to seem unbiased. Measured against the Catholicism of the time, and the divisions current among the faithful in England, the three criticized passages in the *Essay* are scarcely worthy of notice, except in so far as they indicate Pope's too great dependence on his own opinion when it came in conflict with attitudes which seem narrow or lacking in charity.

It is much more probable that it was not the anger of Dennis but the elder Mr. Pope's displeasure and disapproval which explains Pope's absence from London and his usual haunts toward the close of 1711. It is quite possible that, ardent Catholic as he was, Pope's father should have been at variance with his son's liberalism. His mother, too, would in all likelihood be alarmed at Catholic criticism of her son and would make her opinion known to him. Since Pope was devoted to both parents, their desires and opinions would be of enormous weight with him. In all probability Pope's father and mother influenced their son to avoid Button's, or restricted him to an occasional appearance there after 1711.

[64]

It would have been easy enough for Pope's parents and Catholic friends to show Pope the error of his ways in consorting with the little group at Button's coffeehouse, or in seeming weak or liberal about his religious beliefs while he moved among them. Through the influence of Addison, Button's pretended to be a forum for polite literature and Whig opinions. But since politics and religion were closely allied in the struggle for the British throne, and the Whigs of the time were dedicated to upholding the Protestant succession, no Catholic could hope to prosper in such an atmosphere. If he did so, he must deny or endanger his Catholicism in the end. When Queen Anne's health became precarious, and the various factions juggled for power, the repercussions were felt first in the coffeehouses. At Button's Pope could be no more than a "crooked little papist." If he could be used, it would be with a secret laugh at his own simplicity. Any defection from Buttonian orthodoxy and Hanoverian commitment would be the signal for unleashing attacks on Pope's morals and religion, such as he later suffered from the claque at Button's.

Addison himself, whatever his magnificent personal propriety, would be bound to be a participant in the maneuvers for power. It cannot be doubted that his attitude toward Pope would be conditioned by the struggle. That a papist with a "burning quill" should *not* be allowed to become the greatest writer of the day, may very well have sparked the attempts to exalt the *Pastorals* of Philips over those of Pope. It may also have led Addison to assist Tickell in his translation of Homer which was to cause so many alarms. The possibility of these things is implicit in the background of the quarrel between Pope and Addison, and it serves no purpose to ignore them or gloss them over. The eventual animosity between Pope and Addison cannot be understood on literary and personal grounds alone.

[65]

Pope's warm regard for Steele, which was far beyond anything he had ever felt for Addison, was also soured by the
struggle of the times. Though Steele had done Pope many a
favor in persuading him to write and publish his *Ode on St.
Cecelia's Day*, the *Messiah*, and *Hadrian's Address to his Soul*,
Pope saw how little such favors could mean against the larger
struggle for the throne and Protestant succession. That he did
see the implication is shown in Pope's letter to Caryll written
in 1713, at the time when Steele had begun his search for
writers to assist him in publishing the *Englishman*.

> I assure you [Pope wrote to Caryll], I have quite done
> with these papers for the future. The little I have done, and
> the great respect I bear Mr. Steele as a man of wit, has
> rendered me a suspected Whig to some of the over-zealous
> and violent [Catholics]. But as old Dryden said before, it is
> not the violent I design to please, and in very truth, sir,
> they will find me, at the long run, a mere papist.

In 1711 these considerations might well be pointed out to
Pope by his Catholic friends and his parents. Though he had
to learn their full truth in the next four years of bitter experience, he was never again so friendly with the "little senate"
and its overlord. However, Pope was still of sufficient importance to be courted and won for the Whig cause. Addison
asked Pope to write the prologue to *Cato*. It was to be the last
flash of a St. Martin's summer in the relations between the
two men. In 1711, Pope and Addison were still friends of a
sort, while the drama of the Queen's health played out its
first act.

Pope was visiting the Carylls at Ladyholt in the summer of
1711, and probably again in 1712. He now spent more time
with his Catholic and Tory friends than he did with his old
allies the Whigs. There was one exception—Jervas. Pope lived

at the artist's house in Cleveland Court, in a vain attempt to
learn the art of painting. In this effort Pope had little success.
He sent some of his pictures to friends with humorous comments on them, but except for insights into the painter's technique, which he used to advantage in some of his mature
poems, Pope was not a success with the brush.

With the pen Pope had more success in that year. In addition to his *Messiah*, which appeared May 14, 1712, he had the satisfaction of seeing seven of his new pieces in Lintot's volume of
Miscellaneous Poems and Translations. Of these, the first book
of *Thebias* and Ovid's *Vertumnus and Pomona* may be passed
over in the silence which their excessive baroque softness deserves. Among the remaining pieces, three are worthy of comment. The *Letter to a Young Lady* (Martha Blount) indicates
Pope's ability to be at once witty and hard-hitting. His picture
of Voiture toying with life is excellent, but there is a hint of
something more intuitive in the poem:

> The Gods, to curse Pamela with her pray'rs,
> Gave the gilt coach and dappled Flanders mares,
> The shining robes, rich jewels, beds of state,
> And, to complete her bliss, a fool for mate.
> She glares in Balls, front Boxes, and the Ring,
> A vain, unquiet, glitt'ring, wretched thing!
> Pride, Pomp, and State but reach her outward part;
> She sighs, and is no Duchess at her heart. . . .

This is a picture in the best style of Pope's mature portraits
in the *Moral Essays*. Pure notes of descriptive realism are found
in it. These give depth and point to the satire. The realism is
not malicious. The very strokes of the picture seem to ex-
hale a sigh at the waste of human beauty. It is a moral contrast
which is exposed. Against the virtue of integrity Pope sets the
glittering rewards the prince of darkness offered in the tempta-

[67]

tion of Christ: pride of place and pride of the eyes. By pointing out these multiple prides Pope reveals that the unhappy Pamela does not find life the gathering of rosebuds which the epicure suggests it is. Life is, on the contrary, a heavy pose filled with discontent and unhappiness.

Most significant for critics, among the seven pieces published in *Tonson's Miscellany* for 1712 is the first emergence of the *Rape of the Lock*, without the exquisite machinery of the Sylphs. Though its appearance failed to achieve that for which it was designed, it indicated Pope's mastery of the comedy of manners. It is customary for literary rhapsodists to point out the grace and lightness of the *Rape of the Lock*. To them, like Addison, it is *merum sal*, but a thing of spangles and arch gaiety. The serious import of the poem almost always escapes them. Yet its importance as the ancestor of the *Atticus* and *Sporus* portraits and the *Essay on Man* is apparent on close scrutiny. This is the true measure of its real excellence.

When it was first published, the poem lacked the preternatural atmosphere of the Sylphs, and their addition did heighten the drama of the poem, increased its liveliness, and communicated a delightful touch to the humor. The presentation of the Sylphs themselves showed Pope at his best in delicate description and fertile imagination.

These qualities, however, are not the most significant ones to be found in the production. The revelation of an astounding facility for realistic writing and exact portraiture, and the turning of these things to the moral criticism of life signalize the true beginning of a development which, in the *Moral Essays*, made Pope the greatest realistic portraitist and satirist of our language.

In the *Rape of the Lock*, Pope with a smile magnifies the trivialities of life with supreme delicacy and oriental dyes. He richly colors all the preternatural characteristics in the Sylphs;

yet he gives them, at most, only the ineffectual reality and power which they actually could have in human life and human consciousness. There is no confusion of the preternatural and supernatural, such as bedeviled Coleridge and the nineteenth century. Over against this ineffectual quality of the Sylphs, Pope sets a philosophy of value and the mystery of human worth and personality which touches us with thought, with sadness, as we behold the lock:

> A sudden star, it shot thro' liquid Air,
> And drew behind a radiant *Trail of Hair*.
> Not *Bernice's* Locks first rose so bright,
> The heav'ns bespangling with dishevel'd Light.
> The *Sylphs* behold it kindling as it flies,
> And pleas'd pursue its Progress thro' the Skies.

The mystery yawns into both darkness and beauty. That neither may be lost sight of, Pope concludes the poem with a great emphatic chord:

> When, after Millions slain, your self shall die;
> When these fair Suns shall sett, as sett they must,
> And all those Tresses shall be laid in Dust;
> *This Lock* the Muse shall consecrate to Fame,
> And 'midst the Stars inscribe *Belinda's* name.

The immediate cause of the poem was a quarrel between two Catholic families. The quarrel started as a result of Lord Petre's snipping a lock of hair from the head of the beautiful Arabella Fermor. John Caryll suggested that Pope write an epic on the subject in the hope of resolving the quarrel. Though Pope took Caryll at his word and made a superlative masterpiece, the work aggravated the dispute and turned the anger of some of the participants toward Pope.[6] Posterity and

ALEXANDER POPE

the literary public derived the only permanent gain. Pope's
addition of the Sylphs was a stroke of genius. It heightened the
comedy, and it gave the poem a texture and suggestiveness of
greater richness and variety. Far more important to Pope was
the opportunity it gave him for the presentation of a contrast
in value between sprites and spirits.

In the midst of this busy year (1712) Pope was hard at
work on the literary remains of his friend Betterton. He also
labored on his arrangement of the *House of Fame* and a new
poem, *Windsor Forest*. The first part of the latter poem had
been completed as early as 1704; at least Pope said it had.
There seems every reason to believe he had written it during
his early seclusion at Binfield, before London had detected his
genius. It has all the marks of quiet, and the serene observation
of nature, which fit this period of Pope's life and the meditative
weave of his first years among the beauties of Windsor Forest.

It has been said that the final section of the poem, added at
the suggestion of Lord Lansdowne, is inferior to the first part.
Quite the opposite is true. The whole poem is integrated in a
splendid way. Against the serenity of Nature, which opens out
into a wide vista of the skies and eternal felicity, are set the
memorable and precise scenes of the huntsman with his gun:

> He lifts the tube, and levels with his eye:
> Straight a short thunder breaks the frozen sky:
> Oft, as in airy rings they skim the heath,
> The clam'rous lapwings feel the leaden death;
> Oft, as the mounting larks their notes prepare,
> They fall, and leave their little lives in air.

Or the patient fisherman:

> The patient fisher takes his silent stand,
> Intent, his angle trembles in his hand:

With looks unmov'd, he hopes the scaly breed,
And eyes the dancing cork and bending reed.
Our plenteous streams a various race supply,
The bright-eyed perch with fins of Tyrian dye,
The silver eel, in shining volumes roll'd,
The yello carp, in scales bedropp'd with gold,
Swift trouts, diversified with crimson stains,
And pikes, the tyrants of the wat'ry plains.

Beauty is distilled from these, and other sharp portraits which communicate rapidity of movement and realism. The pace of the poem is further accelerated by the inclusion of the legend of Ladona. The sylvan quiet is shattered by the blazing pursuit of Pan. The unfortunate nymph, metamorphosed into a river, escapes her ardent pursuer.

Silence settles down again, and Pope paints his pictures of the river-nymph looking out on the loveliness of the variegated scene from the lisping quiet of her still meanders. Once more the quiet is broken by the discord of civil war. Then "great Anna" appears and imposes peace. So significant is this new peace that the Thames itself in its fruitful valleys becomes a presage of a far-dawning future. It is not a chauvinistic picture Pope drew. In the vision of England as the center of the world, Pope beheld no repressive domination: quiet, civilization, freedom, and peace open into the larger vista of the Christian order:

O stretch thy reign, fair Peace! from shore to shore,
Till conquest cease, and slavery be no more;
Till the freed Indians in their native groves
Reap their own fruits, and woo their sable loves;
Peru once more a race of kings behold,
And other mexicos be roof'd with gold.
Exiled by thee from earth to deepest Hell,

In brazen bonds shall barb'rous Discord dwell:
Gigantic Pride, pale Terror, gloomy Care,
And mad Ambition shall attend her there:
There purple Vengeance, bathed in gore, retires,
Her weapons blunted, and extinct her fires:
There hated Envy her own snakes shall feel,
And Persecution mourn her broken wheel:
There Factions roar, Rebellion bite her chain,
And gasping Furies thirst for blood in vain.

It is the picture of the golden age of the poets, the spiritual reality of the prophets, the new Jerusalem adorned like a bride.

Windsor Forest is an amazing piece of work for a young poet, or for any poet. Its superb qualities are usually ignored by those who should see deeper than the surface. The abrupt contrasts between serenity and turmoil are heightened by the realistic vignettes nicely set at the proper points, and these do not retard but accent the swift pace of the poem. It spirals out to exalted infinity. Precise, like the sonnet, in its form, or like a gallery of pictures—now devastatingly exact, now soft with fancy—the final strophes are colored with the blinding light of the *Apocalypse.*

It is interesting to speculate on the gradual growth of the poem. Pope had a love for animals which was keenly sensitive. One passage of *Windsor Forest:*

To plains with well-breath'd beagles we repair,
And trace the mazes of the circling hare:
(Beasts urg'd us, their fellow beasts pursue,
And learn of men each other to undo) . . .

suggests that Pope may have originally intended the poem to be a protest against the cruel sport of hunting. The suggestion of Lansdowne that Pope turn *Windsor Forest* into a poem in praise of peace at once made Pope realize the full possibilities. The idea of men trained to hunt their fellow men in wartime shows only too close a likeness to the urges of the hunter: The brutalities of war and hunting will not cease to trouble the world until the human heart has disciplined itself through love, and a tenderness toward every living creature.

Pope himself may have realized how important a poem he had written. What interested him most, perhaps, as a suffering Catholic, was the sense of security *Windsor Forest* gave him. It afforded the poet a rich opportunity to express a blunt condemnation of persecuting kings and governments. Using the figure of William the Conqueror, Pope was quite safe from the law in expressing the criticism he did. The Whig sectaries at Button's were quick to point out that Pope's scathing couplets applied with equal force to Henry VIII and his successors:

> What wonder then, a beast or subject slain
> Were equal crimes in a despotic reign. . . .
> The fields are ravished from th' industrious swains,
> From men their cities, and from Gods their fanes;
> The levell'd towns with weeds lie cover'd o'er;
> The hollow winds thro' naked temples roar;
> Round broken columns clasping ivy twin'd;
> O'er heaps of ruin stalk'd the stately hind;
> The fox obscene to gaping tomb retires,
> And savage howlings fill the sacred quires.
> Aw'd by his nobles, by his commons curst,
> Th' Oppressor ruled tyrannic where he durst,
> Stretch'd o'er the poor and church his iron rod,
> And serv'd alike his vassals and his God.

Pope was not less knowing than the "little senate." He knew well that his condemnation was of general and particular application. When town and country accepted the stroke as a particular condemnation and not a general one, Pope knew he was safe. He had found a method of satirical procedure he was to follow to the end of his life; one which assured him freedom of speech on any question without endangering him as a Catholic. And if any point of offense should be indicated by the shrewd or watchful, Pope could in safety maintain his innocence and level the reproach of putting on a shoe which fit.

Once again, Pope was not first in the field with his poem celebrating the peace. Of the many minor poets who wrote voluminous or halting verses on the glowing theme, Thomas Tickell's *On the Prospect of Peace* achieved the most instant popularity and the widest sale. Tickell was a protégé of Addison, and the *Spectator's* cordial praise of his poem, soon after its publication, played a large part in its continued sale.

The publication of *Windsor Forest* achieved three important things for Pope. It brought him the friendship of Swift; it interested both nobility and government in Pope's ability to eulogize; and it proved to Pope that he could say what he liked if he was careful to surround his statements with sufficient concealment and mystification. In one sense, this was to have a bad effect on Pope's character. It encouraged both his boldness and cunning. By nature he had other qualities much more endearing: he was witty, kindhearted, devoted to his friends, and fond of his parents beyond all the demands of duty or tenderness. These were the qualities which endeared him to Gay, Rowe, and Swift, to Spence, Bathurst, and Craggs, and to the other great men of his day. Had he been born with "more than a groat" and not of the persecuted Catholic minority, it is possible Pope might have developed a lovable personality like Dryden's. The political circumstances of the day and his own imperial talents, however, made Pope the perpetual and inevitable opposition. Atterbury might be exiled to France, Oxford be sent to the Tower, Bolingbroke be forced to flight—Pope remained. But Pope remained only by trusting no man; he kept his place by cultivating the arts of concealment and through the fabrication of unwithering satire.

Once the poet had discovered, in *Windsor Forest*, a safe method of political satire, the stronger elements of Pope's character, boldness and cunning, became the dominating forces of his life. From this point forward his rise and satirical development were confident and rapid.

The initial signs of his complete confidence in himself and his newly discovered freedom to say what he liked were expressed in two actions. The first of these was his revenge on Dennis for his brutal attack on the *Essay on Criticism*. At the time, Pope had published nothing in reply. He had pretended to be highly amused at the insane rage of the pamphlet. His friends, like Gay, had defended him. Circumstances now played into Pope's hands. They gave him a chance to prepare a complete revenge which was well suited to the brutality of the blows he had suffered.

Addison was still the literary arbiter of the day. Looking about him for a poet to write the prologue to his play, *Cato*, he selected Pope. Pope wrote the prologue and was "clapt into a Whig" for the night. He watched from the pit the abounding triumph of Addison, who sat in a box sipping champagne with George Berkeley and some other friends.

The political and dramatic success of *Cato*, which violated some of the classical dramatic proprieties, filled John Dennis with critical disgust. In his incautious way he condemned the play in a grave pamphlet, *Remarks upon the Tragedy of Cato*. Those who still admired Dennis for his integrity of speech and action did everything they could to deter him from publishing his *Remarks*. He did hesitate, but in that moment Bernard Lintot interposed.

[75]

Lintot, who may have been stimulated by Pope, persuaded Dennis to publish his condemnation of *Cato*. The play had taken the town by storm. Anything written on it was almost certain to have a vogue, and Dennis was usually in need of ready cash. Dennis did publish his pamphlet, but the only result it achieved was the alienation of his last partisans. He had made a complete fool of himself.

It cannot be proved that Pope engineered the situation in which Dennis found himself, but whether he had or not, Pope was quick to take advantage of it. In all probability his friends Arbuthnot, Steele, and Gay aided him in composing his now famous *Narrative of Dr. Robert Norris, concerning the deplorable Frenzy of Mr. John Denn-s*. It was advertised in the *Post Boy*, July 28, 1713.

In the *Narrative*, Dr. Norris describes with care his sudden summons to the room of Mr. Dennis. The description of the frenzy in which he found Dennis, and the ensuing compounded misunderstandings and cross purposes of the actors, are carried off in the most robustious vein of low comedy. The pandemonium, bloodshed, and complete rout of Dr. Norris and Lintot make amusing reading, even today.

Pope at once denied any part in the pamphlet. Good manners demanded such a denial, particularly because the pamphlet contained some excellent strokes on Pope's friends Henry Cromwell and Lintot, who were pictured in conference with Dennis at the opening of the scene in his lodgings. Though Pope later in his life admitted some share in the production, it is not necessary to presume that he was in entire agreement with the manner in which Cromwell and Lintot had been treated. Dennis was the real butt of the joke. In paying him off with the assistance of his friends, Pope was not likely to be squeamish about the manner of doing it.

Once the joke had been perpetrated, Steele, at Addison's

direction, wrote a frigid note to Lintot. It voiced his disapproval of the horseplay:

Aug. 4, 1713

Mr. Lintot,——Mr. Addison desired me to tell you that he disapproves of the manner of treating Mr. Dennis in a little pamphlet by the way of Dr. Norris's account. When he thinks fit to take notice of Mr. Dennis's objections to his writings he will do it in a way Mr. Dennis shall have no just reason to complain of. But when the papers above mentioned were offered to be communicated to him, he said he could not, either in honour or conscience, be privy to such treatment, and was sorry to hear of it.

By his own admission Addison had advance knowledge of the pamphlet, but he suffered it to appear in silence without making too early a protest. Addison's late attempt to exculpate himself and retain his pose of magnificent serenity and propriety fails to be convincing. He could not have been human had he not enjoyed the broad joke which ministered to his vanity in the same thorough way it purged Pope of his spleen.

It is customary for biographers to fancy that Addison tolerated Pope and only cooled toward him until a break in their relations was inevitable. The facts and imponderables would seem to prove the direct opposite. Pope had the greater genius of the two, and could not have been held forever in the docile admiration Addison demanded from those who frequented his company and made up his select coterie of Whig writers.

4

Jove and Vulcan

The whispered word in Gath and slander's spite
Must stand the inquisition of the light.

THE gradual alienation of Pope and Addison has been ascribed to many small annoyances. Some scholars have been eager to lay the blame on Pope. They have said that his double-dealing and lack of gentility were the first causes which ultimately killed the friendship.

Pope was no gentleman in the priggish sense of the term. The most magnificent nobility of blood and brains; dukes and lords, the intellectual and the daring, the genuine wits, and the most lovable personalities of Pope's time, sought out his company and acknowledged his brilliance and talent. If he was sometimes "drunk as a lord," or furious with rage, he was living perhaps unwisely; but a man who makes no mistakes is either a saint or a madman: Pope was neither. His high spirits carried him away on occasions. He could be rash and vulgar, and his precarious situation under the raised axe of the penal laws made double-dealing less a crime than a necessity—that is, if he meant to prosper, and he was determined to do so with every nerve and muscle of his "crazy little carcase." He loved his fashionable world of nobles and wits. He wanted to play a colorful part in their mannered magnificence. But in order to cut such a swath he would require plenty of hard cash.

The amazing story of Pope's business sharpness[1] makes excellent reading. Pope's disgust with publishers; his direct dealing with printers; his return to publishers or printers as they suited his purposes, are astonishing signs of his genius for affairs. Nineteenth-century hypocrisy which had to pretend a contempt for filthy lucre found no place here. Pope was tougher. He was almost untouched by all the "art for art's sake" nonsense. He wrote with the whole complicated force of his creative mind and heart. Business affairs brought another side of his nature into focus, and this facet of his being was of equal brilliance.

It was this magnificence of Pope's talent on several levels which Addison tried to hold in check. To Addison, the gain of keeping Pope in the Whig camp was obvious. Addison was shrewd enough to realize something of Pope's rich talents and possible political usefulness *if* he could control Pope's ebullience of spirit and direct it into party channels. The *Prologue to Cato* was a last attempt to keep Pope in the fold. Addison tried hard to direct Pope to the purposes for which he employed Tickell and Budgell, Philips and Burnet. But Pope knew he was superior to these party wheel horses, this tight little coterie which struck in the dark with hints and innuendoes, or employed men of integrity, like Dennis, who fought for them in the daylight.

Addison cultivated an Olympian easiness with his subordinates, which Pope once described to Spence:

Addison's chief companions, before he married Lady Warwick, were Steele, Budgell, Philips, Carey, Davenant and Colonel Brett. He used to breakfast with one or other of them at his lodgings in St. James's Place, dine at taverns with them, then to Button's, and then to some tavern again for supper in the evening: and this was then the usual round of his life.[2]

The patronizing cordiality of Addison seemed all the more hateful to his adoring circle while they watched their great friend doing his utmost to charm the "crooked little papist." It was the more infuriating since they all knew or felt what Burnet confessed to Duckett, that Addison hated Pope "worse than Beelzebub."

Windsor Forest and *The Rape of the Lock* had confirmed Pope in his convictions of maturity and confidence. This frame of mind gave him an opportunity to examine his life for the purpose of striking some sort of balance. He had punished Dennis, and the time was ripe to consider his relations with Addison himself.

There were wrongs on both sides. Pope felt there was, among Addison's intimates, a conspiracy to prevent his rise. He remembered the inimical attitude of the little coterie toward his *Pastorals*. Any critic with an ounce of feeling or training could see at once, in the same *Miscellany*, the dullness and un-inspired quality of Philips's *Pastorals* contrasted with the fine music and aspiring energy of Pope's work. Yet Addison, who stood well as a poet, and was called the best prose writer of the time, sanctioned a continued stream of articles which magnified the pastoral poems of Philips and largely ignored those of Pope. It is not necessary to presume malice in these articles in praise of Philips's work. The men who wrote them were close friends of Philips: he had a more complete meaning to them than Pope had. This circumstance communicated to Philips's poems qualities superior to anything in Pope's verse. Their feelings warped their critical judgments. In any choice which had to be made between a Protestant Whig and a

Catholic Tory, the Whig was fated to win. The critics were not evil, but men. Considering the bitterness of the time and the close connection between religion and politics, it was hardly possible for them to make any other choice or take any other attitude than the one they did.

Such objective views are expected of us today, but had we stood in Pope's slippers the view we took of these things could hardly have been objective, if we had any essential humanity about us. He felt, possibly, less aggrieved for personal than practical reasons. The *Tatler, Spectator* and *Guardian* were the most popular pages of the period, perhaps of any period. If you felt yourself to be the greatest poet of the time—and Pope did—it was hateful to think that, except for cautious commendations, your work was ignored in such important journals, while the poems of a less capable artist were puffed up and magnified beyond their just deserts.

There is in the mind of every supreme artist a profound sense of the fleeting character of time. "This subtle thief of life, this paltry Time," Pope called it. Such feeling among great artists stems from the complete harmony of their out- ward- and inward-looking consciousness. Dullness, tedium, and *accedia* have no part in their existence. The world is some- thing which can be interpreted—must be interpreted. Places, circumstances, manners, people, are, in consequence, all in- vested with thrilling life not seen by those less talented, less aware, or less skilled in communication and interpretation. The real tragedy of time for all artists is its fleetness. Pope had this feeling in an exaggerated degree. Time was running away in glittering couplets, while the wide audience he might have was denied him.

He was restive under the slight to his *Pastorals*. It is probable that the same treatment of *Windsor Forest* moved him into action. The *Narrative of Dr. Robert Norris* had obviously broken the glossy surface Addison sought to maintain among his friends and subordinates at Button's. It upset all the apple-carts of prudence and fine manners. Pope could be relied upon to contribute a paper or poem to the organ of the party; he could be depended upon for a prologue; yet in the final analysis he could not be trusted. Unlike the other docile members of the little circle, he was unpredictable.

Pope could never pass up an occasion for a witticism; he was skilled in detecting pomposity, or the refractions of a situation which made it seem rotten-ripe for comment. *Cato* afforded one of these occasions. All the probabilities point to Pope as the originator of two vulgar and well-circulated epigrams which made light of the play. Addison was not one to appreciate epigrams reflecting upon his work; the vulgarity of these must have outraged his sense of propriety which, in public at least, was extremely nice.

Each man had adequate cause for suspicion of the other: Pope in his intuition of a plot to exalt his rivals, which must have become almost a certainty upon Addison's advice not to include the Sylphs in a revised version of the *Rape of the Lock;* Addison in his feeling that Pope was ungrateful for his patronage, and far too unstable to be of service to the Whigs.

By the year 1714 there was almost open war between the two men. The publication of the revised *Lock* in five cantos gained new reputation for Pope and confirmed him in the bad opinion he entertained of Addison's double-dealing. Addison had advised Pope not to include the Sylphs in the new production. Pope had ignored the advice, and now that the poem was a success, he thought he detected a plot in Addison's original objection.

In 1714 Gay published his *Shepherd's Week*. It was intended to be a satire on Philips's *Pastorals* and was detected as such by the wits, but Gay found himself in the enviable position of having written a satire in Pope's behalf which appealed to the general reading public on its own merits.

It is not astonishing: the "Proeme to the Courteous Reader," with its sly charm in the appeal to patriotism and learning, is shot with satire directed toward the critics at Button's. The silly exclamations and ridiculous climaxes of the *Pastorals* themselves, and the heavy footnotes in Greek and Latin, all added to the hilarious fun of the piece. But in writing the work, something of the graceful gaiety of the poet came to the surface of the satire. It abounds with artless and charming touches. The praise of Arbuthnot and the court in the Prologue has a ravishing simplicity which is reflected in other parts of the work:

> Quoth I, please God, I'll hye with Glee
> To Court, this Arbuthnot to see,
> I sold my sheep and Lambkins too,
> For silver loops and Garment blue;
> My boxen Haut-boy sweet of sound,
> For lace that edg'd mine Hat around;
> For *Lightfoot* and my Script I got
> A gorgeous Sword and eke a Knot.

It is satire much like the *Beggar's Opera*. Observed as a whole it is devastating, yet the good humor and grace of the various parts give Gay's pastorals an abounding life of their own which is independent of their satirical intent.

Shortly after Gay's astonishing success with his burlesque shepherds, Parnell, the Irish poet, composed his "Bookworm." It too was directed against Dennis and Philips. These were minor winds before the impending storm, but they indicated —with the epigrams on *Cato*—that Pope and his friends had declared open war against the claque at Button's.

Sometime during the winter of 1713–14 Pope and his intimates formed a club of wits. They called their new organization the Scriblerus Club. The regular members and the most active spirits in the club were Arbuthnot, Gay, Parnell, Swift, and Pope himself. The meetings were held in Arbuthnot's rooms or elsewhere, and the purpose of the club was to ridicule false taste and the antics of ponderous pedants.

Many of the meetings generated nothing more than spontaneous persiflage and witty conversation. If the club had achieved no more than this, it would not deserve to be so long remembered. Actually in some of the meetings the gay company laid plans for future books and projects. From such serious sessions came *Martinus Scriblerus*, the *Art of Sinking*, and part of the design for the *Duncaid* and *Gulliver's Travels*.

Favored guests were sometimes asked to attend special meetings. Among these was the Earl of Oxford, prime minister at the time of the club's greatest activity.

For those who are acquainted with the arch drollery of the little circle, an invitation in rhyme—rescued by Norman Ault from the papers of Lord Oxford—deserves to be quoted. It is in Pope's autograph.

Tho the Dean has run from us in manner uncivil;
The Doctor, and He that's nam'd next to the Devil,
With Gay, who Petition'd you once on a time,
And Parnell, that would, if he had but a Rhyme.
(That Gay the poor Sec. and that arch Chaplain Parnell,
As Spiritual one, as the other is Carnal),
Forgetting their Interest, now humbly sollicit
You'd at present do nothing but give us a Visit.

A. Pope.
That all this true is   T. Parnell
Witness E. Lewis   Jo: Arbuthnot
                                            I. Gay.[3]

The immediate cause of the complete alienation of Pope and Addison was, of course, the translation of *Homer*. Originally Addison had encouraged Pope in the project, but once the subscription was under way he did little or nothing to forward it. Pope had assumed the task because of his desire to make money and enlarge his fame. He was at first appalled by the difficulties. Pope read little Greek, if he read it at all. This was not the complete handicap some have imagined. There was an abundance of good translations, in Latin, Italian, French, and English. Chapman, in particular, had given, more or less, a translation of the exact sense of Homer, and Mme. Dacier, whose edition of Homer Pope had, provided all the necessary material for comments and footnotes. But it was a scholarly time in which Pope lived: he had determined to match the spirit of the age with Greek and Latin footnotes. For these he required the services of precise scholars. The engaging Parnell helped him through the maze of three volumes of Dacier and Valerie, two of Barnes, and the critical labyrinth of "Eustathius, Cuperus, Leo Allatius, Macrobius and Aulus Gellius." When Parnell found it imperative to return to Ireland, Pope by constant importunity of his friends was fortunate enough to find other helpers like Broome.

Pope had determined to make a free translation of *Homer*. It was tedious work but, in the beginning, not too much of a strain. The poet's health was not good, but he wrote many of the couplets while still abed, or even in the middle of the night, and then revised them at leisure, polishing both the sense and the animated flow of the verse.

In all probability, Pope no longer frequented Button's coffeehouse after 1714. It must have been evident to him that Addison's followers were losing no chance to attack him in papers and broadsheets. He could hardly be blamed for feeling that Addison, who ruled the little group with a firm hand, was inimical to his interests. What interested him far more than the old quarrels was the rumor of a rival translation of the first book of the *Iliad* being made by Thomas Tickell and Addison.

This suspicion had become a certainty by 1715. If other evidence were wanting, confirmation of Pope's belief is to be found in the second edition of *A Key to the Lock*. This pamphlet was first published by Pope in April 1715. The *Key* was a rather obvious satire on the *Rape of the Lock*. Pope under the name of Esdras Barnivelt pretended to discover a popish plot behind the airy beauty of the events and characters delineated in his comedy.

In the second edition of the *Key*, published June 1, 1715, the humor of the original production was heightened by dedicatory poems to Mr. Barnivelt. These verses praised him for his services to the nation in exposing the machinations of the new "Popish Plot."

One of these poems, entitled "To my ingenious Friend, the author of the key of the Lock," bears poetic witness of Pope's suspicions of Addison:

> Tho' many a wit from time to time has rose
> T' inform the world of what it *better knows*,
> Yet 'tis a praise that few their own can call,
> To tell Men things they never *knew at all*.
> This was reserved Great *Barnivelt* for Thee,
> To save this land from dangerous Mystery.
> But thou too gently hast laid on thy Satyr;
> What awes the World is *envy* and *ill Nature*.
> Can Popish writings do the Nation good?
> Each drop of ink demands a drop of blood.
> A Papist wears the lawrel? is it fit?
> O Button! summon all thy Sons of Wit!
> Join in the common Cause, e'er 'tis too late;

Rack your Inventions some *in time* translate.
If all this fail, let Faggot, Cart and Rope
Revenge our Wits and Statesman on a Pope.

                     The Grumbler.

In this doggerel Pope states his grievances. "Envy and ill nature" have combined to thwart his ambition and talent. The source of the enmity is his religion, and the plots against him emanate from the clique at Button's. The three lines:

Oh Button! summon all thy Sons of Wit!
Join in the common Cause, e'er 'tis too late;
Rack your Inventions some *in time* translate.

challenged Addison and his friends to do their worst.

Pope was not as brave as his words promised. There was too much at stake. His real friends, like Swift and Caryll, had bustled about the country building a subscription list for his *Homer* which was like a *Who's Who* of the times: 1 princess, 17 dukes, 3 marquises, 49 earls, 7 duchesses, 1 marchioness, and 8 countesses; 9 generals, 10 colonels, and 2 captains; an Irish bishop and 19 members of the clergy; Booth, Cibber, Wilks, Addison, Congreve, Hughes, Rowe, Steele, Swift, Jervas, Newton, Pepush, Meade, and—Courthope maintains—the King and the Prince of Wales. It was a glittering array balanced by the learned world, from which Dublin University and ten Oxford Colleges had subscribed.[4]

If Pope's first volume was successful, he stood to gain some five thousand pounds, but if he failed . . . it was horrible to contemplate. It was necessary to be cautious with Addison.

Pope proceeded cautiously. Burnet had already attacked him in 1714 in his first *Homerides*. His second edition of the same work proved to be not a second edition at all but a new attack. Duckett and others followed the lead of Burnet. These envious sallies Pope could afford to endure in peace until such time as he chose to answer them, or revenge himself. Tickell's translation was another matter, for it was being whispered that Addison was helping with the work. A translation by two Oxford dons offered more than a mere threat to Pope's *Homer*. Addison was at home with Greek and Latin; he was one of the ripest scholars of the times. His translation of the *Metamorphoses* had demonstrated his ability to be colorful, clever —and erotic, a fact too often overlooked in our adulation of his character. He was a far greater threat than the less talented Tickell.

Pope's *Homer*, scheduled to appear in March, was deferred, probably in the hope that Tickell might publish his translation first. When it became apparent he would not, Pope brought out his first book of the *Iliad*, June 6, 1715. Two days later Tickell produced his version with a preface of which Sherburn says: "After all that had passed, it was now somewhat naïve of Tickell and Addison to disclaim rivalry with Pope." (The statement in large type inserted at the front of Tickell's translation said in part: "I must inform the reader, that when I begun this First Book I had some thought of being diverted from the Design by finding that the work was fallen into a much abler hand.")

It was not merely Pope and his friends who were suspicious of the strange coincidence of the simultaneous appearance of the two translations of *Homer:* the whole town was talking. On June 4, before the publication of the rival books, the *Weekly Journal* had declared:

> The Discourse at present among the Learned, is upon the publication of the first Volume of *Homer*, done by the most ingenious Mr. Pope, who had already given us Many Testimonies as he has written Poems, that he alone is equal to so great an undertaking; and this Pleasure is heightened by a Con-

sideration, that those Enemies of Wit who would get a Name
by finding Fault with any Perfection they cannot attain to,
are likely to meet with such Discouragement as Mr. Pope will
with Honour and Applause: We are however advised from
Button's That as their party have engrossed to themselves
the whole Art of Politics, so they will now advance with
Vigour and will continue to make violent Incursions into all
the Provinces of Literature, till they have laid waste all good
Sense as well as Honesty. But as the Fort of *Homer* is the
first Place they set upon, and seems impregnable by Art and
Nature, 'tis believ'd the Siege will be razed and the besiegers
quit with Shame, so heedless a Project, and so unpromising
an Undertaking.

Not satisfied with such a plain statement, on June 11, one
week after the first notice, the *Weekly Journal* returned to
the charge with an item which called Steele and Addison the
inspirers of the plot against Pope.

The *Weekly Journal* paid Pope the compliment of coming
next to Homer himself in rendering the sense and effect of
the *Iliad*. Tickell was dismissed with a satirical reference: he
had imitated Homer in but one thing, his blindness. The notice
concluded with the following epigram:

> As some harsh Critics, who are too severe,
> And verse by Judgment try, as well as Ear,
> 'Gainst *Tickel* as a *Rhiming Falstaff* plead
> For Murth'ring Homer, after he was dead;
> And say our *Isle* could for no pardon hope,
> Were not th' absolving Words bestowed by Pope:
> So by more *Civil* Judges it is said,
> That not ev'n Pope could without *Tickel's* Aid,
> Have rais'd *entire* Homer from the Dead.
> 'Tis plain to reconcile the Difference,
> *This* Bard his *Blindness* shews, and *that* his *Sense*.

[89]

That there had been a patent cabal against Pope can be proved now in the letters and journals of Addison's circle which have come down to us. It is obvious that Addison played some part in the plot. Just how much he had helped in Tickell's translation remains a mystery. Tickell, who knew the whole story, remained silent on the subject all his life. He did not deny, however, that Addison had had a hand in the composition.

Pope was justly incensed against the Buttonians and Joseph Addison. In his moment of triumph, in which facts and precise comparison demonstrated Pope's enormous superiority in translation, Pope's seething rage led him to compose the famous "Atticus sketch," which is one of the finest and most devastating portraits he ever drew. Pope's enemies implied that Pope wrote the lines after Addison's death, which would suggest Pope's cowardice in this act toward a man who was dead and could not answer him. Pope maintained to Spence that he had sent the "Atticus sketch" to Addison about three years before his death and "was used very civilly by Addison ever after." There is every reason to believe Pope rather than his enemies. Several persons, including Lady Mary Wortley Montagu— she was Pope's enemy at the time—have testified they saw the lines in question in Addison's lifetime.

There is further evidence. In 1716 the Buttonians, for no apparent reason, stopped all the attacks against Pope. Addison himself in the *Free-holder* of May 7, 1716, also attempted to make some amends for his conduct by complimenting Pope's *Homer*. In a paper dealing with the hazards of literature and the courage it requires to follow it, Addison said:

The illiterate among our countrymen may learn to judge from Dryden's *Virgil* of the most epic performance: and those parts of *Homer*, which have already been published by

Mr. *Pope*, give us reason to think that the *Iliad* will appear in *English* with as little *disadvantage* to that immortal poem.

Speaking of Rowe's *Lucan* and Pope's *Homer*, Addison remarked at the close, "If the two works last mentioned are finished by those masterly hands, which are now employed in them, we may despair of seeing them attempted by others."

Never had the apostle of good form been shown to such mean advantage as he appeared in his quarrel with Pope. The nineteenth-century biographers of Pope, for the most part, took sides with Addison against Pope, however suspicious the circumstances. Today, with the emergence of additional facts and written evidence, it is obvious that Pope suffered great injustice at the hands of many who wrote about him.

In the characters of Pope and Addison there were qualities which made the struggle between them inevitable. With the death of Dryden, Addison was the undisputed emperor of the literary scene. He had all the outward qualities of cool magnificence which went with the position. With the emergence of Pope, Addison's prominence was challenged by one who, in his shape and background, could have been little more than contemptible to a man of Addison's environment, training, and experience.

From the days of his youth Addison had been an ardent believer in Protestantism. In 1702, while making the "grand tour" of Italy and the Continent, he demonstrated his precise attitude toward religion. In Venice he observed that the end of the state was "to encourage idleness and luxury in the Nobility, to cherish ignorance and licentiousness in the Clergy . . . to connive at the viciousness and debauchery of the convents."

His dislike of the monks is reflected in many places in his journal. He was not astonished at the poverty of the papal kingdom, which "shuts up in the cloisters such an incredible multitude of young and lusty beggars."

The convents were equally ridiculous and evil, the nuns were vicious and time-wasting in following "gross and absurd traditions." Monasteries served one good purpose, like the madhouse, for "all men of bad tempers, according to their degree of melancholy or enthusiasm, may find convents fitted to their humors and meet with companions as gloomy as themselves." In conclusion, Addison was revolted by the "abuse of Indulgencies, the folly and impertinence of Votaries and in Short the Superstition, credulity and childishness of the Roman Catholic Religion." A sense of obvious relief colored his writing when he reached the Protestant parts of Switzerland.

This attitude was intensified in the years which followed Addison's "grand tour." After his poem on Marlborough's campaign, Addison "awoke one morning to find himself famous." He had been made by the *idea* of the Protestant succession; not because he was a hypocrite, but because he ardently believed in that succession, and was willing to prove his belief with deeds.

To see his convictions threatened by a papist and a half-concealed Jacobite (Pope's satire on Settle proved that) was more than a casual challenge to Addison's vanity. It touched him in the secret springs of his being.

But even though the facts which have come to light show Addison at a disadvantage in his final dealings with Pope, it is not necessary to presume that Addison was acting like a cad in treating Pope as he did; he was in truth acting from deepest principle. That paradox should read a lesson to all of us.

A mistake some biographers make is in fancying that Pope was not acting on equally valid principle in opposing Addison. Pope knew he was a genius. The position of subordination offered him by Addison was not acceptable.

And, whatever defects there were in Pope's nature, a narrow outlook on religion was not one of them. He joked about his own faith. He tried to minimize its importance for others out of charity for their weakness and intemperateness. But no man could ever accuse him of slighting the religion of any person.

Yet, in a way, he felt himself to be the actual champion of enlightened Catholicism; his first criticisms of Dennis and Settle are strong proofs of this. His sweeping condemnation of religious persecution in *Windsor Forest*, condemnation which had passed largely unnoticed, is more telling evidence of the same thing. Pope, in 1714, felt capable of forcing an issue with Addison; he did not show himself wanting in bravery by acting on that conviction.

In the quarrel which ensued, Addison made two mistakes: first, he fancied it was he who threw down the gage, and it never occurred to him that there could be any doubt of the outcome of the struggle; second, he thought he was selecting the field on which the battle was to be fought. In entering the field of great poetry, he demonstrated a fatuousness which caused him to underestimate his own and Pope's capabilities. Had he selected religion and politics instead of literature, he would have won the struggle with the same bland ease which characterized his usual conduct.

It must have occasioned Addison considerable chagrin to find that Pope had won the contest not merely because he was the greater poet, but because he was the better man.

5

The Cautious Venus

Love seldom haunts the breast where learning lies.
The Wife of Bath

POPE'S triumph was complete—perfect as supreme things
are perfect! He had played a game of fence with one who was
thought to have all the odds on his side. Now, more than ever,
the victorious poet knew with every curve of his mind and
every twist of his body that it was dangerous to be so intelligent without that pinch of the serpent to safeguard the flight
of the dove into the sun. Yet, remembering the shadows of
recent terror, Pope realized also there was more than a flash of
the providential about his success. His assiduous reading of the
Psalms and the Wisdom of Solomon drove that point home
to his consciousness. The world is full of traps and gins—it is
also pregnant with surprises.

But, of course, Pope's triumph was far more than a personal
one. It had a touch of the immortal in the work he had spun,
and labored, and hammered, and wrought; that would stand
witness to him while music, balance, and beauty were dear to
the children of men. The work itself—it was good. It was perfect after the fashion of a Greek temple. If you chose to walk
around it or saunter through it, you marveled at its simplicity
of line and obvious rhythms of balance. But ever and anon

as you contemplated the regular march of its columns and the
evenly set tympanums, the light struck a great chord from it.

The town read the glittering couplets, and praise poured
upon Pope in a bright stream. Gay and Swift were pleased;
his noble friends took to themselves some credit for the
achievement; his Catholic intimates and acquaintances, who
had subscribed at the insistence of Caryll, found themselves
proud of "one of their own."

Addison, because of his close connection with Dryden, had
considered himself the heir apparent to the throne of poetry.
Now he was thrust aside and disinherited. The whole fashionable world went running after the funny little papist with the
hunched back. Whigs, Tories, Garters, ancient names, great
lineage of blood, ladies in waiting, their pert, patched faces
lifted under the glow of the candles, all went to look on the
wonderful little monster, and were taken captive by his wit and
awareness.

Pope had demonstrated his superiority over Tickell, Addison, and the Buttonians. The result was more a revelation than
a demonstration; he had, in fact, produced in verse an English
edition of *Homer* which has stood unrivaled ever since. Other
poets have translated, perhaps, more accurately the exact sense
of Homer. Precision of language itself is no absolute guarantee
of supreme excellence in translation. A feeling for the movement and texture of an author is important: it suggests something of the intuitions of genius to be able to see into the mind
of the original creator. This is Pope's excellence. Uninhibited
by the necessity of translating Homer word for word, he was
free to put into his translation the feeling and movement
characteristic of the blind bard himself. Pope had a further
advantage. Casting aside the obvious temptation to imitate in
English the musical pattern of Homer, Pope translated in
heroic couplets. The couplet had become in his hands a supple

instrument which made its employment easy, varied, and musical in the extreme.

The nineteenth-century romantics would admit none of this excellence. They were content to scorn the "mechanical flatness" of Pope's verse. The heroic couplet was precise—exact as geometrical forms are exact. Within its artful repetitions ideas took memorable shape. Sometimes they had the precise beauty of snow crystals; sometimes they were baroque and exuberant. In consequence, Pope transferred much of the inscape of his author, not set to its old music but to new combinations of sounds equally valid and equally amazing. A man bent on translating the exact sense of an author labors under one obvious handicap. If, in addition to this, he should attempt to catch the precise texture of the original music in its nearest English verse equivalent, he is burdened in a double sense: the best he can hope for is an imitation, of lesser intensity. By escaping both temptations Pope produced a new work of art, essentially his own, yet essentially Homer's.

Until 1720, Pope was to be more or less chained to his work of translation. It grew oppressive to him as the years flew swiftly by.

Pope's letters to his friends are loud with complaints. He did not gain in health from the long confinement which flouted Radcliffe's prescription. The migraine half blinded his great eyes, the curvature of his spine grew worse, he lost his beloved father, and his mother's illness delayed the final book of the *Iliad*, which did not appear until 1720.

Not all Pope's problems were concerned with his own family or his own bad health. The Jacobite conspiracy of 1715 and its suppression led to a renewed and bitter outcry against Catholics. Once more the bonfires were lit. Men marched with knives and muskets; faces of neighbors and friends were twisted in disdain or hatred while the great bells jangled and set men's teeth on edge. Stringent new laws were passed against the papists. They were required to take the revised oaths of allegiance or suffer the usual penalties. Such was the continued alarm that many frightened Catholics took the oaths and conformed. Pope was not one of these: he refused the oaths and prepared for the worst. The Popes, like other Catholics, were thrown into a panic by a new measure before Parliament. The new law required Catholics to register their estates for the purpose of levying special taxes to defray the expenses of putting down the Scottish rebellion. Let the English Catholics pay for the war touched off by their Jacobite brethren across the border! Many Catholics sold their houses and lands in order to escape the crushing new levies. A considerable number emigrated to the Continent.

Pope's father disposed of his beloved refuge at Binfield, and early in 1716 transferred his family to Chiswick under the protection of the magnificent Lord Burlington. Pope seems to hint at Burlington's interest in a letter to Caryll:

> My father and mother having disposed of their little estate at Binfield, I was concerned to find out some asylum for their old age: and these cares of settling and furnishing a house have employed me till yesterday, when we fixed at Chiswick under the wing of my Lord Burlington.[1]

This letter is cheerful. It demonstrates Pope's natural optimism and the possible assurance he had received from his noble friend of personal security against molestation. There is evidence that Catholics and nonjurors living in Windsor Forest were under some particular threat from the new laws. In their seclusion and fancied security, they had perhaps grown a shade careless in expressing their opinions, and now feared to be called a nest of suspects.

Something of the tremendous apprehension of Pope and

those living in the Forest is mirrored in a letter Pope wrote to Caryll at this time:

> If the whole religious business of mankind be included in resignation to our Maker, and charity to our fellow creatures, there are now some people who give us the opportunity of affording as bright an example in practising one, as themselves have given an infamous instance of the violation of the other. Whoever is really brave has always this comfort, when he is oppressed, that he knows himself to be superior to those who injure him; for the greatest power on earth can no sooner do him that injury, but the brave man can make himself greater by forgiving it. If it were generous to seek for alleviating consolations in a calamity of so much glory, one might say that to be ruined thus in the gross with a whole people is but like perishing in the general conflagration, where nothing we can value has been left behind us.
>
> Methinks, in our present condition, the most heroic thing we are left capable of doing is to endeavour to lighten each other's load, and, oppressed as we are, to succour such as are yet more oppressed. If there are too many who cannot be assisted by what we cannot give, our money, there are yet others who may be relieved by our counsel, by our countenance and even by our cheerfulness. The misfortunate of private families, the misunderstandings [of people] whom distress makes suspicious, the coldness of relations whom change of religion may disunite, or the necessities of half-ruined estates render unkind to each other,—these at least may be softened some degree by a general well-managed humanity among ourselves, if all those who have your principles had also your sense and conduct. But indeed most of them have given lamentable proofs of the contrary: and it may be apprehended that they who want sense are only religious through fear, and good-natured through shame. These are narrow-minded creatures, that never deal in essentials; their faith never looks beyond ceremonials, nor their [char-

ity] beyond relations. As poor as I am, I would gladly relieve any distressed conscientious French refugee at this instant. What must my concern then be, when I perceive so many anxieties just now springing up in those hearts which I have desired a place in, and such clouds of melancholy rising on those faces I have so long looked upon with affection? I begin already to feel both what some apprehend, and what others are yet too stupid to apprehend. I grieve with the old for so many additional inconveniences and chagrins, more than their small remains of life was to undergo; and with the young for so much of those gaieties and pleasures, the portion of youth, as they will by this means be deprived of. This brings into my mind one or other I love best, the widow and fatherless late of Mapledurham. As I am certain no people living had an earlier and truer sense of other's misfortunes, or a more generous resignation as to what might be their own, so I earnestly wish that whatever part they must bear of these may be rendered as supportable to them as it is in power of any friend to make it. They are beforehand with us in being out of house and home by their brother's marriage; and I wish they had not some cause already to look upon Mapledurham with such sort of melancholy as we may upon our seats when we lose them.

I write this from Windsor Forest, to which I am come to take my last look and leave of. We here bid our papist neighbors adieu, much as those who go to be hanged do their fellow prisoners, who are condemned to follow them a few weeks after. . . . I parted from honest Mr. Dancastle with tenderness and from old Sir William Trumbull as from a venerable prophet, foretelling with lifted hands the miseries to come upon posterity, which he was just going to be removed from. Perhaps now I have learned so far as *Nos dulcia linquimus arva*, the next may be *Nos patriam fugimus*. Let that, and all else be as Heaven pleases! For the rest, I shall ever be, dear sir, most faithfully and gratefully yours, and all your family's.[2]

It is not necessary to presume that Pope was dramatizing himself or was playing upon the sympathies of his favorite correspondent. He had refused the oaths; anything might happen. He may have considered emigration or the possibility of it.

In April, 1716, the Popes were settled in Mawson's Buildings at Chiswick. The same old currents of anonymous attack, in pasquinades and newspapers, had once again begun to flow over the unhappy shoulders of Homer's translator. Likely as not, the event of that unhappy year most satisfactory to Pope was his action in giving an emetic to Curll, the publisher. That worthy gentleman had added another terror to his reputation by publishing without authority a series of satires called *Court Poems*.

In the preface to the *Court Poems*, Curll had boldly ascribed the satirical verses to Pope, Gay, and "a lady of quality." The publication of pirated poems of this sort containing strictures on Court personages was of particular danger to Pope, since the poems had appeared in the midst of a new persecution of papists. This, alone, may well have been the source of Pope's determination to punish Curll, though his decision to do so must certainly have been strengthened by his chivalrous regard for Lady Mary Wortley Montagu and John Gay.

Whether it was Pope's own danger or his romantic feeling which fired him, he took swift revenge. With the aid of Arbuthnot and the connivance of Lintot, he met Curll at Lintot's shop, and reproached him for publishing the poems. Curll apologized and they drank a glass of sack together. Into this potion Pope had conveyed a purge and an emetic. The moment Curll was in the throes of agony, a pamphlet was hawked about the streets. It must have been prepared in advance. It retailed for the public the complete story of Curll's mischance, and

was entitled *A Full and True Account of a Horrid and Bar-
barous Revenge by Poison on the Body of Mr. Edmund Curll.*

History furnishes us with examples of satyrical authors
who have fallen sacrifices to revenge, but not of any booksellers that I know of, except the unfortunate subject of the
following paper; I mean Mr. Edmund Curll, at the Bible
and Dial in Fleet-street, who was yesterday poisoned by Mr.
Pope, after having lived many years an instance of the mild
temper of the British nation.

Every body knows that the said Mr. Edmund Curll, on
Monday, the 26th instant published a satyrical piece, entitled Court-poems in the preface whereof they were attributed to a lady of quality, Mr. Pope or Mr. Gay; by which
indiscreet method, though he had escaped one revenge, there
were still two behind in reserve.

Now on the Wednesday ensuing, between the hours of ten
and eleven, Mr. Lintot a neighbouring bookseller, desired a
conference with Mr. Curll about settling a title-page, inviting him at the same time to take a whet together, Mr. Pope,
who is not the only instance how persons of bright parts
may be carried away by the instigation of the devil, found
means to convey himself into the same room, under the pretense of business with Mr. Lintot, who, it seems, is the printer
of his Homer. This gentleman with a seeming coolness,
reprimanded Mr. Curll wrongly ascribing to him the afore-
said poems; he excused himself by declaring, that one of his
authors (Mr. Oldmixon by name) gave the copies to the press
and wrote the preface. Upon this Mr. Pope, being to all appearances reconciled, very civilly drank a glass of sack to
Mr. Curll, which he as civilly pledged; and though the
liquor, in colour and taste, differed not from common sack,
yet it was plain, by the pangs this unhappy stationer felt
soon after, that some poisonous drug had been secretly in-
fused therein.

What follows the introductory paragraphs is not on so high a plane. Indeed, Pope descends to vulgarity, which, in a sense, distracts from the comical parts of the production.

The will evoked by Curll's conviction that he is really dying is very well done. It has felicitous touches such as the aside, "Only God bless Sir Richard Blackmore! you know he takes no copy money." Lintot's question to Oldmixon when he is certain Curll will die is equally comical: "Why not find another bookseller, brother Oldmixon?" and then took Mr. Oldmixon aside and whispered to him: "Sir as soon as Curll is dead I shall be glad to talk with you over a pint at the Devil." It is a sterling example of the ways of eighteenth-century publishers.

Pope had exceeded in the vulgar details of his pamphlet, but it is interesting to know that Curll remembered the emetic for years, and the rumor of it frightened Oldmixon into a lying denial of being the author of the preface to the *Court Poems* or the instrument of having purveyed the poems themselves.

Curll was punished, but the results of that punishment were to haunt Pope for some decades. Curll was to gather up and publish every scrap of the "men's-room" poetry Pope wrote in his most exuberant moments. In addition to this, Curll became the solid core of the opposition to Pope which, after the failure of the Buttonian conspiracy against him, might have fallen away into something scattered and sporadic. In purging Curll, Pope in a sense had purged himself.

Being a papist and a satirist, it was inevitable that Pope should have had enemies. Many of Pope's enemies were party men and hack writers who lacked Pope's intuition in detecting the tragic flaws in men, or those exaggerations in manners, posture, and dress, which are the only stuff of valid satire. Pope's enemies used things more understandable to the mob.

Their efforts, in consequence, have not the immortal qualities found in Pope's best personal satire. In their own fashion, however, they have an immortality of sorts—the immortality of mud. Pope was abused for being a papist, a crooked and ungrateful friend, a liar, an atheist, and a rake. These accusations were not made first in generalities: they appeared in pamphlets and reported conversations, in scandalous chronicles such as Eliza Heywood's *Memoirs of a certain Island adjacent to the Kingdom of Utopia*, and an anonymous publication, *The Life of the late Celebrated Mrs. Elizabeth Wisebourn, vulgarly call'd Mother Wybourn*. They suggested, by implication, innuendo, and double-meaning, actions and attitudes of mind for which any confirmation was lacking, beyond that of gossip or the suspicions of dirty minds.

Of all such accusations, two have had the longest life: Pope's "deism," and his "immorality." However, as patient modern scholars turn over the letters and diaries of the time, as new facts emerge into the light of day, it is becoming more obvious that Pope's immorality was a figment in the minds of men who disliked him.

His relations with women were conditioned by two things. The first of these was his misshapen body: he was humpbacked and emaciated, his legs were spindles, and he had to be laced into a canvas corset every day of his life. He was only four and a half feet tall, and though his face was fine, as Joshua Reynolds attests, and his comments on life showed devastating wit, yet almost everything about his person unfitted him for affairs of gallantry. In his early youth he went about in the company of young sparks and gallants; he loved to think himself daring and rakish. Although his spine and his headaches unfitted him for such a life he could brag and talk about it, he could make rhymed jokes, vulgar in the extreme, but seldom more vulgar than witty.

The second quality which conditioned his dealings with "the fair" was an incredible mannered gallantry, like the love dance of the praying mantis. Pope had fed his mind with the highly spiced effusions of the Renaissance: the Lauras and Beatrices, the dukes and the duchesses of sixteenth-century England and fourteenth-century Italy. For him, woman was still on the pedestal she had usurped from the Virgin. She was still worthy of the whole complicated ritual with which the intellectual amorists had replaced the ceremonial dedicated to the Mother of God. In Pope's age woman had become an end in herself. She had come down from her pedestal to become a female wit, or a beauty whose love had monetary value because of its uses for pleasure. But, for Pope, she was still enthroned.

His tenderness toward his mother and Mary Beech declared part of Pope's mind; his gallant letters to the Duchess of Marlborough, certainly long past the age for love or gallantry, were a telling commentary on Pope's romanticism, which reached a climax in his complimentary letters to Lady Mary Wortley Montagu, and in his poems, *To the Memory of an Unfortunate Lady* and *Eloisa to Abelard*.

Had Pope been blessed with bodily vigor, we can see from the sugar and flame of his romantic poems how entirely he would have committed himself to the experience of human love. *To the Memory of an Unfortunate Lady* falls merely within the realm of the pathetic, but in *Eloisa* the revelation goes much deeper. As G. Wilson Knight has indicated, this poem is intensely dramatic; it occupies the same level of tragedy, and exposes the same elements of eros-exaltation as those found in Shakespeare's *Antony and Cleopatra*. It is all for love in Antony's mind, the denial of an empire for the sake of love; in the mind of Eloise the denial of God himself, if Abelard were to ask it. Pope showed considerable psychological subtlety in his analyses of the heart and mind of woman in his *Eloisa*, but the poem is a still greater revelation of Pope's own personal psychology and his whole outlook on love.

In Shakespeare's *Antony and Cleopatra* we have the existence and enjoyment of warm passionate love and sexual ecstasy. These realities give to the two chief characters natural depth and richness. We are forced to believe in them. They awaken our sympathy with their philosophy: all for love, nothing without love.

Pope's Eloisa and Abelard function against a total dissimilarity of background. They are absent from each other, and the whole burden of the poem rests upon Eloisa's recollection of Abelard's love and its ultimate meaning. Most important of all, we see that it is an intellectual conception of love which Pope is drawing. It differs from Antony's because Eloisa has not physical possession of the loved one, and as a consequence has nothing to renounce but her own exotic imagination. This is the weakness of Pope's conception of love. It is an intellectual conception which demands exaggerated imaginative contrasts to warm its coldness, such as Eloisa's appeal to Abelard "to aid the fiend and tear me from my God."

Such exaggeration, without its natural background of love and passion, does not measure up to the idea of genuine drama which is supposed to hold a mirror up to nature. It is, rather, a conceit. Any attempt to make of this poem a mysticism of love is destined to failure. *Eloisa* does not express a true mysticism but a conceit of love.

Eloisa should be of special interest to Pope scholars in that it reveals the secret of Pope's dealings with women. When writing or acting as a great poet he employed the conceit: drama, high-flown language, exaggerated compliment. These sum up an intellectual conception of what love could be in the grand style, not what love is in fact.

There was another element in Pope's understanding of woman: a corollary of the first. Women elicited a tender response from him, such as he had toward puppies and feeble things which required his protection. It was an attitude of gallant kindness. This attitude is demonstrated in his love for his mother and Mary Beech, and for Martha Blount, and in his ready sympathy for Mrs. Weston and Mrs. Cope.

Pope did write bawdy occasional verse which was picked up in "pocketbooks" and elsewhere, and published without his consent. Pointing to this as a background of immorality, his enemies (and some of his biographers as well) sieved his life, letters, and poems for anything which would deepen the picture of the poet's moral weakness.

With the publication of the poem *Elegy to the Memory of an Unfortunate Lady*, the fashionable world, and even the unfashionable world of Pope's friend Caryll, began to ask Pope questions about the lady he had portrayed. Pope ignored the queries, for of course he had got the whole story out of his own lively imagination. Shorn of its special circumstances, it is related to any of the thousand stories which float about in romantic novels, like those read in servants' quarters or hid under the mattresses of adolescent girls to whom love is still a speculative *frisson*.

Pope's failure to answer Caryll's questions, significant enough in itself, led to the construction of a romance between himself and the Lady. Warburton gave a suggestion of reality to the affair by saying in a note to the poem, published after Pope's death: "See the duke of Buckingham's verses to a Lady designing to retire into a monastery, compared with Mr. Pope's letters to several ladies. . . . She seems to be the same person whose unfortunate death is the subject of the poem."

Taking Warburton's clue, Ayre in his life of Pope[3] embroidered a lively tale in which the poet himself became the hero. Sir John Hawkins later produced the name of the woman: "The unfortunate lady's name was Withinbury pronounced Winbury." Bowles took these hints and others to deepen the mystery surrounding the story by substituting a French Lord in place of Pope, thus exalting the story to the snobbish level of romance popular in his own day. All this nonsense, including the speculations of Courthope, who desired to deal with the subject on a reasonable basis, are entirely nugatory.

Apply the same reasoning to other famous authors and the stupidity of the method becomes at once apparent. Shakespeare must have known Malvolio, Antony, Juliet, Othello, Desdemona, and all the crowded humanity of his scenes. Chaucer must have looked into the eyes of the forsaken Criseyde and walked the walls of Troy.

Shakespeare had known his characters well and so had Chaucer. They knew them in their own imaginations, minds, and intuitions, in the same way that Pope knew the unfortunate lady. There were real women in his life: his mother, his aunt, Mary Beech, Teresa and Martha Blount, Mary Lapel, and the unforgetable Lady Mary Wortley Montagu. There is no necessity to look for imaginary women between the lines of

Of Mrs. Weston and Mrs. Cope, it is sufficient to say that Pope considered them abused by their husbands. The interest he took in attempting to aid them had nothing in it but the purest altruism. Pope was perhaps a shade meddlesome in the affairs of Mrs. Weston, and his ready sympathy with her sorrow may have lengthened the misunderstanding between her husband and herself.[4]

The aid he gave to Mrs. Cope was amply justified. Her husband had forsaken her and had bigamously married a French woman, Eulalia Morell. Pope did everything possible to alleviate Mrs. Cope's anguish, and he made her a small allowance up to the time of her death in France.[5] His intense sympathy with wronged or suffering women often led him to lend too willing an ear to their stories and tears.

Pope's relations with Lady Mary Wortley Montagu gave considerable fuel to enemies who had an itch to blacken his character. Very likely she was one of the social lights who thronged about the little poet in 1715, when his *Iliad*, the *Rape of the Lock*, and his witty conversation had made him the most sought-after person in England. The rich and the noble, whose sated lives are often dull, were glad of a chance to meet a stimulating personality, and Pope was more than willing to oblige their importunity. He was particularly willing to cultivate them if they were or had been in the government: not from snobbishness, which some have too readily believed, but because, as a papist, those in power and sympathetic to him could afford him protection in moments of danger or crisis. Trumbull, Lansdowne, Harley, Craggs, Bolingbroke, the Caesars, Harcourt, Fortescue, and, best of all, Mrs. Howard, later Countess of Suffolk, could reassure "the highest quarters" of Pope's virtue and constancy. Probably Pope met Wortley Montagu through some of his government friends and in turn was introduced to his wife, Lady Mary. She was then at the height of her wit and beauty. Her conversation and repartee made her companionship delightful to one of Pope's quickness and sharp wit. They became close friends at once, with a summer swiftness.

In the portraits of Lady Mary which have come down to us, she is shown as a somewhat cow-eyed young person, with a saucy twist of nose and lips. In her youth she was considered one of the great beauties of her time.

It is not necessary to abuse Lady Mary for the sake of arriving at definite conclusions regarding her friendship with

Pope. This seems to have been decorous enough, and received the full encouragement of her husband. Then, when her husband became ambassador to the Sublime Porte and Lady Mary departed to join him, Pope was to all appearances affected by the interruption. He followed the lady with a shower of letters which revealed his own inner attitude toward love. In a sense the letters to Lady Mary *sound* like genuine love letters, but they are in truth a mere form, filled to the brim with compliment and florid comparisons. Pope spent less ink bewailing the agonies of separation than he did in attempting to be witty, entertaining, and passionate in the grand style of some minor poet of the *quattrocento*. The letters are, like his *Eloisa*, a conceit of love. Noble love expects such agonies, and Pope did his best to live up to the rules of the game. The letters are tortured and artificial; not in any sense the passionate torrent flowing from the pen of an actual lover. In his letters Pope compared the Lady to the stock divinities of the court poets; like a true papist he invoked her guardian angel and the saints in her behalf. Lady Mary's factual answers were not designed to put an end to the game but to stimulate it. She clearly loved Pope's flattery and recognized it as such. In appearing to dismiss Pope's flatteries, Lady Mary inspired him to further flights of fancy.

Theirs was a literary friendship which demanded conceits. The publication of the pirated *Court Ballads* was a good instance of the community of interests on which the friendship with Lady Mary was based. Had George I been handsome, witty, or attractive, had he possessed one iota of the fatal charm of the Stuarts, Pope would have suffered for the satire in the *Court Ballads*. For the sake of the Protestant succession the ruling oligarchy was content to put up with many things. In public, and hedged in by the trappings of state, Hanoverian royalty was not too unkingly; but behind the scenes, in the discreet upper circles, it was laughable. The dull court provided ample fuel for satire. Pope's punishment of Curll could be accepted by the oligarchy as a gallant gesture in defense of "a lady of quality" who had implied what everyone in the inner circle was saying. The publication itself was not malign, but indiscreet.

Whatever its implications for the public and the oligarchy, *Court Ballads* is valid early evidence of the similarity of tastes and personality which drew Lady Mary into close friendship with Pope, Gay, and their circle.

Dante's friendship and adoration of Beatrice had stimulated him to composition. Lady Mary also impelled Pope toward the expression of the conceits of love. The *Elegy*, *Eloise to Abelard*, and *On Two Lovers Struck Dead by Lightning* are the best fruits of Pope's literary admiration of his lady. They express his feeling of what should be, rather than what was. They are defective because of their excessive sentimentality, but they are excellent in their intellectual appreciation of what love for love's sake should expect and possibly demand.

By the time Lady Mary had returned from Constantinople, Pope was living at Twickenham. A thousand schemes were dancing in his head. He wanted to create a little paradise in which he could be the center of fashionable and witty life. Nothing would serve but that Lady Mary should take a house in the vicinity. Readily falling in with the idea, Lady Mary rented a place, which Pope himself had found, where she and Pope and Gay could consult about their writings and be witty over the world and its foibles. It all promised high comedy and happy hours.

This physical propinquity marked the beginning of the end of the friendship. To serve a divinity in absence makes it possible to preserve all the highest and holiest elements of adoration. Daily service at close range begets all those contemptible things of contemptuous familiarity. If, as the wit has said, "a martyr is one who lives with a saint," it may be alleged with equal validity that a cynic is one who lives with a divinity.

Whether the cause of the break was the sheets Lady Mary borrowed (she was penurious in the extreme), or the harpsichord Pope was not allowed to lend her for a concert, or the lady's widening the bases of her satire to threaten the security of those who protected Pope cannot be determined today from the conflicting evidence which has come down to us. Pope loved his mother deeply. Her unlettered common sense would not have a high opinion of Lady Mary's wit, brilliance, and careless good breeding. The affair of the borrowed sheets or the unborrowed harpsichord would seem to indicate there was bad blood between the two women.

After examining the facts, Sherburn suggests that the friendship was terminated by Lady Mary's satire on Mrs. Murray; a callous attack on a friend of Pope's who had been saved from rape through her quick presence of mind. Pope's enemies had at once attributed the anonymous satire to Pope. Sherburn also implies that Lady Mary's satires or jibes at Pope's powerful Tory protectors and Lady Mary's failure to own her satirical performances, once they had got into print, may have been contributing causes in the rapid decline of their friendship.[6]

Pope's security depended far less on his Tory friends than on the great Whig Lords and the Whigs in the government, such as Secretary Craggs. These were friends and correspondents of his who, like the Master of the Rolls, gave him assistance in secret financial transactions. A cordial friendship with Lady Mary, whose husband was an intimate member of the Whig oligarchy, was sure to provide a ready channel for carrying malicious gossip or satirical performances got up in moments of fun. Reports of such trivial things might have the direst consequences, and cut at the very roots of Pope's safety.

Foundation for this inference is seen in Pope's subsequent actions toward Lady Mary. The moment their friendship was over, Pope in devious ways took particular pains to warn Sir Robert Walpole against the satirical slights of the lady:

> I have seen Sir R.W. but once since you left [Pope wrote to his friend Fortescue]. I made him then my confidant in a complaint against a lady, of his, and once of my acquaintance, who is libelling me, as she certainly one day will him, if she has not already. You will easily guess I am speaking of Lady Mary. I should be sorry if she had any credit or influence with him, for she would infallibly use it to belie me; though my only fault towards her was, leaving off her conversation when I found it dangerous.[7]

Lady Mary was not at all discreet in publicizing what she maintained was the cause of the break between herself and Pope. According to her version of the affair, Pope had made a romantic declaration of love, which had occasioned her immediate laughter, which in turn had hurt the little poet. Being a woman, Lady Mary could safely advance such reasons with every hope of having them believed.

Her actions belied her words: there is evidence in them of the fury of a woman scorned. This may indicate her inability to determine on what grounds she had offended the poet. The brazen circulation of her defense and the surreptitious strokes against Pope's personality did not originate in the quiet confidence of the innocent, but in the fury of the scorned.

In the beginning, Pope let her gossip and personalities pass in silence. When he first lashed out against her in the second book of the *Dunciad*, it was in an oblique fashion, a threat of what he might do rather than being an actual execution:

> (Whence hapless Monsieur much complains at Paris
> Of wrongs from Duchesses and Lady Maries);

The aside referred to an accusation that Lady Mary had defrauded Rémond, a French gallant, of a considerable sum of money in the bursting of the South Sea Bubble. The gossip was known only to a few of Lady Mary's intimate friends. Pope's glancing reference could have done little harm had Lady Mary been wise enough to remain silent or had she feigned indifference.

Undeterred by the threat, Lady Mary with the aid of Lord Hervey perpetuated the *Verses Addressed to the Imitator of Horace*, and the *Popp upon Pope*. Pope eventually retorted in kind with his scathing portraits of Lady Mary as "Sappho" and of her helper, Lord Hervey, as "Sporus."

The verses to the imitator of Horace and the *Popp upon Pope* are cruelly personal: they abuse Pope's poetry, lineage, habits, and person. In answering such vituperation with personalities which were a combination of vitriol and hot lead, Pope should not be blamed. The white heat of fury was deserved, and if the portraits of "Sporus" and "Sappho" are thought undignified or revengeful, the abusive climate of Pope's age should be recalled, and the perpetual shower of bitter shafts, most of them anonymous, which fell upon his crippled shoulders year after year, many times for no better reason than his religious affiliation. These slurs could be endured from venal writers who had no social standing; but to suffer such "slings and arrows" from persons in the highest stratum of society, and, in the case of Lord Hervey, from the very court circle itself, was not to be thought of. The immortal spleen of Pope's "Sporus" and "Sappho" does not prove Pope's bad manners or eternal hatred. Those characters are rather prime examples of a hard-hitting age which did not believe in fighting the devil with rose water.

To Lady Mary's scornful nobility, Pope was no better than a "link boy." She paired him with Swift in using this term of complete nonentity. They were nullities like the automatons that lit her to her barge or stood impassive in courtyards where her coach waited. Pope would be quick to pour out the depths of his wrath upon such bourgeois complacency. Why bow and cringe to such an adversary? There were other modes for such inhumanists. Fight the devil with fire! Sandalwood and attar of roses for the fair, but for the foul—sulphur and hellish brimstone.

The curious things about this much-discussed quarrel are some of the succeeding circumstances. Pope always kept portraits of Lady Mary on his walls: a painting in the room facing the Thames, and a drawing in the great parlor. Of course, they were valuable, and Pope was stingy about destroying things of value. Lady Mary made no attempt to harm Pope by lying about factual things which might have hurt him irreparably; her witness to the existence of the Addison portrait proves that. Her attacks on Pope were more personal than harmful.

The complete story of their love and hate has remained and will probably remain a mystery, but whatever the unknown facts may be concerning the friendship of Pope and the lady, their ultimate quarrel arose in a large part from conflicts of personality. The real harm came when the goddess descended from her pedestal. In doing so she proved to be a mere woman, and a malicious female wit at that.[8]

Yet in those secret places of the poet's heart where ideals kept their spacious halls intact among the ruin about them, pictures of Lady Mary, the goddess, still shone out from the walls, speaking of what had been or what might have been, though all the world, even the goddess herself, denied the dogmas that made her what she was.

In spite of the bitter experience, Pope sped on to new triumphs as a translator and philosopher, while Lady Mary gradually went downhill. She spent her final year on the continent, an untidy old woman with a disfiguring sore on her face, among other eccentric females such as Molly Skerret and Lady Pomfret. Ruins of beauty on both sides: neither justice nor truth is served in abuse of either party.

Of the other women in Pope's life, the two who have most engrossed the attention of Pope's enemies and inimical biographers are the sisters, Teresa and Martha Blount. In his childhood acquaintance with these young girls, Pope was at first attracted to the lively Teresa. She was beautiful and quick, while Martha was of an opposite disposition: shy and retiring, but invariably good-humored. Pope's letters to the two girls in the early stages of their friendship are, on the whole, some of the most natural letters he ever wrote. The only artificial passages in them occur in the parts where Pope fancied it incumbent upon him to pay extravagant compliments, such as he paid the Duchess of Marlborough and Lady Mary.

All that was happiest in Pope's life looks out through the bars of gracious gaiety in his early epistles to the two sisters: life in the chequered sun and shade of Mapledurham and Whiteknights; the charm of virtues enjoyed, confidences and private jokes shared among them.

The death of their father and the marriage of their elder brother changed the tranquil character of the girls' lives. It was necessary now for them to leave Mapledurham, and they transferred to Bolton Street, London. Pope was tireless in his offers of assistance and help: he knew their fortunes were constricted by the move, and that after 1715 their very safety was threatened by the revived and strengthened penal laws. He visited them often and sent them presents, multiplied their money in South Sea stock, and became woven into the fabric of their existence.

A capricious strain in her nature, and a sensitive strain in Pope's disposition, ultimately caused coldness and enmity between Pope and Teresa. In her straitened circumstances she had apparently suggested to the poet some need of an allowance. Pope took her suggestion in earnest and found upon its execution that he had offended her pride. He was bitterly hurt by her attitude, but after apologies had been made, the poet returned again to the family circle on something of the old carefree footing.

In the course of the misunderstanding, Pope had come to value the good-natured temper of Martha more than the intellectual dash and style of her sister Teresa. Perhaps his obvious preference for Martha may have accentuated the misunderstanding between himself and Teresa, or, like as not, it gained further force from the fact that enmity feeds on the consciousness of guilt. One injustice breeds another. In any event, Pope learned to distrust Teresa more and more. Well before the close of his life, the poet concluded she had slandered him in many ways.

With Martha, it was different. In her, Pope found the good humor and understanding he relied on among his men friends. He found it in an exaggerated sense; for, wanting her sister's brilliance, Martha expected nothing from him but sincerity.

The friendship deepened with the years. Time with his scythe took away the father Pope loved; Gay, with his merry heart; and Pope's dearly adored mother. Only in Martha did he find the ready sympathy and ease of friendship his heart craved. With the rich and the noble, Pope was always on show: the "crooked monkey" performing. He was expected to be witty and animated; he was called upon to give perpetual evidence of the genius within him. But there was nothing to love.

As a consequence, Martha Blount became a necessity to him: she followed him about the country when he visited his powerful, noble, or witty friends. She was not necessary to him as a wife is to a husband, or as a mistress is to a lover, but as one human being is to another: for confidences, for solace, for all those thousand arts of understanding which make a man's closest friends at once a relaxation and a fortress. Pope's letters to Martha Blount show the progress of the relationship and its gradual deepening and enrichment. They lack the fluid artificiality of the letters he wrote to other women: women who touched his gallantry and stimulated him to the conceits of love so obvious in his letters to Teresa, to Lady Mary, and to Judith Cowper.

Most of Pope's friends seem to have understood the poet's fondness for Martha and his need of her, but there were some who found the affair suspect. There is every indication that Martha Blount traveled with her maid and usually saw Pope in the presence of others. His reliance on her was obvious; he was a cripple and depended on a great many kindnesses of hosts and servants for even the shreds of comfort.

But there was considerable talk, it is evident; not all Pope's friends were as civilized as Gay, Bathurst, and Swift, who loved and admired Martha Blount. The jealous Teresa, perhaps, seeing herself deposed from the triumvirate, whispered gossip about Pope and Martha. Pope suspected she had done so, and there were many of his enemies and some of his friends who found in the whispered gossip some crystallization of their own suspicions.

Among those who were suspicious of his relations with "Mrs. Martha," apart from the venal hacks who accused him of every crime in the calendar, was Mrs. Ralph Allen. Pope's acquaintance with the Allens came late in his life, after the pirated publication of his letters. Reading them and being struck with their benevolence and high tone, Allen conceived a deep admiration for Pope. A complimentary correspondence ensued, and a friendship sprang up.

Allen was a wealthy man. He had started life as a postal

clerk, but his rise had been rapid, owing to his own observing ways and good manners. Seeing the necessity of cross posts to connect with the great postal system running the length of the islands, Allen had put his idea into practical execution. He had provided a genuine public service which brought him a large income. As evidence of his success Allen had begun to build a great mansion at Prior Park, near Bath. Pope and Allen visited each other with some degree of frequency. Allen often advanced money to Pope for his needs or charities.

Affairs were in this happy state when Pope and Martha Blount arrived at Prior Park in the spring of 1743. Contrary to her usual amiability, Mrs. Allen received Pope and the "lady" with coldness and constraint. In this she was abetted by Warburton and her reluctant husband, who demonstrated a surliness and ill nature quite at variance with his usual sunny disposition and kind heart.

It is alleged that the misunderstanding between Martha and Mrs. Allen arose over Martha's insistence that a means of transportation be provided for her attendance at Mass on Sunday. Such gossip, which was whispered to save face for Mrs. Allen, does not appear anywhere in the letters between Pope and Martha. Had the quarrel developed on such slight grounds, one would not be impressed with Mrs. Allen's good breeding, or her enlightened tolerance, since it is one of the marks of a good hostess to see to the comforts of her guests regardless of their faith or lack of it. However, considerable allowance must be made for the persecuting spirit and the universal bias of the time.

The cause of the coldness went deeper. Pope was in all probability expected to arrive alone. When he appeared with Miss Blount in tow, his hostess was probably outraged to be a party to a liaison which she might already have heard discussed at considerable length. Mrs. Allen could be expected to be sensi-

tive regarding the proprieties. She was herself the illegitimate
daughter of General Wade, who had been Allen's first patron
and the architect of his fortune.

What ensued at Prior Park was one of those comedies of
manners which could have happened only in a country which
prided itself equally on its Puritanism and good breeding. No
doubt it was decided *in camera* to treat the whole situation
with a frigid politeness which would terminate it at the earliest
possible moment.

Pope at first noticed nothing out of the ordinary in his hosts.
He was used to calling on his friends for unusual favors and,
from all that can be gathered, never expected to find mean suspicions in those he admired and trusted. He was undisturbed
until Martha pointed out her suspicions to him. Pope at once
decided to leave Prior Park for a friend's house. He probably
expected Martha to return to London in the coach of Lord
Archibald Hamilton, who was staying near by at Lincombe.

Pope departed, but Martha was forced to remain at the Allens' and was compelled to suffer further coldness and slights
not to be endured by any woman. A letter to Pope indicates
something of her anguish:

> I hope you are well. I am not. My spirits are quite down,
> though they should not, for these people deserve so much
> to be despised. One should do nothing but laugh. I packed
> up my things yesterday; the servants knew it. Mr. and Mrs.
> Allen never said a word, nor so much as asked me how I
> went, where, or when. In short from every one of them
> much greater inhumanity [than] I could conceive anybody
> could show. Mr. Warburton took no notice of me—'tis most
> wonderful. They have not one of them named your name,
> nor drunk your health since you went. They talk to one
> another without putting me at all in the conversation. Lord
> Archibald [Hamilton] is come [to Lincombe]. I was to have

gone this morning in his coach, but, unluckily, he keeps it here. I shall go and contrive something with them today, for I do really think these people would shove me out, if I did not go soon. I would run all inconveniences, and drink the waters,* if I thought they would do me good. My present state is deplorable—I'll get out of it as soon as I can.[9]

The letter brought great pain to Pope. It was probably all the more infuriating when he recalled his great friends, the Duchess of Marlborough, Mrs. Howard, and the Duchess of Hamilton, who liked Mrs. Martha and were glad to welcome her and Pope at any time, while these *nouveaux riches* took it upon themselves to display their bad manners and narrow respectability. The poet's words are burning in his reply to Martha. The very unexpectedness of the experience was a terrible blow to Pope:

So strange a disappointment as I met with, the extreme sensibility which I know is in your nature, of such monstrous treatment, and the bitter reflection that I was wholly the unhappy cause of it, did really so distract me, while with you, that I could neither speak, nor move, nor act, nor think. I was like a man stunned or stabbed, where he had expected an embrace; and I was dejected to death, seeing I could do or say nothing to comfort, but every thing rather to hurt you. But for God's sake, know that I understood it was goodness and generosity you showed me, under the appearance of anger itself. When you bid me first go to Lord B's from them, and then, hasten thither, I was sensible it was in resentment of their conduct to me, and to remove me from such treatment, though you stayed alone to suffer it yourself. But I depended you would not have been a *day* longer in the house after I left you last; and of all I have endured, nothing gave me so much pain of heart, as to find by your letters you were still under their roof.[10]

* At Bath.

Pope advised Martha to ignore the whole incident, and he carefully outlined the various ways in which she could leave the Allen house and return to London without troubling her disagreeable hosts. One thing was certain, she must leave as soon as possible.

The final sentences in the letter are highly amusing: "I should not wonder if listeners at doors should open letters. W. [Warburton] is a sneaking parson and I told him he flattered." They show Pope's particular resentment at Warburton's part in the affair and the whole small complexion of the disagreeable episode.

Pope, in his last letter on the subject, told Martha of a visit from Mr. Allen in which he tried to adjust the unpleasantness which had occurred. Allen arrived on Holy Thursday, 1744, and "proposed to have stayed only to dinner; but recollecting the next day was Good Friday, he said he would take a bed here, and fast with me."[11]

The date of Allen's visit is particularly interesting in the oblique evidence it gives of Pope's observance of Lent and Holy Week. It is obvious that the poet still kept the fasts of the Church. This is a curious circumstance in the life of a man who was said to have been a deist in his final years.

Allen's visit led to a formal reconciliation between the two men. Allen insisted the affair at Prior Park was a misunderstanding which concerned his wife and Martha alone, but Pope suspected his excuses and was resolved to have little to do with the Allens in the future.

Pope, with true insight, already realized the fatal nature of his illness (dropsical asthma) and the short span of life remaining to him. His whole concern was for Martha:

I assure you I do not think half so much what will become of me, as of you; and when I grow worst, I find the anxiety for you doubled. Would to God you would quicken your haste to settle, by reflecting what a pleasure it would be to me just to see it, and to see you at ease; and then I could *contentedly leave you to the providence of God in this life and resign myself to it in the other.** I have little to say to you when we meet, but I love you upon unalterable principles, which makes me feel my heart the same to you as if I saw you every hour.[12]

In the final days of Pope's illness, when he was playing out the comedy of dying like an antique philosopher, it was Martha Blount alone who could raise his spirits and bring a breath of air and sunshine into an existence which Bolingbroke had attempted to dominate too long with his fatal charm and theatrical talents.

Pope left a life interest in his house and fortune to Martha Blount, and there were tongues that were quick to hint she had been either Pope's mistress or his wife. There is no factual evidence to prove either assertion.

Martha Blount was admired by all Pope's closest friends like Gay, Swift, and Arbuthnot; and his oldest friends among the nobility seemed to have been pleased to have her in their houses. They sometimes bought special gifts for her, such as the exquisite wines she and Pope enjoyed. Warburton and Bolingbroke, however, demonstrated a sharp dislike of the lady. Martha's blunt, common sense must have been something of a standing reproach to the theatrical charm Bolingbroke turned on and off like a windmill, and naturally Warburton, who was out to make his fortune as well as his fame by his association with Pope, found his expectations considerably reduced by the care Pope expressed to see Martha settled and secure for life.

In spite of all their sneers, Martha remained the last human

* Italics the author's.

being, as she had been one of the first, in whom Pope had explicit confidence.

Malice remained after Pope's death to whisper, to point, to footnote with bland suggestion what has never had a shred of genuine evidence to bear it out. It was a vain attempt to turn one of the finest things in Pope's life into the appearance of something calculating and evil.

Today, from the poems and letters, and the gradual sifting of time, it is at least morally certain that Pope loved no women as a husband loves a wife. He knew his shape was ridiculous, and he often referred to his insuperable handicaps for love, as he and his age understood it. His ardent compliments were reserved for those romantic souls, like Lady Mary, who could see how the game should be played, and who, like Teresa Blount, made the game worth while by playing out the gambit to its arch and negative conclusion.

Pope was never really at home with women unless he treated them like romantic idols or pampered them like his sister Magdalen: running their errands, investing their money, amusing their dull and idle hours with witty sayings, droll poetry, and fanciful speculation upon the small things which made up their constricted lives.

Rich as he was, he might easily have found women who would have endured "a man of his make," for the larger honor of spending his money and being hostess for the best genius of the age. But Pope showed caution on each occasion such a match was suggested to him. He had in his nature too lofty an idea of love to compromise it; an admirable integrity prevented him from ever enduring in a moment of anger the smile of pity or the grimace of disgust which he knew too well lay in the hazard of the experience. He charmed all the ladies with wit and wisdom, he turned his energies into couplets, gardening, and a cursory study of philosophy. He was most at home with his men companions; the coarseness of some of his jests shows it. What understanding and sympathy he craved, he found in two women: his mother and the smiling Martha.

In the conjunction of stars at his birth, whatever aspect Venus showed, it was none of those known to legend or antiquity: neither the froth-born goddess, nor she of the melting languors and brazen charms. This was a new manifestation: a Venus who did not pursue or lie in wait. She was a cautious jade who mouthed of love but shuddered at the reality which was incapable of realization like the scoriac imaginings of a housemaid's Heloise.

6

Achilles and the Myrmidons

A man of many talents is undone
By things as light as motes that ride the sun.

WITH the completion of the *Iliad* in 1720, Pope was, in many ways, a free man. He now had time to play, to indulge to the full his love for company and good conversation. Pope was also free in the sense that he was a rich man. He had made £5,000–£6,000 by his translation of the *Iliad*. Through wise investments, and annuities purchased from reliable friends, Pope, in some measure, insured financial safety for himself and his mother. Yet there was money to spare over and above those sums set aside for a provident security.

Pope was not a penurious man. He spared paper, and occasionally spared the roast or the wine, but he had a child's delight in gold and magnificence of every sort. He took pleasure in his own importance and the dignity which went with it. Mr. Pope, the translator of Homer, must have his proper setting. With such thoughts in mind, Pope decided to move from his cramped quarters at Chiswick to something more in keeping with his fame.

At first he was bursting with excited ideas of building himself a Venetian *palazzotto* in London. Plans for this tantalizing dream were hurriedly drawn up by Gibbs, the fashionable architect. The more Pope pored over the plans, the more he was in love with the idea of a smart town house. His friend Lord Bathurst, to whom he revealed his dream, turned his mind away from the project by indicating archly just how fast Pope's money would fly away to the tune of saws and hammers.[1]

Bathurst's caution made Pope thoughtful. Perhaps imagination could achieve what mere wealth could not. It was clear a lord of language was still only a Pontius Pilate of gold. He could not hope to vie with the imperial magnificence of the oligarchy, who shared the plunder of the state. Instead of building a new house, then, Pope took from Vernon, a "Turkey Merchant," a long lease on a villa at Twickenham.[2]

This acquired domain soon engrossed his whole interest as the former scheme to build a town house had done. Pope himself superintended the improvement and perfection of his newly leased estate with his unusual nervous energy and creative imagination. There was much to be done. The villa faced the Thames. At the front of the house there were sunny stretches of green lawn sloping down to the bright water. Behind the main edifice and outbuildings, a path to Hampton Court Road cut across the property and divided the larger part of the gardens from the land on which Pope's villa stood. With a poet's sublime scorn of obstacles, Pope surmounted this difficulty by making under the road a grotto which connected both parts of his estate.

This was the grotto of which Dr. Johnson hoped no more than an "ague," yet it set something of a fashion, which the Prince of Wales himself emulated at Richmond House. Pope ornamented the walls and ceiling of the grotto with bits of looking glass cut in bizarre shapes. His noble and scientific friends manifested their interest and approval of the project by sending samples of bright ores and unusual stones, which were added to the galaxy of mirrors. In the flickering light shed by an alabaster lamp which hung from the center of the ceiling, the grotto seemed, at approach of evening, like the glittering cave of Aladdin. By day the pleasure was more enchanting. The light and shade in the atmosphere worked their miracles in the mirrors, as passing sails or drowsing trees caught the refracted light from the water.

This *"camera obscura"* was a mere prelude to that other and greater achievement—Pope's gardens. In laying them out he had, with a poet's originality, turned away from the fashionable French and Dutch styles of gardening perfected by Le Nôtre and Wise. Instead of following a rigidly prevailing geometrical order, Pope's little lawns were casual in their artistry. Paths wound from them to other lawns and other vistas. The bordering thickets were planted with trees of heavier and darker foliage in the foreground, receding into lighter shades and verdure beyond. This trick of planting gave to the eye a false sense of spaciousness and added perspective. In this particular instance, Pope had adapted a hint from Le Nôtre, who had edged the *tapis vert* at Versailles in the same fashion, leading the eye and imagination into a seeming eternity of distance.

Pope was successful in propagating his Italianate style of ordered disarray. Hardly a peer or newly rich commoner built an estate or planned a garden without consulting the "sage of Twickenham." The King's mistress, the Prince of Wales, Bathurst, Burlington, Chandos, Allen . . . all wanted his advice. In landscape gardening and in his verse, Pope set fashions which predominated long after his death. The idiom of his verse and the style of his gardening had much in common. In laying out his gardens Pope "twirled his paths" and gave his lawns a casual air of unplanned beauty. Every vista which might tire the eye was broken up into smaller and more varied units. This was approximately the same method Pope employed in his heroic couplet. The form, used by any but a master, can be monotonous and mechanical. But Pope was a master: he calculated the pauses in his couplets in an artful fashion which minimized their metronomic tendencies; he varied and contrasted the vowel sounds and colors. These calculated effects gave his couplets variety of pace and variety of music. In gardening and prosody Pope was a supreme artist.

Twickenham was a wild success in every way. One of its chief advantages was the fairly wide freedom of movement it gave Pope. By barge he could move up or down the Thames. He could be met by the coaches of his noble friends at any designated point. In his gilded nest at Twickenham, Pope was in a convenient spot to return their hospitality.

It was not penny-pinching or fear of the future which prevented Pope from owning a coach of his own. The penal laws forbade papists to possess such a vehicle. It was part of the state strategy employed to immobilize Catholics. When his friend Lord Halifax offered Pope a pension of £300 a year that he might have a coach, the poet refused. The reason he gave was his reluctance to get used to a comfort which he might later have to forego, should the pension be withdrawn. The comfort of a coach—we can smile at the phrase today— would have been of enormous service to Pope.

He was perpetually in flight, like the actors in the plot of a bad film. He loved to travel to the country houses of his great friends, or on a sudden to set out for London and the fashionable acquaintances and excitements there. A coach would have given him the freedom to go where he desired without wasting interminable hours waiting on the vehicles of friends. Yet, had Pope owned a coach, his enemies would have been able to point to his open flouting of the penal laws. They suspected him of ignoring the law secretly in his investments and transfers of property, but nothing could be proved: his friends Pigott, Fortescue, Craggs, and Bathurst were much too shrewd and co-operative for that. Pope's enemies also suspected him of being a Jacobite, but any references in his poems which touched on that delicate subject were of such an oblique nature that Pope might have disowned them with a smile. To own horses and a coach, however, would have been an obvious breach of the laws, one which would have admitted the possibility of incredible enlargement by his enemies. It would have given them an imaginative field day; freedom among plotters, fancied journeys by night, conferences in transit without fear of listening ears.

Pope must have realized he was much more fortunate in being made dependent upon the kindness of noble friends with their Flanders mares and houses on wheels. It was far better to have their word of corroborating proof in case there were any hints or direct accusations of treason. At Twickenham he was secure and very comfortable. The law might confiscate his coach and horses if he were foolish enough to buy them. His river they could not take from him. It was open to the sky, and secret, like his own mind.

One of Pope's fascinating Twickenham friends was Francis Atterbury, Bishop of Rochester. Atterbury had been an intimate associate of the poet in the last years of Queen Anne's reign, at a time when they were both members of the Scriblerus Club under the harum-scarum leadership of Swift. The beginning of Pope's extant correspondence with Atterbury dates from 1716, and is, for the most part, of a literary and critical nature, in all probability a continuation of their original Scriblerian roles.

Atterbury was a man of taste and action. His loyalty to the Stuarts was the guiding principle of his life. He has been unduly criticized for disloyalty to the Hanoverians. The idea of a Protestant succession probably meant nothing to his enlightened mind, compared with the Stuart kings, whose personal charm and genuine talents gave them some right to a man's loyalty and admiration. From a point of law, theirs *was* the first right to the throne, and his mind was logical enough to see this. Had Atterbury been a duke instead of a bishop, he might have *done* something radical about his convictions. In his role of Bishop he moved Heaven and earth to encourage decision and action. But in the closing years of Queen Anne's reign it was the Whig lords and their followers who showed all the energy. The Tory lords vacillated: they made and unmade decisions, while time ran away with opportunity.

At the time of Queen Anne's death, Atterbury was the sole Tory leader who showed an inspired decision which might well have carried the day. With a careless disregard for the popular portents he went to the Duke of Ormonde and offered to proceed to Charing Cross to proclaim the Pretender in lawn sleeves. The uncertain leaders of the Tory party ignored Atterbury's boldness. While they talked and talked, while they dreamed and spun theories, Hanover was *over*.

Atterbury seemed to accept the inevitable. He lived a retired life in the diocese of Rochester, but in his capacity as Dean of Westminster he still had ample opportunity to impress the public with his eloquence, taste, and culture.

The extant correspondence which passed between Pope and the Bishop bears witness that Atterbury was more than a little flattered to be the intimate correspondent of the most famous poet and wit of the day. They were both close friends of the lively Bathurst, and at his house, St. Paul's Deanery in London, and "Twitnam," the friendship between the Bishop and the poet warmed into something of genuine intimacy. Atterbury was proud to claim a part in suggesting ideas to

Pope's genius; moreover he had, it appears, some hope of converting Pope to the Established Church.

This hope unmasked itself at the death of Pope's father. Atterbury was one of the first to offer Pope sympathy. With his usual active genius, Atterbury also suggested in the letter, with some indecent haste, that now the time was ripe for Pope to change his religion. Many of those who have commented on this episode have presumed that Atterbury made the suggestion from a desire to secure the glory of converting a great poet, thus adding to his own not inconsiderable fame as a persuader of men.

The circumstances surrounding the suggestion make this over-simplification untenable: Atterbury was much larger, much more urbane than that supposition would indicate. Pope's conversion would have been of much more value to Pope than the Bishop. Had Pope gone over to the Established Church, the constricting penal laws would have ceased to affect his peace and safety. He would have been free in his movements, his fortune, his lands, and his life. In addition to these enlargements his papistry would no longer be the chief stick which Grub Street could use to beat him. A golden future of government patronage, pensions—the very laureateship itself—would be spread out enticingly before him. These advantages were in Atterbury's mind as they were in Pope's. The Bishop's gesture was in keeping with his decisive habits of mind and the genuine affection he had for his friend.

Atterbury's letter to Pope on the occasion of his father's death is worth quoting, for many reasons. In his easy intercourse with Pope, Atterbury may have fancied he detected in Pope's jokes concerning pious things, and in his condemnation of all sectarian narrowness and persecutions, a latitudinarianism which indicated that Pope was merely a formal or traditional Catholic, without genuine roots of conviction.

These thoughts prompted Atterbury to write Pope the following letter upon the death of his father:

I have nothing to say to you on that melancholy subject, with an account of which the printed papers have furnished me, but what you have already said to yourself.

When you have paid the debt of tenderness you owe to the memory of a father, I doubt not but you will turn your thoughts toward improving that accident to your own ease and happiness. You have it now in your power to pursue that method of thinking and living which you like best. Give me leave, if I am not a little too early in my applications of this kind, to congratulate you upon it; and to assure you that there is no man living who wishes you better, or would be more pleased to contribute any ways to your satisfaction or service.[3]

Pope's reply, in spite of its diffuse length, is an exact expression of his mind as it was reflected in the actions of his life. Pope took Atterbury's reasons, one by one, and he indicated in what manner they were inapplicable to himself. The close of the letter is a dignified rebuke to Atterbury for his inability to understand Pope's integrity as a Catholic, and it hints at the Bishop's failure to concentrate on the *spiritual* aspects of the case. Yet Pope managed to temper his words to the shorn cleric:

My Lord,—I am truly obliged by your kind condolence on my father's death, and the desire you express that I should improve this incident to my advantage. I know your lordship's friendship to me is so extensive that you include in that wish both my spiritual and my temporal advantage; and it is what I owe to that friendship, to open my mind unreservedly to you on this head. It is true, I have lost a parent for whom no gains I could make would be any equivalent. But that was not my only tie: I thank God another still remains (and long may it remain) of the same tender nature. *Genetrix est mihi:* and excuse me if I say with Euryalus,

Nequeam lacrymas preferre parentis.

A rigid divine may call it carnal tie, but sure it is a virtuous one. At least I am more certain that it is a duty of nature to preserve a good parent's life and happiness, than I am of any speculative point whatever.

Ignaram hujus quodcunque pericli
Hanc ego, nunc, linquam?

For she, my lord would think this separation more grievous than any other, and I, for my part, know as little as poor Euryalus did, of the success of such an adventure; for an adventure it is, and no small one, in spite of the most positive divinity. Whether the change would be to my spiritual advantage God only knows: this I know, that *I mean as well in the religion I now profess as I can possibly ever do in another.* Can a man who thinks so justify a change, *even if he thought** both equally good? To such an one the part of *joining* with any one body of Christians might perhaps be easy, but I think it would not be so, to *renounce* the other. Your lordship has formerly advised me to read the best controversies between the churches. Shall I tell you a secret? I did so at fourteen years old, for I loved reading, and my father had no other books; there was a collection of all that had been written on both sides in the reign of King James the Second. I warmed my head with them, and the consequence was, that I found myself a Papist and a Protestant by turns, according to the last book I read. I am afraid most seekers are in the same case, and when they stop, they are not so properly converted, as outwitted. You see how little glory you would gain by my conversion. And after all, I verily believe your Lordship and I are both of the same religion, if we were thoroughly understood by one another; and that all honest and reasonable Christians would be so, if they did

* Italics the author's.

[133]

but talk enough together every day, and had nothing to do together, but to serve God, and live in peace with their neighbour. As to the *temporal* side of the question, I can have no dispute with you; it is certain, all the beneficial circumstances of life, and all the shining ones, lie on the part you would invite me to. But, if I could bring myself to fancy, that I have any talents for active life, I want health for it; and besides it is a real truth, I have less inclination (if possible) than ability. Contemplative life is not only my scene, but it is my habit too. I begun my life where most people end theirs, with a disrelish of all that the world call ambition. I do not know why it is called so, for to me it always seemed to be rather *stooping* than *climbing*. I will tell you my politic and religious sentiments in a few words. In my politics, I think no further than how to preserve the peace of my life, in any government under which I live; nor in my religion, than to preserve the peace of my conscience in any church with which I communicate. I hope all churches and all governments are so far of God, as they are rightly understood, and rightly administered: and where they are, or may be wrong, I leave it to God alone to mend or reform them, which whenever he does, it must be by greater instruments than I am. I am not a papist, for I renounce the temporal invasions of the papal power, and detest their arrogated authority over princes and states. *I am a Catholic in the strictest sense of the word.** If I was born under an absolute prince, I would be a quiet subject; but I thank God I was not. I have a due sense of the excellence of the British constitution. In a word, the things I have always wished to see, are not a Roman Catholic, or a French Catholic, or a Spanish Catholic, but a true Catholic: not a king of Whigs, or a king of Tories, but a King of England; which God of his mercy grant his present Majesty may be, and all future Majesties. You see, my lord I end like a preacher: that is *Sermo ad clerum* not *ad populum.*[4]

* Italics the author's.

[134]

This is a good, honest letter, though it seems to have shocked some Catholics, who consider it disloyal to the Church. There is nothing disloyal in it: quite the opposite is true, if Pope is placed in proper historical perspective. Atterbury wrote to Pope in haste and out of pure kindness. Pope's reply put the Bishop in his place with firmness, but he restricted himself to arguments which a man of common sense, an intimate of the inner circle, would understand. Atterbury spoke of Pope's father, the poet countered with his mother; the Bishop suggested worldly advantage, Pope rebuked him by denying the possibility of any *spiritual* gain in such a change—a thing which should have been first in Atterbury's mind, because of his calling. Pope's analysis of his outlook on religion was accurate: he followed Erasmus, he denied the temporal power of the Church, as most of the clergy of France did at the time; he despised the narrow nationalism and the parochial outlook which men were attempting to foist on the Church. He was, none the less, a true Catholic, who believed first in charity and the doctrines of the creed. Considering the age, considering the background, Pope emerges from the encounter with a sort of splendor.

Atterbury's lack of success in converting Pope had no adverse affect on their friendship. The poet's reasons for remaining what he was in fact shine out from the letters he edited—with still greater brightness from those which were not smoothed or refined or changed for the public, and which have come down to us by other hands than Pope's or Warburton's.

In reality Pope was an aggressive Catholic. His aggressiveness revealed itself in his words and actions at many points of his life. He frequently schemed to present Catholicism in a good light and he made timid but positive attempts to convert others to his religion. Pope maintained that Wycherley

and Garth were eleventh-hour Catholics, and he recommended
to the Duchess of Hamilton the company of Dr. Legg (a
Catholic priest) who had entered on his "function this winter
at Mrs. Blount's." Pope's delightful letter to the Duchess was
a shy attempt to interest Her Grace in the Catholic Church.
Of Dr. Legg [Pope thought or pretended his name was Logg],
the poet said:

> They [the Blounts] have chosen this innocent man for
> their confessor; and I believe most Roman Catholic ladies,
> that have any sins, will follow their example. This good priest
> will be of the order of the Melchisedec, a priest for ever and
> serve a family from generation to generation. He will stand
> in a corner as quietly as a clock, and being wound up once a
> week, strike up a loud alarum to sin on a Sunday morning.
> Nay, if the Christian religion should be abolished (as indeed
> there is great reason to expect it from the wisdom of the
> legislature), he might at worst make an excellent bonfire,
> which is all that, upon a change of religion, can be desired
> from a heretic. I do not hope your grace should be converted,
> but however I wish you would call at Mrs. B.'s out of
> curiosity. To meet people one likes, is thought by some the
> best reason for going to church, and I dare promise you will
> like one another.[5]

The letter written by the Duchess in reply to Pope's suggestion displays something of her cordial affection for Pope.
It is also a striking revelation of her impetuous and charming
nature. The Duchess had taken the poet's advice and had got
in touch with Dr. Legg,[6] but there is scant evidence that Pope
was any more successful with Thackeray's beautiful Duchess
than Atterbury was in attempting to convert the translator
of Homer. True, all the golden reasons were against the conversion of Her Grace of Hamilton: she was lovely and young
and she was getting an intense pleasure from the mere joy of

being alive. In her own eyes she required amusements rather
than constraints.

If these observations could be doubted, the final extant
letter of the Duchess to Pope offers a delightful and definitive
expression of her casual enjoyment of life. The main part of
the letter was written by Maddison, her amanuensis. A postscript, added in the impetuous style of the Duchess, is a charming question mark which makes one sorry so few of her letters
to Pope have survived:

> Sir—[Maddison writes] My Lady Dutchess being drunk at
> this present, and not able to write herself, has commanded
> me to acquaint you that there is to be musick on the water on
> Thursday next, therefore desires you to be that evening at
> her house in Bond Street by Six o'Clock at farthest, and her
> Grace will call of you there, to take you in her barge, which
> she has ordered to be ready at that time at White Hall with
> Provisions, and shall land you [on] the wish'd for shoare. I
> am, Yr. most humble servant, Maddison.

To which the Duchess—revived briefly, one presumes, or only
joking in Maddison's epistle—added with imperious directness,
"Out of ye abundance of ye heart ye mouth speaketh, so Pope
is the word, a disappointment is not to be endured."[7]

Pope may have had little success in attempting to convert
the Duchess, but the reasons which he advanced to Atterbury
for remaining a Catholic were not mere rhetorical reasons.
Writing Mrs. Knight, the sister of Secretary Craggs, in 1731,
ten years after Atterbury's attempt to bring him over to
Anglicanism, Pope declared without equivocation his personal
outlook on Catholicism. It is one of the few unguarded expressions to be found in his letters:

> My next journey is to Southampton, to Lord Peterborough,
> where I also have a Catholic friend who will take care of my

soul; and shall dine with a Jesuit, thrice a week, worth all the priests in Essex, if you accept Mr. Tripsack.

In Pope's other letters to Mrs. Knight there are additional signs that the poet tried to interest her in Catholicism through Martha Blount: cautious examples of Pope's proselytizing zeal, which are the strongest possible proof of his Catholicism and his ardent love for it.

Bishop Atterbury's failure to turn Pope to the Established Church was balanced by his success in two other matters: the translation of the *Odyssey*, and the ill-starred edition of Shakespeare's works. Pope, it is clear, undertook the labors at the insistence of Atterbury and other close friends. These consuming tasks, and the edition of Buckingham's works, were to keep Pope busy until 1726. By this time the conclusion of his labors was an eruption of terror and vexation.

In setting out to edit Shakespeare, Pope was ill advised. He lacked the habits of mind, the brutal application, and the complicated knowledge which the task required. Pope knew this himself, for in his preface he said with genuine modesty: "In what I have done I have rather given proof of my willingness and desire, than of my ability to do him [Shakespeare] justice."

From Pope's letters to Broome and Fenton, it is obvious now that Pope worked on his edition of Shakespeare and the *Odyssey* at the same time. Gay and Fenton assisted him with the Shakespeare. In addition to their aid, Pope had other help for certain emendations which he made.

But before Pope's *Odyssey* and his edition of Shakespeare had been brought to completion, the poet endured a disagreeable experience which was to linger in his imagination for many years. Upon the death of the Duke of Buckingham, Pope was persuaded to undertake the task of editing the

Duke's works for publication. Atterbury and the Duchess of Buckingham, it seems, persuaded him to assume the burden.

Katherine, Duchess of Buckingham, a natural daughter of James II, was a vain woman. She was so conscious of her position that she spent a fortune in the attempt to outdo for her husband, and again for her son, the funeral of the great Marlborough, which had been of almost incredible splendor. When she applied to the tart Duchess of Marlborough for permission to use, for young Buckingham's funeral, the hearse which had conveyed the old warrior to his grave, she was told, "It carried my Lord Marlborough and shall never be used for anyone else."

"Very well," the magnificent Katherine is said to have retorted, "I have consulted the undertaker and he tells me I may have a finer for twenty pounds."

John Sheffield, Duke of Buckingham, and Pope had been on easy terms since about the time of the publication of the *Essay on Criticism*. Sheffield was an ardent Tory by conviction, but he found it convenient to fraternize with the Whigs when it suited the purposes of his own ambitions. He had prospered under Mary and Anne and had seemed an ardent partisan of Hanover, but once George I was seated on the throne Buckingham's loyalty was, at best, suspect. He seems to have been an avowed opportunist; he also posed as a literary man and a Maecenas. Buckingham's relations with Dryden had been cordial, and he demonstrated toward Pope and Prior a friendliness and interest in keeping with the roles he had marked out for himself: he enjoyed their company at times, as well as the superficial discussions of philosophy and literature which animated the clubs and newspapers of the day and found a flamboyant echo at the dinner table at Buckingham House.

The appetite for posthumous fame which slashed and disfigured the Abbey in the eighteenth century also made it fashionable to employ noted figures for the fabrication of epitaphs and the editing of family papers—in particular, when such papers had some credit in the world of literature. Sheffield's unquestionably had. The Duchess of Buckingham, no doubt, was delighted to secure Pope's services in editing her husband's papers. Aside from the monetary advantage implied in the transaction, Pope himself would lose no prestige among the nobility through his employment. Vitally concerned as he was in the translation of the Odyssey and the editing of Shakespeare, it may be taken for granted that Pope spent more time and care on these tasks than he poured into the editing of Buckingham's papers. Yet Pope had an artist's conception of such labors, and he would see to it that his edition of Buckingham was careful and beautiful. We may presume he supervised every step of the task.

A letter to his friend Caryll, at the time, would seem to indicate that Pope chortled over the Jacobite tendencies of some of Buckingham's memoirs, notably "Some account of the Revolution" and the satire on European royalty entitled "A Feast of the Gods."

> Though I can give you no good account of myself as to anything of my own, [Pope wrote to Caryll] yet I am very busy in doing justice to a far greater poet [Shakespeare] of whose works I am giving a new edition. Besides this, I have the care of overlooking the Duke of Buckingham's papers, and correcting the press. That will be a very beautiful book, and has many things in it you will be particularly glad to see in relation to some former reigns.[8]

Everything seemed propitious for the publication of Buckingham's works until the discovery of a plot to bring over the Pretender electrified and changed the whole political atmosphere. Bishop Atterbury had been the center of this new intrigue, at the very time when Pope was thought to be his closest friend. Atterbury's guilt is certain today, since the publication of the Stuart Papers; yet, at the time the plot was discovered, he had so thoroughly covered his tracks that the Lords were unable to convict him of treason.

The discovery of the Atterbury plot gave rise to the usual "no popery" excitement. The Whig party writers increased the uproar by their usual wild accusations and veiled innuendoes. Pope provided a ready target for their barbed shafts of ridicule and suspicion.

The two quarto volumes of Buckingham's works, which were beautiful beyond Pope's promise to Caryll, were published on January 24, 1723. Three days later, without warning, the Black Staff appeared at the printers and seized the entire edition, by the King's order. This circumstance provided Pope's enemies with fuel for their usual accusations of trickery and lies, but it would appear that government inspection of the volumes led to no more drastic action than the excision of some offending pages of Volume II (68–103 and 159–171), and permission later to restore them. Careful perusal of the volumes today proves that there was little in them which was more than suggestive of disloyalty. Their actual danger lay in the explosive political situation, especially alarming since the discovery of Atterbury's plot against the regime.

In writing his account of the Revolution of 1688, Buckingham probably came nearer to the truth than most supposed writers of factual history. His careful analysis of the character of James II and his ungrateful daughters, and the high comedy of the King's downfall, make fascinating reading today. In 1723, however, the Whigs and the Hanoverians were more intent on retaining the throne than they were zealous for truth. Buckingham's account of the Revolution made tatters of the fine fustian of the popular accounts of the "glorious" aspect of the struggle; and, as such, his account was disquieting and dangerous. "A Feast of the Gods," with its disapproving glance at the power politics of the day and the kings of Europe, also contained incendiary possibilities.

Early in 1721, Pope had tried to abandon the task of editing Buckingham's works in favor of Alderman Barber. A letter to Tonson indicates this fact. It is quite possible that some of Pope's friends in the government had warned the poet of the danger which threatened.

Whatever the reason for Pope's hesitation in 1721, the Duchess of Buckingham and Bishop Atterbury somehow persuaded Pope to continue the work, but the poet went his way with caution and in the end the license and the risk were assumed by Barber.

Probably the only misrepresentation Pope made, after the government seizure of Buckingham's works, was his reassurance to Lord Carteret that he had "never look'd into those papers or was privy to the contents of them when the License was procured by Mr. Barber to secure his own property." Without doubt Pope had seen every page of the books. They had seemed innocuous before the discovery of Atterbury's plot to bring over the Pretender. This and the excitement attendant upon such a discovery had played him a scurvy trick in magnifying a molehill into mountainous proportions.

It is easy to sneer at Pope's lie to Carteret. It is simple enough to fancy that it is another instance of his insincerity, as his enemies have alleged. The circumstances surrounding this instance, however, give it a particular complexion which considerably alters Pope's culpability. His statement to Lord Carteret was an untruth, but had Pope's detractors stood in his imminent peril they might have been willing to trifle with truth.

That Pope felt himself in actual danger there can be no

doubt. Bishop Atterbury, accused of high treason, was taken to the Tower in August, 1722. He lay there awaiting trial during the period in which the seizure of Buckingham's works had taken place. In May, 1723, his trial began. Pope was called before the House of Lords as a character witness for the Bishop.

The prospect of this interrogation frightened the poet beyond measure, although most of the members of the august court were his friends or acquaintances. It was the penal laws he feared; the hazard of a misstatement which would bring down the full force of them on his undefended head and his mother's.

His genuine fear and confusion are illustrated in the letter he wrote to Lord Harcourt, on May 5, 1723:

> I resolve to take any opportunity of declaring (even upon oath) how different I am from what a *reputed** Papist is. I could almost wish I were ask'd if I am not a Papist. Would it be proper in such a case to reply, that I don't perfectly know the import of the word, and would not answer anything that might, for ought I know, be prejudicial to me, during the bill against such, which is depending. But that *if to be a Papist be to profess and hold many such tenets of faith as are ascribed to Papists, I am not a Papist; and if to be a Papist be to hold any that are averse to or destructive of the present Government, King, or Constitution, I am no Papist.*[9]

He had worried himself into a state of near idiocy when the actual day arrived, and he made a very poor showing, which he described to Spence:

> When I was to appear for the Bishop of Rochester, in his trial, though I had but ten words to say, and that on a plain point (how that bishop spent his time whilst I was with him at Bromley), I made two or three blunders in it: and that not

* Italics the author's.

withstanding the first row of lords (which was all I could see) were mostly of my acquaintance.[10]

Pope's testimony was not worth much, but Atterbury escaped the death penalty. He was deprived of all his ecclesiastical honors and banished for life. He wore out his days in uneasy exile in France, still yearning for his old influences and the good opinion of his own people. Correspondence with him was forbidden, but Pope communicated with him from time to time until the Bishop's death.

The newspapers and the pasquinades of the time were quick to accuse Pope of participation in the Atterbury plot. From the general tenor of his correspondence with Atterbury there is no evidence which would bear out this suspicion, or tend to show that Pope was involved in the intrigue. The Bishop and Pope had a genuine community of interests: these were literary and artistic. There is no suspicion that Pope was ever trusted with any of the intimate political secrets of Atterbury's life.

The trial, the public excitement, and the rash of anonymous accusations against Pope made it wise for him to defer the advertisements of Shakespeare and the subscription list for the *Odyssey*. Of the two works, the *Odyssey* was of first importance to Pope. There was little financial advantage to be gained in editing Shakespeare's plays. In making an edition of the *Odyssey* there was a fair possibility he might do well financially. Those who possessed the first half of the translation of Homer would wish to complete their sets.

In 1725, when the cry on papists no longer echoed in print, and the Atterbury plot had been fairly well forgotten, Pope launched his two new projects by advertising them in the newspapers. The edition of Shakespeare was the first to appear, in six quarto volumes published by Tonson.

There were some small immediate criticisms of the work,

but the great blow to Pope's credit as a Shakespearian scholar came in 1726 with the publication of Lewis Theobald's *Shakespeare Restored*, a more or less scholarly attack upon Pope's edition. In this work Theobald suggested important emendations of the test. They were obvious improvements on Pope's work, but in truth many of the emendations pointed out were improvements in printing.

A modern critic has clarified this point:

There can be no doubt of Theobald's superior knowledge and technique as compared with Pope's, but it may be urged that modern attempts to exalt Theobald's reputation have exaggerated somewhat the merits of *Shakespeare Restored*. About a third of its corrections are based on appeal to early texts—a 1632 folio, a 1637 quarto, and Hughes's edition of 1703. More than another third are conjectural emendations, and many are corrections in pointing and printing. These last probably annoyed Pope most; for many of them simply make the text slightly easier to read, but do not change the meaning in the least: they at times merely represent the eighteenth-century love for commas. The corrections most commonly accepted by later editors are those based on 'various readings' of texts neglected by Pope. Of the first fifty emendations about twenty are conjectural in nature, and seventeen of these have *not* been accepted by recent editors. Some of these are almost as absurd as Pope's howlers; others would irritate a *bel esprit* by their excessive technique.[11]

Theobald's praise of Pope in his Preface is usually brought forward in proof of his scholarly poise and ardent desire not to offend Pope. Careful examination of Theobald's panegyrics, however, leads one to believe they are pseudo-panegyrics rather than the stuff of real praise. Like Hamlet one would say of them, "The lady doth protest too much." They are too extreme, too overloaded with fulsome praise, especially when we recall Theobald's purpose in publishing his book, and the extravagant claims he made for his learning and his method.

It was no small satisfaction therefore to me, when I first heard Mr. *Pope* had taken upon him the publication of Shakespeare. I very reasonably expected, from his own Talents and Abilities, from his uncommon Sagacity and Discernment, and from his unwearied Diligence and care of informing himself by an happy and extensive Conversation, we should have had our author come out as perfect, as the want of *Manuscripts* and *original Copies* could give us a possibility of hoping. I may dare to say, a great number of *Shakespeare's* admirers, and of Mr. Pope's too, (both which I sincerely declare myself), concurred in the Expectation: for there is a certain *curiosa felicitas*, as was said of an eminent *Roman* Poet, in that Gentleman's Way of working, which, we presumed, would have laid itself out largely in such a Province; and that he would not have sate down contented with performing, as he calls it himself the dull *Duty* of an *Editor* only.

I have so great an esteem for Mr. Pope, and so high an opinion of his genius and Excellencies, that I beg to be excused from the least Intention of derogating from his merits, in this attempt to restore the true reading of Shakespeare. Tho' I confess a Veneration, almost rising to Idolatry, for the writing of this inimitable Poet, I would be very loth even to do *him* Justice at the expense of *that other* Gentleman's Character.[12]

This may sound like true praise, but it is nearer to irony, especially when, on page 75 of his work, Theobald points up his simulated praise of Pope into something more like a "Bronx cheer":

There are many passages of such intolerable Carelessness interspers'd thro' all six Volumes, that, were not a few of Mr. Pope's *Notes* scatter'd here and there too, I should be induced to believe that the Words in the Title Page of the *First* Volume . . . *COLLATED* and *CORRECTED* by the former *EDITIONS, by Mr.* Pope . . . were placed there by the *Bookseller* to enhaunce the *Credit* of his *Edition;* but that he had play'd false with his *Editor*, and never sent him the Sheets to revise.

Theobald seemed to praise Pope in the Preface, in order that he might tear his critical reputation to tatters in the text. His manner of attack was marvelously successful; so much so, in fact, that Pope's excellences were lost sight of, if not completely obscured.

Theobald had long planned to make an edition of his own, quite probably before Pope took up the project. He had not responded to Pope's public advertisements inserted in the *Evening Post* (October 21, 1721, and in the same paper in 1722), for anything which might aid the work. Now, having bided his time, he was able to demonstrate Pope's unfitness for the task. His own demonstration of superiority, however, was marked by considerable malice. It went much beyond facts, and there can be little doubt Pope was hurt by such a staggering condemnation of his efforts, and marked Theobald for the revenge he later executed on him in the *Dunciad*.

Theobald's *Shakespeare Restored* has had a tendency to make people forget the good parts of Pope's edition. The Preface is excellent, some of the best prose Pope ever wrote. From a critical point of view it adumbrates, for the first time, the canons which resulted in the critical editions of the plays, and a basic text of some undoubted correctness. Dr. Johnson commended Pope's critical introduction for its style and content, and justly said of it in conclusion: "He was the first that knew, at least the first that told, by what helps the text might be improved. If he inspected the early editions negligently, he taught others to be more accurate."[13]

Later, in making his own edition of Shakespeare, Theobald showed none of the boldness he used in attacking Pope's work. On the contrary, he paid William Warburton to help him with his work, and in writing his Preface began with the same figure of a house and rooms with which Pope had concluded his introduction.

It has been often asserted that Theobald's *Shakespeare Restored* was the beginning of Pope's enmity with Theobald and the reason for exalting him to the empery of Dullness in the *Dunciad*. Perhaps this is not entirely true. There is a possibility that in *Shakespeare Restored* Pope recognized the hard weave of the satires on him which appeared in *Mist's Journal* from time to time, and found his suspicion of Theobald verified rather than first created. In Pope's enmities there were always secondary reasons behind those adduced by enemies and certain biographers who have shown a distaste either for the man or his works.

The publication of Pope's translation of the *Odyssey* was also attended with annoying vexations. Like those attending the appearance of Shakespeare, they were to last for years. The work on the *Odyssey* had proceeded quietly. Because of the delay in launching the subscription, the entire task of the translation was finished before the printing of the first volume.

The task of collaboration started with utmost good humor among Pope and his assistants. At first they fought an amiable battle for the privilege of translating certain favorite books. There seemed to be every prospect of a happy and speedy termination of their labors.

In planning the work, Pope had decided to save himself the exhausting labor which had been his in the translation of the *Iliad*. Courthope maintains that the reflective and narrative qualities of the *Odyssey* were not suited to Pope's genius as the brisk movement and oratorical splendor of the *Iliad* had

been, and that this had, in consequence, suggested the employment of Fenton and Broome in the translation of a great
portion of the *Odyssey*. Courthope's kind surmise does not
seem plausible. Pope enjoyed writing description and nar-
ration: *Windsor Forest* alone is proof of it, and after his wide
experience in translating the *Iliad* he was skilled in handling
any type of translation. Much more likely, Pope was sick to
death of translation. After five years of grueling work, it was
the reward of such labor which glittered in his sight. In consequence, he employed Broome and Fenton on a different basis
from that which had governed his relations with those who
assisted him with the *Iliad*.

Pope apparently decided to employ Fenton and Broome
more or less completely, giving them a share in the work and
the honor which went with the labor. Both were excellent
scholars; both had a poetic reputation of sorts. They were
each to translate a complete portion of the *Odyssey*. In keeping with justice and the roles they were to play, Pope took
twelve books, Broome eight, and the plump and lazy Fenton
was satisfied with four books.

The collaboration, begun in 1721 or 1722, was not to be
more than a "genteel equivocation." The complete extent of
Pope's work and revision was not to be made public until the
critics had declared themselves, and payment had been made
by the subscribers. Such an arrangement commended itself to
Broome and Fenton. The amount of money involved was not
small. More desirable than that was the eminence they would
attain as Pope's collaborators. Though no precise financial
arrangements had been made in 1723, Pope had, it is probable,
planned to reward Broome and Fenton with the copy money
for books which they had translated, in addition to any further
sums obtained for subscriptions among their friends. Had
the scheme succeeded in the way Pope planned it, Broome

and Fenton would have achieved a great deal more in honor than they received in money. The gain to their literary future promised to be very great.

In order that Pope might have his jibe at the critics and achieve his financial ends, absolute secrecy was necessary. In the early correspondence between the three men, Pope and Fenton entreated Broome to be silent and keep the secret. Pope and Fenton kept it well, but Broome was unable to do so because poetic fame meant so much to him. He was Rector at Sturston in Suffolk, a plush benefice; he had married a wealthy wife and could not be said to look forward to the monetary reward of his labors. He did have a rabid itch for poetic fame.

Fenton, who was both needy and indolent, was a very silent man; Broome was not. He talked of his task to many people. His indiscretion was such that it became noised about London that Pope was not the sole author of the new translation. Such talk threatened to injure Pope where it hurt him most, in his purse. He cautioned Broome to a more discreet silence, and asked Fenton to use his influence with Broome to keep the secret better. This was the beginning of an acrimonious correspondence between the three men in which Pope and Broome prevaricated roundly and suspected each other's motives.

Broome, in particular, felt angry and defrauded, for it now seemed to him Pope was bent on taking the whole credit for the work, or at least sought to give the impression he had thoroughly corrected and emended the work of his helpers before giving it to the press. This would have minimized the labors of the two assistants and taken away their chief credit as independent translators. A state of angry resentment persisted until the publication of the *Odyssey* in 1726. Yet, in spite of the bitterness between Pope and Broome, possibly by sheer power of invective or threat of failure, Pope persuaded Broome to affix a statement to the last book of the *Odyssey* which was anything but the truth. In this extraordinary effort, Broome said:

> I have used Madam *Dacier* as she has done others, in transcribing some of her Remarks without particularizing them; but indeed it was through inadvertency only that her name is sometimes omitted at the bottom of the note. If my performance has merit, either in these, or in any part of the translation (namely in the sixth, eleventh, and eighteenth books) it is but just to attribute it to the judgement and care of Mr. Pope, by whose hand every sheet was corrected. His other and much more able assistant, was Mr. Fenton, in the fourth and twentieth books. It was our particular request, that our several parts might not be made known to the world till the end of it: and if they have had the good fortune not to be distinguished from His, we ought to be less vain. Since the resemblance proceeds much less from our diligence and study to copy his manner, than from his own daily revisal and correction. . . .
>
> I must not conclude without declaring our mutual satisfaction in Mr. Pope's acceptance of our best endeavours, which have contributed at least to his more speedy execution of this great undertaking. If ever my name be numbered with the learned, I must ascribe it to his friendship, in transmitting it to posterity by participation in his labors.[14]

Broome added to the force of the statement by breaking out into a gushing hymn of praise to Pope, which said in part:

> 'Tis thine, on ev'ry heart to grave thy praise,
> A monument which Worth alone can raise;
> Sure to survive when time shall whelm in dust
> The arch, the marble, and the mimic bust:
> Nor 'till the volumes of th' expanded sky
> Blaze in one flame, shalt thou and Homer dye:

Then sink together in the world's last fires,
What heav'n created, and what heav'n inspires . . .
To verse like thine fierce savages attend,
And men more fierce: when Orpheus tunes the lay
Ev'n fiends relenting bear their rage away.[15]

Such admiring couplets, when compared with Broome's shrill abuse of the poet in his letters to Fenton, can hardly be understood or condoned.

Although the *Odyssey* appeared in 1726, it was almost a year before Pope's assistants were paid. Fenton would not face Pope alone; and Broome, in spite of his lush couplets of praise to Pope, sulked at Sturston. Finally payment was made: Broome received £500, plus £70 14s. for the fourteen subscriptions he had obtained; Fenton got £200 for his share of the work in translating four books.

Fenton and Broome, it is obvious, had hoped that Pope would give them a larger share from his own profit of some £5,000. They felt they had "hunted with the lion." Once they had been defrauded of the fame commensurate with their labors, they looked forward to a monetary compensation for their loss in prestige. Pope serenely ignored this hope. His fame and the exertion of his friends had built up his own subscription list; Pope felt no generous impulse to share the golden shower with his myrmidons.

The resentment of Fenton and Broome grew the more they talked of the affair and wrote of it to each other. The whole controversy gave Pope endless trouble, because of the weapon it put in the hands of his detractors. They now called him mean and penurious, in addition to the other vilifying epithets they were accustomed to apply to him.

At the time of Fenton's death in 1730, Broome and Pope were reconciled and took up again their complimentary correspondence. Broome was still affected with his yearning for poetic fame, and he asked Pope's help in getting his collected poems published. In a letter dated October 29, 1735, Broome admitted the precise amount of work each man had done. It is unfortunate that he said nothing which would enable us to determine the exact amount of correction Pope had given the work of his assistants. The matter has continued to be clouded in mystery. Because it is mysterious, there is strong suspicion that Pope made very few corrections in the work of Fenton or Broome.

A survey of all the evidence concerning the translation of the *Odyssey* and the ultimate disagreement and ill humor of the three translators gives us an unflattering glimpse of both Pope and Broome. However, it would appear that Pope has been too bitterly blamed for the *whole* unfortunate situation. Analysis of the existing correspondence between Pope, Broome, and Fenton indicates that there was from the first some sort of loose verbal understanding between the translators which specified, perhaps in a general way, the literary credit and the monetary reward which was to be the share of each of the co-workers. In working out the verbal contract, it seems certain the money guaranteed Pope's assistants was that which was paid them: the copy money for each book translated, plus any sums realized through the subscriptions of their friends. A share in the glory of the work was also to be one of the rewards, *once the edition was safely produced and paid for.*

This second clause, much more attractive than mere money, hinged on the necessity of keeping secret the precise conditions of collaboration until after the public and the critics had been bit. By his careless talk Broome had endangered the success of the whole project. In forcing or convincing Broome to make an untrue statement, if Pope did either (it has not been proved that Broome did not volunteer the service), Pope and Broome participated in an evasion unworthy of them and their work. It must be remembered, however, that the project does not seem to have been planned that way in the beginning. Broome's indiscretion, in Pope's mind, justified the consequent deception: this latter was a bungling attempt to carry through the original plan.

Pope's helpers had received as much, or nearly as much, as they had originally been promised. Pope took the lion's share of the proceeds, because he and his friends had built up the subscription list on the basis of Pope's performance in the *Iliad* and his widely admired personality. Broome and Fenton were well paid, but they had some justification for feeling cheated financially after Broome's evasive statements had deprived them of their proper share of glory.

The ten years Pope labored as a "mere editor," 1720–1730, are the least creditable portion of his whole life. They were also the most troubled. So much concealment of his life and business affairs was forced on Pope by coercive and discriminative laws, that he should not be too harshly blamed for having an equivocating mentality where his financial security was concerned—and, in a sense, his reputation as a translator. The constant stream of unjust attack, most of it anonymous, was sufficient to be a challenge to Pope to maintain his eminence and enlarge his fortune by whatever weapons came easiest to his hand. He retained his place and went on to new triumphs, perhaps only because he was fitted to survive at a period when any weapon seemed valuable in the struggle between Whigs and Tories, between genius and the dunces.

7

The Scourge of God

Before her Fancy's gilded clouds decay,
And all its varying rainbows die away.
The Dunciad

THE years spent in drudging as a "mere editor" had been
of no credit to Pope's creative genius. He was uneasy: a consuming restlessness possessed him. The old flight from himself
went on: the procession to glittering country houses, the jolt-
ing journeys to Bath and Oxford. There were wit and good
manners and bright entertainment of celebrities at Twickenham. The lawns and gardens greened and prospered, but the
poetic reputation of Pope showed no perceptible increase.
The appearance of Buckingham's *Works* had bared for a
moment the sharp-edged sword of justice; the reception of
Pope's edition of Shakespeare had been obscured by envy and
malice, masked behind the bland face of scholarship; the
Odyssey had led to accusations which seemed to lower Pope's
work to the level of Broome's and Fenton's. A brilliant stroke
was wanted: something of breath-taking splendor to light up
the battlements on the towers of literature; something blazing
aloft to catch the fancy of the town with the force of a
dazzling comet, crying a portent to Pope's age, or any age, in
the endless void of the future. The genius of Pope was equal
to the demands of the times and the clamoring of circum-

stances. In composing the *Dunciad*, Pope evinced, as he had in *Windsor Forest* and the *Rape of the Lock*, a universal quality which took its life from the depths of his roots in his own period.

Just how early Pope had begun to form his first plan of the *Dunciad* is debatable. It may have dated from his Scriblerian days, but it had taken some definite shape by 1725. In a letter to Swift, dated "Twickenham near Hampton Court, Oct. 15, 1725," Pope observed:

> I am sorry poor P [Philips] is not promoted in this age: for certainly if his reward be of the next, he is of all poets the most miserable. I am also sorry for another reason; if they do not promote him, they will spoil a very good conclusion of one of my Satires, where, having endeavoured to correct the taste of the town in wit and criticism I end thus:
> But what avails to lay down rules for sense?
> In [George]'s reign these fruitless lines were writ
> When Ambrose Philips was preferred for wit.[1]

This playful letter reached Swift in Ireland. The meditative quiet of his deanery gave him the opportunities for that devouring scrutiny of humanity which led him to denounce it for its insanities and hypocrisies. Well, then—Pope was making ready to step into a field traveled by the Drapier and Gulliver. Let him not step into it with his eyes closed. It was no May Fair suited to a day or a week of idle fun. Pope must be cautioned—and so he was with shrewdest wisdom—in the reply the Dean wrote him:

> Take care the bad poets do not outwit you, as they have served the good ones in every age, whom they have provoked to transmit their names to posterity. Maevius is as well known as Virgil, and Gildon will be as well known as you, if his name gets into your verses: and as to the difference between good fame and bad fame, it is a perfect trifle.[2]

[156]

Swift's incisive comments commended themselves to Pope. It would be gratifying to show the town how witty he could be. The time was hungry for personalities. If he were to assuage that hunger, his enemies would be struck down for a time. But on the mountains of the future, what would show to posterity? The faces of those who hated him, carved in the immortal granite of words. The personalized direction of his satire must be changed. He must lift it and elevate it to a plane of universality and poetic brilliance worthy of himself and his talent. This change of direction was somewhat coarsely foreshadowed in his answer to the Dean's cautions:

> To vindicate one's self against such nasty slanders, is much as wise as it was in your countryman, when the people imputed a stink to him, to prove the contrary by showing his backside. So let Gildon and Philips rest in peace! What Virgil had to do with Maevius, that he should wear him upon his sleeve to all eternity, I do not know, 'but I think a bright author should put an end to slanders only as the sun does to stinks—by shining out exhale them to nothing.'[3]

Pope's quick appreciation of Swift's meaning gives us an interesting insight into the workings of the poetic mind. In speculating on Swift's summary, Pope's imagination compared the case of Virgil and Maevius to his own situation, and he apprehended truly that genius, if it merely descends, has but the eternity of its detractors; it is only when a poet's talent shines out with full coruscation that the noxious odors rising from the fens and swamps of literature are dispersed in the healthy light of day. Had Pope elected to bedevil his adversaries in a smart, timely *Dunciad* it would have had the immortality of his detractors' works: the immortality of those winking insects in the river mud which perish when the sun goes down.

Within three months of Swift's first warning, the Dean had

[157]

come over to England. Judging from his letters to Pope, after returning to Ireland, the time spent in England was interesting and crowded with activity. There were journeys back and forth to London and the "digs" of John Gay, which were Swift's headquarters there: hours on the Thames and in the gardens of Twickenham and Dawley, crammed with the witty badinage of Gay, Bolingbroke, Arbuthnot, and Pope himself —the finest wits and raconteurs of a malicious and witty period.

Swift, as always, found things to his liking in the larger atmosphere of England. It gave him scope for impudence; ample fuel for his devastating indignation. It made him forget for hours the roaring in his ears, like the clamor of a thousand bores in the narrow fiords of his brain.

Dear lazy Gay and his nonsense; Bolingbroke, with his long actor's hands and carefully landscaped conversation in the best French style; and Pope, a delighted moth fluttering about him—they loved Swift in their own way. They lighted fresh fires in their hearts to do him honor.

Swift particularly enjoyed Mrs. Pope's company. He played endless games of ombre with her and chuckled over the cards and her open attempts to convert him to Catholicism. Martha Blount, too, appealed to Swift, because of her straightforward honesty and her lack of the simper and pose of the women of her day. Reading over and pondering the letters between Swift and Pope, Bolingbroke, and Gay, one is struck with the kindliness of Swift and a deep religious strain in him, so well hidden by his impudent approach to life and his perpetual habits of joking and making satirical references.

With people, good honest folk, Swift was himself. Unlike the philanthropist and pietist, he despised humanity but loved people. In the mass Swift found humanity loathsome. In his expression of this loathing, he seems a shade more honest than those who pay lip service to humanity and hate people.

Swift was not of this sort. No Walpurgis Night of the psychoanalyst, or the curdled sallies of the clerical ghouls who have commented on his letters in the Elwin and Courthope edition of Pope's works can obliterate the gentle, tenderhearted, absolute honesty which flashes out from the letters he wrote his trusted friends.

Swift spent about four months in England, most of this time in Twickenham. Not all the hours were given over to scintillating talk and broad jokes which casual conversation suggested. There was a serious purpose in Swift's visit. He had returned to gather the humorous and satirical works of the little circle for publication in several miscellanies. He was anxious also to destroy pieces not worthy of publication, which might drift into the hands of Curll. There was much sorting of papers; hours devoted to uproarious reading of past work; improvements to be suggested and planned, criticism to be made.

According to Pope's story in the appendix to the first *Dunciad Variorum* of 1729, it was probably in one of these critical sessions that Pope first showed Swift the "Dullness," as it was first called.

> For when he together with Mr. *Pope* (for reasons specified in their preface to the Miscellanies) had determin'd to own the most trifling pieces in which they had any hand, and to destroy all that remained in their power, the first sketch of this poem was snatch'd from the fire by Dr. Swift, who persuaded his friend to proceed in it and to him it was therefor inscribed.[4]

After four charming months in the society he loved and in which he shone, Swift hurried back to his distracted and despairing Ireland, with a head full of happy memories to warm his heart. Almost immediately upon his return to Ireland, the Dean sent a bundle of his lighter verse to Pope, with full power to burn, blot, or correct his works for the completion of the *Miscellanies* they had planned together.

Pope published the first two volumes of the *Miscellanies* in June, 1727, almost a year after Swift's visit. The third volume, containing the "Bathous," or the art of sinking in poetry, was not published until the following March. Courthope believes there was a reason for delaying the publication of the "Bathous." According to his inference, Pope laid a plot to make the extremely personal satire of the *Dunciad* acceptable to the public, which might have otherwise resented Pope's rough handling of many characters in his poem. Courthope further surmises that Pope had inserted into the "Bathous" Chapter VI, which groups the lesser lights of "sinking into the profound" under the guise of flying fishes, swallows, ostriches, parrots, didappers, porpoises, frogs, and eels. Not content with this literary bestiary, Pope audaciously set down the initials of authors at the end of each category, so that there should be no reasonable doubt of his meaning or intent.

It is not in any sense necessary to evolve a theory of Pope's "nice plotting" as Courthope does. No preparation was necessary to make Pope's satire acceptable to the taste of his age, which battened on personalities.

It is equally unprofitable to infer that Pope waited to enlarge the "Bathous" with more apt quotations of authors who had excelled in the "art of sinking." It is even possible to suspect, if suspicions have any value, that the "Bathous" originally ended with Chapter VI. The remaining chapters may well have been added after the first two books of the *Miscellanies* had been published, in one of those flashes of fun which sometimes convulsed Pope.

There were other good, solid, factual reasons for delaying the "Bathous." Pope was shrewd enough to know that the publication of the "Bathous," with its apt examples of stupidity and its menagerie of performing animals, was certain to bring down upon his head the full fury of the hacks and tenth-rate writers of Grub Street. It was of the essence of strategy to allow the mob no breathing space. Before their attacks on the "Bathous" could assume the complexion of a triumph, Pope must be prepared to meet them with a counterblow which would annihilate them. The "Bathous" was good fun, but if it served to release a flood of stupid spleen, his countergesture must have that elevation in conception and execution which would move the whole discussion to a plane in keeping with the concept of eternal genius surrounded by the gadflies of envy and dullness.

There were other things to be considered; things which took up time and suggested cautious preparation before giving the "Bathous" to the public. There were laws of libel to be weighed and the brutal force of the penal laws. Careful preparation was imperative before Pope could be sure he might proceed with the project in some degree of safety. Pope without doubt consulted his legal friend Pigott, "who always kept him out of law," and Fortescue, the Master of the Rolls —one of the channels to the ear of Sir Robert Walpole—and equally learned in the law. Doubtless, as a result of their advice, Pope planned the careful strategy he pursued in publishing the *Dunciad*.

Meanwhile, Swift in Ireland was spoiling to see Pope's "Dullness," which the poem was called in 1727. Pope, it would seem, did not inform Swift of his full intentions, or the causes for delaying the appearance of the third *Miscellany*, perhaps because Swift had inoculated Pope with some of his own mistrust of prying postal officials. Pope did, however, give hints which piqued Swift's curiosity. In one of the joint letters written to the Dean by Pope and Gay, Pope made a long comment on court intrigues, a subject which Swift followed with perennial interest until his giddiness and the roaring in his ears reduced him to caring as little for courts as he did for human companionship. Gay had recently been offered the post of gentleman-usher to Princess Louisa. He had killed any hope of court preferment by refusing the sinecure. Commenting on his act, in a short note at the end of one of Gay's letters, Pope observed:

> Gay is a free man, and I writ him a long congratulatory letter upon it. Do you the same: it will mend him, and make him a better man than a court could do. Horace might keep his coach in Augustus's time if he pleased; but I will not in the time of our Augustus. My poem [*Dunciad*] (which it grieves me that I dare not send you a copy of, for fear of the Curlls and the Dennises of Ireland, and still more for the fear of the worst of traitors, our friends and admirers), my poem, I say, will show you what a distinguishing age we lived in. Your name is in it, with some others, under a mark of such ignominy as you will not much grieve to wear in that company. Adieu, and God bless you, and give you health and spirits.

> > Whether thou choose Cervantes' serious air,
> > Or laugh and shake in Rab'lais' easy chair;
> > > Or in the graver gown instruct mankind,
> > Or, silent, let thy morals tell thy mind.

> These two verses are over and above what I have said of you in the poem.[5]

In January Pope gave Swift further intimation of the "Dullness," and sent the completed dedication, of which he had given the Dean a sample in the foregoing letter. By early February the *Dunciad* was nearly finished. Bolingbroke inferred that in one of his balanced epistles to the Dean. "Dulness grows and flourishes . . . It will indeed be a noble work; the many will stare at it, the few will smile, and all his patrons from Bickerstaffe to Gulliver will rejoice, to see themselves adorned in that immortal piece."[6]

The advance accounts and the atmosphere of secrecy captivated Swift. They made him cry impatiently at the end of February: "Now why does not Mr. Pope publish his Dulness? The rogues he mawls will die of themselves in peace and so will his friends, and so there will be neither punishment nor reward."[7]

The third volume of the *Miscellanies* was published in March, 1728. It included the "Bathous," which Pope had rewritten. In spite of the success of Gay's musical comedy, *The Beggar's Opera*, which had the town by the ears and ran for "forty nights," the "Bathous" soon made the welkin ring with the furious shouts of the Grub Street poets who resented their inclusion in the "art of sinking."

On March 23, Pope indicated to Swift that he had altered the title of his forthcoming poem:

As for those scribblers for whom you apprehend I would suppress my Dulness (which, by the way, for the future, you are to call by a more pompous name, the Dunciad), how much that nest of hornets are my regard will easily appear to you when you read the Treatise of the Bathos.[8]

The "Bathous" *had* stirred the hornets. In poems, pasquinades, and broadsheets they came at Pope from every direction. Burnet, Oldmixon, Dennis, and "Tibbald" flamed into print: the air was thick with the old malice. The best of the satire and abuse against Swift and Pope was gathered in a *Miscellany* purporting to be a fourth volume of the Swift-Pope Miscellanies. It was the work of Swift's enemy Smedley, the other Jonathan and Dean of Clougher. It was published in 1728, after the appearance of the *Dunciad*.

This "fourth volume" was divided into two sections:

"Gulliveriana," a collection of vituperation against Swift; and an appended smaller section entitled "Alexanderiana." The "Gulliveriana" starts out with high good humor in the clever introduction, but it degenerates into the dull abuse Swift and Pope usually received from their enemies, who had to resort to name calling in defect of satire. The section dealing with Pope begins with the usual tirade against his religion: a comparison between the ecclesiastical and poetical Popes. It is significant, as one of the possible early sources for the persistent accusation that Pope was a deist and an unbeliever:

> The two Popes profess the same Religion, but 'tis doubted whether either of them believe in Christ. *The Great Foreigner* pretends to forgive all manner of Sins: *The Little Britan* does not think there is such a Thing, as *Sin* in the World.
>
> They both set up for infallibility, but shew it in nothing but *Bulls* and *Blunders:*
>
> They both set themselves at the Head of their Profession, and dictate and insult, altho' all the world knows they carry visible Marks about them, of *Cheats*, *Impostures* and *Pretenders* and do daily discover innumerable Signs of *false Prophecy* and *false Poetry*. They both usurp over greater, wiser, wittier and better men than themselves . . .

The dull and abusive indictment goes on to its duller conclusion:

> The Breviary of the one can, no more make you a Saint than the *Criticism* of the *other* can make you a *poet.* Both these performances are equally, dull, cantering and fustian stuff; that a confused Plagiary from the *Bible:* This, from *Vida* and others.[9]

Much of the other material in this Miscellany, by far the greater part of it, is composed of selections from newspapers;

indignant letters and ephemeral attempts at epigram. Wit flounders in the furious waves of billingsgate.

While the wasps of Grub Street had rallied their half-wits to a struggle against the "Bathous," Pope dropped his literary D.D.T. in the anonymous publication of the *Dunciad*, May 28, 1728. It was published anonymously, primarily for reasons of caution, but for the fun of the thing as well. Pope did not publish the dedication to Swift in the first edition, and the title page was arranged to suggest that the London issue was a mere reprint of a Dublin edition. The names of persons involved in the satire were indicated by initials, the same method Pope had employed with success in the "Bathous."

The pretense of a Dublin edition was of course a subterfuge to protect the printer and publisher against legal action. Pope could not—even had they been co-operative or willing—employ any of his usual publishers or printers, if he were to follow a path at once secret and safe. He found a way out. In the anonymous reprint of the fictitious Dublin edition, Bettenham, the son-in-law of Bowyer, who printed the *Iliad*, was his printer; but when a publisher was selected with the exclusive privilege of publishing the *Dunciad*, the name of Lawton Gilliver appeared on the title page and was so registered at Stationer's Hall.

Gilliver was an apprentice of John Bowyer. He gradually worked himself into the book trade. He first emerged as a publisher in 1729, undoubtedly under Pope's patronage.[10] In all likelihood Pope selected a young man because of his willingness to run the hazard of publishing a work as explosive as the *Dunciad*. Pope further protected himself and Gilliver by having Burlington, Oxford, and Bathurst assign Gilliver the copyright of the *Dunciad* for fourteen years. Had the scheme misfired in any way, through an unfavorable attitude of the court, government, or aristocracy, Gilliver would have suffered the full force of the laws. In assuming the risk he did, Gilliver showed a shrewd trust in himself and Pope which was a good earnest of his eventual success.

Gilliver's wager was accurate: the town went mad over the *Dunciad*; everyone wanted to identify the initials in the poem. The noble and the witty were relieved at not discovering their own initials, and in consequence found themselves allied with Pope against the forces of dullness and reaction.

Once he was assured of the *Dunciad's* success and the inaction of those he had satirized, Pope proceeded to arrange a handsome variorum edition of the poem, which was published in 1729. In the preface to it he appended the long letter from William Cleland. This was at once an apology for the *Dunciad* and a stratagem which provided Pope an excuse for introducing copious notes and quotations. It was this machinery which lifted the satire into the realm of the impersonal, by demonstrating with thundering conclusiveness that Pope's enemies were of the same ilk and used much the same material as the enemies of Dryden, and by implication, of any great literary figure who might blaze up on their gray horizon. Pope also used this machinery to indicate that noted critics and fair critics had not hesitated to admit his eminence.

The publication of the first *Dunciad Variorum* took on a tinge of Renaissance splendor such as attended the first showing of a work of art by Michelangelo or Leonardo. The King and Queen were each presented a copy of the poem by their Prime Minister, Sir Robert Walpole; the court buzzed with rumor, throbbed with laughter. The ruling clique went thumbing from the index of persons celebrated in the poem to the episodes which satirized them. The booksellers were besieged for copies they didn't have.

Though he had tickled the fancy of the highest, Pope was careful to take no chances. The copyright was first vested in three of Pope's patrons: Lord Bathurst, and the Earls of Oxford and Burlington. They distributed the books to the purchasers. The booksellers were allowed to have no hand in the affair until it was certain all danger of persecution had passed.

The laughter of the Court and the protection of some of the most respected titles and greatest monied interests of the Kingdom frightened the dunces from taking revenge at law. Pope had silenced them for the moment. James Ralph and his other old enemies tried their usual abusive tactics, but they withered in the laughter of the town. Some dunces were frightened at a prospective loss of employment by the booksellers. In moments of fear they wrote Pope abject notes of repentance. They cringed before him. It was a great triumph.

The *Dunciad*, in general, owed much to Dante and Milton, and in particular to Dryden's *Mac Flecknoe*. Curiously enough, however, some individualizing notes of Pope's satires may have been derived from a passage in *Kit-Cats*, a satirical poem written by Pope's archenemy, Sir Richard Blackmore, and first published about 1700. It must have been one of the poems Pope read in forming his satirical style, and since it so far surpasses all of Blackmore's other efforts in the same genre it may have commended itself to Pope's attention. It contains some excellent satirical strokes, quite at variance with the usual style of the "Father of the art of sinking":

In famed Hibernia on the Northern Main,
Where Wits unknown, and Schools are built in Vain,
Between two hills that rise with equal pride,
And with their Tops the floating Clouds divide;
Secure from Storms, extended lies asleep. . . .
On the dark Margin of the Stagnant Flood,
The Temple of the God of Dullness stood.
With rude magnificence high in the Air
Thick Walls of Mud the pond'rous Roof did bear.

Of Birds the formal Owl, of Beasts the Ass
Dear to the God, did dark the Niches grace.
And on the Dome's high Front ill cut in Wood,
Scottish *Silenus*, and Dull Morpheus Stood,
Irregular it seemed in every Part,
Which as in *China*, here is perfect Art.
In Gouty Pillars, thick unlightsome Walls,
With windows at the Top, like Pigeon Holes,
It imitates our hideous Church of Paul's.
Such is the Skill, that all the parts appear,
Contriv'd from dull and blind Devotion here.
Sleep pamper'd Priests beneath the Altar snore,
And stretch't at Ease, their stupid God adore.
The vot'ries here Eternal Silence keep,
And unreproach'd their worship pay asleep.
The Idol is compos'd of massy Lead.
And wreaths of Poppy-Flowers Adorn his Head.
Lolling and yawning in his Chair of State,
And dropping down his Head the drowsy Figure sate.
For incense here instead of Indian Gums,
Paetum and Poppies spread their grateful Fumes;
Which lull'd the Senses vext with Care and Pain,
Blunt the sharp Edge of Thought and Kindly cloud the Brain.

The owl, the ass, the dome, and the whole background of
the poem are very much like the *Dunciad*. The general atmosphere suggests Pope's original "Dulness."

Whether Pope took the germ of his idea from Blackmore
and Dryden or not, he ultimately made it something in accord
with his own genius. It may have been something other than
he had intended it, but it was mysteriously beautiful, like those
secret forces within him which from nothing had raised him
to be the first figure of his age. Courthope and many others
have maintained that Pope's satire is too personal to give the
Dunciad the moral force which valid satire demands. These

accusations may be true of the anonymous editions of 1728, but they evaporate before the revised edition of 1729. In the first *Dunciad Variorum* the malice, inadequacy, meanness, and mental poverty of the dunces are condemned out of their halting, half-mad mouths by extensive quotations from their own works. They happen to be Pope's enemies, but they were also Dryden's. In any age the dunces will always hate eminence and genius, or anything light which makes a reproach of their darkness. What does it matter whether "Tibbald" reign or Cibber? "Dunce the second follows dunce the first." The supply of dunces is inexhaustible. Their names will be Cibber and James tomorrow. In the dark grab bag of time they will be called Smith or Jones, Lockhart or Elwin; any tag which may give to envy "a local habitation and a name."

The poem itself is superbly organized. It is as well integrated as Dante's *Inferno* and is a much better-natured poem in every way. Against the heavy strokes of darkness in the background of the poem, the action is executed with brilliance. Distaste for the *Dunciad* usually springs from a critical misconception of it; a misconception which grows from a willful misjudgment of Pope himself.

The first quality of the poem was not its personalities, but something objective: a good-tempered arraignment of mediocrity and envy. Because of this end, Pope had no need to be either cruel or unjust. Tibbald, Welsted, Curll, Moore, and Blackmore were temporary manifestations of something as old as time itself. Not men but Dullness *herself* is the chief burden of Pope's song:

> The Mighty Mother and her Son who brings
> The Smithfield Muses to the ear of Kings.

Here is both generalization and particularization which set the tone of the satire. It is made to fit all humanity; it narrows to its present manifestation in England and in Pope's own decade is personified in particular men.

Malice has asserted that the poem lacks sufficient action to be properly called an epic, but that criticism, too, is of a carping nature. The action in the poem is obvious to those who wish to see it.

From her cloud-hung gloom above rag fair, Dullness surveys her growing empire in England. She sees it deepening into ever greater gloom with the multiplied presses, cliques, booksellers, and false scholars. Her eyes light up as she beholds her favorite son Tibbald, supperless in the Gothic Vatican of his Library. Tibbald offers a sacrifice of his books to the goddess. They flame up toward her and she descends with just one monolithic page of Ambrose Philips's *Thule* and puts out the fire. Dullness instructs Tibbald to meet her in her palace. He obeys her command, and with opium is anointed "King Log," to the plaudits of Smithfield and Grub Street.

The physical pitch of the action accelerates in Book II. Dullness proclaims triumphant games to celebrate Tibbald's enthronement. To these contests the hacks and the booksellers eagerly throng from all the moldy corners of London. A plump well-fed poet is offered as a prize in the first race. Lintot and Curll volunteer to run. They speed forward in the best style of the twenty-third *Iliad*. Curll flounders in cloacal mud while Lintot hurries on, but Curll prays to Jove; his prayer is heard by the god and Curll, refreshed from his bath of ordure, flashes forward to win the race.

As he attempts to seize his prize where "The Tall Nothing stood or seemed to stand," the form vanishes. In order to add a frolic note to the scene, Curll runs about after one or other of the pretended poets disguised by Dullness in the likeness of the great. Then, to console the disconsolate publisher, Dullness gives him another prize in place of the poet he had hoped to win: a tapestry woven with scenes of cudgeling, vomiting, and tossing in blankets. Curll receives it avidly, like one who glories in his shame.

The next contest is a trial of strength in voiding urine. The prizes offered are a chamber pot and Eliza Heywood. Curll's son Henry competes in this contest with Chetwood, another raffish stationer. Chetwood meets with an ignominious mischance and Curll the younger, like an animated geyser, wins. He walks off with the lady, while Chetwood consoles himself with the "jordan."

Following the "water sports" are a tickling contest with a noble lord for a prize, a braying contest, and a diving contest in the sewer-ooze of Fleet-ditch, all farcically described. The final game is an endurance contest between the soporific works of Henley and Blackmore. While the eager hacks gather around appointed readers, alternate ponderous passages are droned out, until every one achieves the equal prize in this contest—sleep.

Many of the hack poets are off at once in Walpurgis dreams, but King Tibbald sleeps with his anointed head in the lap of Dullness. In Tibbald's dream the goddess herself takes him to the Elysian fields. There he meets his great father Settle and is shown all the past glories of Dulness. With something of the stage terror felt in the implacable march of the apparitions in Macbeth, Tibbald is whirled about the terrestrial globe, through the ages and centuries. It is action of the intensest sort, so large in its outlines that the careless reader may lose sight of it. King Tibbald beholds the Goths, Huns, and Visigoths sweeping over the antique learning of the world: sacking libraries, burning and pillaging the civilization and learning of antiquity. He beholds the formal condemnation of the classics by some of the early Christians and Popes, the quarrying of the artistic monuments of Greece and Rome to raise Christian churches and statues.

Next Dullness reveals to Tibbald his future glory, taking shape in England. He sees the crowds of venal and stupid writers exalted to eminence while Pope, Gay, and Swift are ignored in the honors of state and court. King Tibbald becomes a portent which ushers in the new Saturnian age of lead, in which "none but himself can be his parallel"; where Ambrose Philips is "preferr'd for wit"; where the great works of architecture—the labors of Wren, Boyle, and Inigo Jones—are already falling into decay for want of repair. The universities, the schools, art and philosophy, physics and mathematics, perish in a Stygian darkness which "buries all."

Here is a prodigality of action! From the individual Tibbald in the first book, to the crowd of stationers and hacks seeking fame and laurels in the second, to the world and eternity in the third, it is a widening-out into a series of ever greater vistas and more grandiose conceptions of darkness, flight, and distance.

There are some critics who seem perturbed that Pope should have resorted to broad vulgarity in most of the games described in the second book. In his defense, it may be said that Pope, unlike Addison, was almost untouched by Puritanism. He was one with Shakespeare in believing that the foulness and mire of existence are a part of living. As a consequence, Pope makes the punishment fit the crime. Curll, Chetwood, Mrs. Heywood, Oldmixon, and the others were purveyors of garbage literature. They habitually dealt in moral slime and character assassination. Those who continue to see all things through the spectacles of Victorian prudery may wince at Pope's use of vulgar words, which, as far as one can determine, caused no blush in the candlelighted drawing-rooms of his day; nowhere in fact, except from the very people of his period who reveled in squinting wickedness hiding behind anonymity, the screen of the fan, or the luster of hammered words.

The *Dunciad* is not a tour de force fabricated to punish Pope's personal enemies. It is of a piece with the *Essay on Criticism*,[11] the *Rape of the Lock*, and *Windsor Forest*. It is a creative defense of the very fabric of Western culture and civilization, which sees in man himself, and in keeping the traditions, not a slavery but a freedom from slavery. The *Dunciad* is a positive statement in favor of order, human qualities, tolerance, and virtue. It is an inspired diatribe against the mechanistic evil of men who are so busy agitating, hating, and annotating that they have lost all conception of the honest face of truth: the truth of beauty and the truth of tolerance.

The background of the poem is tinctured with darkness, saturated with gloom. A world of grisaille emerges in which the trumpets in the landscape are muted like the notes blown from a hatted cornet. Dullness is the daughter of Chaos and Night; her majesty is a clouded one, like some bright architectural marvel of London coated with fog and soot; she looks out on a chaos dark and deep, where "nameless Somethings in their Causes sleep." Mud, filth, darkness, opium; a kingdom of owls and asses! Yet it would be false to fancy Pope has failed to show us beautiful things against this murky tapestry. In the same way in which Dante intensifies the sulphurous caverns of the *Inferno* by introducing lovely pictures of the beautiful world he has left behind, Pope, too, makes this universe of dullness come into more vivid darkness by equally valid contrasts. Against the squalor and darkness of the first book, a warm picture of the Lord Mayor's procession:

Pomps without guilt, of bloodless swords and maces,—
Glad chains, warm furs, broad banners and broad faces,

[173]

Pope's silkworm spinning its slender store, and his weighted
clock, are lovely against the gloom.

In the second book, the rumors of beauty grow in frequency. The senate of Leo, the urn of Eridanus, the noble lord
in his sedan chair preceded by six huntsmen and followed by
four jockeys, Hill metamorphosed to a swan—are in Pope's
best sparkling manner. These touches of splendor multiply
with the unfolding of the third book. The immediate atmosphere is lovely: Tibbald is curtained with "vapours blue"
sprinkled with "Cimmerian dew," the volumes spawned by
hack writers are seen "thick as stars of night or morning dews."
Such glimpses are intensified in the vision of the future opened
out before the new-made King of Dullness:

> See round the pole where keener spangles shine
> Where spices smoke beneath the burning line.

The last images are akin to the metaphysical poets and Shakespeare: at once amazingly precise, yet thrown wide for the
imagination to make of them a whole speculation of beauty.

> Lo where Meotis sleeps and hardly flows
> The freezing Tanais thro' a waste of snows. . . .
> Yet would thou more? In yonder cloud behold
> Whose Sarcenet shirts are edg'd with flamy gold,
> A matchless youth; his nod these worlds controuls
> Wings the red lightning and the thunder rolls.

The beauty carries through to the inspired conclusion, and it
is coupled with a kind of exaltation. Here is to be found no
scorpion condemnation of one who hates the world and loves
to voice his hatred. Pope savors the splendor of wind and star
and flower. It is with freezing horror that he beholds the
quenching of the pulsing stars, not in the blaze of day, but in
eternal darkness.

The organization of the poem is well planned. Reality and

objectiveness are held up for our admiration, and there is complete correspondence between these universals and the figures which refract them into life. The *Dunciad* can hardly be called criticism at all; it is rather an extended intuition of values. The only hatred it expresses is a compelling distaste for the furious envies of the bourgeois mentality.

Nor is the fun in it icily bitter, as Swift's humor often is. Pope enjoyed himself in the *Dunciad*. He didn't make the fatal mistake of thinking all men are hideous. But when men turn aside from polite learning and genius, they are certainly ridiculous and in a sense even inhuman in a comical way, yet never completely loathsome. Pope's description of Curll, Moore, Lintot, and Theobald were created to make the poet laugh: he was not in a pet, not morose. He was rather like a precocious child who is naughty in an amusing fashion and who first of all enjoys the fun himself.

The nineteenth-century critics, on the whole, found the *Dunciad* too rich and too realistic for their nice stomachs. In their pursuit of the pretty, they too often forgot that life in its compelling, coarse, and vital aspects must also show itself in valid and eternal literature.

Pope's clairvoyant qualities are stunningly revealed in the *Dunciad*. His prophetic excellence is obvious to any man who is honest enough to make a comprehensive survey of our own literary horizons.

8

A Case for Sherlock Holmes

Hath Bolingbroke
Deposed thine intellect? hath he been in thy heart?
Richard II, Act V, Scene I

IN the *Dunciad* Pope offered up a hecatomb of authors to the god of mirth. He exposed the poisonous malice of the bourgeois and untalented in a vision which went from age to age. Those of his enemies not reduced to silence were kept within some bounds by the goodnatured pages of the *Grub-Street Journal*. In this paper, under the able editorship of John Martyn and Richard Russell, Pope, it is believed by many of his biographers, extended the scope of his purge on dullness.

It has often been said that Pope's wit and humor were malicious and scornful. Their objectivity has eluded many of the well-disposed commentators of Pope's works, chiefly because Pope's enemies, during his lifetime, ascribed motives to the poet which had a tendency to obscure for posterity either a fair or critical estimate on his satirical work. If the pages of the *Grub-Street Journal* reflect the temper of Pope it is possible to examine a larger picture of his good humor; a kind of pixy side of his nature which delighted in epigrams and pranks, less for the harm they might do than for the sake of the wit in them.

The *Grub-Street Journal* may well have sprung from Pope's desire to enlarge the good effects of the *Dunciad*, but there is little in its pages which would suggest that it was brought into being to pursue the poet's private vendettas. Pope's personal enemies happened to be the *Journal's*. His enemies were the most active of the disciples of Dullness, her greatest dark-bearers. They hated Pope as they hated Swift or Gay or Arbuthnot. Pope, the most exalted literary success of the day, was attacked with greater fury because of his eminence and the obvious target he offered in his personal and civic disabilities.

Close investigation has revealed little of the actual background or ownership of the *Grub-Street Journal*.[1] Circumstances, however, point to its control and ownership by someone who had the good will of Walpole, as Pope had. The *Journal* could not have hoped to remain in existence without the toleration of those in authority. The persistent compliments to Walpole, some of them almost fulsome, would seem to indicate his knowledge of the *Journal* and its true owners.

In all probability the *Journal* was organized on the model of the Scriblerus Club, each issue taking its final form after discussion and group suggestion. Many of the contributions which are said to be Pope's contain touches not in his style, and some skits not attributed to him show flashes of his best manner.

Considering the complexion of the times, the *Journal* displayed balance and good temper. It admitted correspondence on both sides of almost every question, and in its early numbers pursued its way with a joyous verve which is reminiscent of Pope and his nervous good spirits. It became, in time, the most popular paper of the decade because of its wit and objectivity.

Many telling circumstances point to Pope's influence with the paper until it ceased publication. Though the later numbers were less high-spirited, its original purpose persisted. Pope used the *Journal* for his personal announcements, such as that of his mother's death. He also found it of service in denying some of the most stupid accusations against him; notably that concerning his "illegitimate children." The irreligion of Wollaston was often held up to scorn, and there were persistent satires on Bentley, Dennis, Moore, and Curll, and on the weekly papers in which Pope most often suffered attack.

Like all such efforts, the satires published in the *Grub-Street Journal* prodded Pope's enemies into renewed activity. These enemies indicated their respect for Pope and the *Journal* by cloaking their names in false initials or in complete anonymity. Where they had once been specific in their charges against the "little viper," they now resorted to generalities. Pope was penurious, a treacherous friend, unduly sensitive and bad-tempered, a liar, a lecher, a deist, or an atheist. As Sherburn has said:

> Nothing (usually) is proved; the most sensational charges are made in the vaguest possible terms; and by reiteration the charges have been made to pass as an authentic source of light on Pope's character. The more general charges . . . those involving moral traits . . . assert his ingratitude, treachery, ill-nature and malice. If the concrete accusations were proved, these traits could safely be imputed to Pope.[2]

In the following pages of his biography (154–161) Sherburn examined some of the concrete accusations against Pope, sifting them out, and showing on what flimsy grounds of fact most of them rested. Yet this is not enough to kill the canards, which continue to be current.

If Pope sometimes seemed penurious, he was also magnificent: he entertained at Twickenham in a superb manner, played cards for high stakes with Bathurst and Duke Disney, drank expensive Madeira and port, and was charitable to a great many people, such as the Blounts, Mrs. Cope, and Deane, to mention but a few of those for whom he opened his purse. His quarrels with Addison and Dennis, his ultimate dislike for Lady Mary and Lord Hervey, the temporary misunderstandings with Wycherley and Broome, are seen to be trivial evidences of Pope's bad temper compared with his friendship for Gay, Swift, Garth, Parnell, Fortescue, Bathurst, Craggs, Harley, Atterbury, and a thousand other notables. In the case of Atterbury, Pope defended him when such defense could not possibly serve his own interests.

The *Narrative of Dr. Norris*, the account of Curll's purge, the *Dunciad* itself, and the amusing fun of the *Grub-Street Journal*, are a good indication of Pope's humorous amiability, which was obviously his true nature, for it was reflected in the faces of the Scriblerus Club, in Gay, Swift, the Blounts, and in his early friendship with Lady Mary. He preferred dashing, high-spirited friends like himself.

His sharp portraits of Addison, Lord Hervey, and a few others were less personal than general. They were sharp attacks on jealousy, female boldness, insinuating evil in high places, and the impudent folly of the titled and eminent. The seeming malice in them arises from their tight form and the striking, intellectualized phrases which clothed the thought.

In those affairs which threatened his fortune or safety, or which brought him into conflict with the penal laws, Pope was less truthful than provident in looking to his own hide and safety at a time of crying injustice. In things outside this sphere, his "genteel equivocations" were not any more glaring than the subterfuges and sharp practices which appear in the life of any public man.

Some of Pope's enemies maintained he was a master of smut; an immoralist who used his pen to debauch and ruin women. Of course such assertions are ridiculous. There is every sign that Pope had a pure love for two women: his mother and Martha Blount. His bawdy poems, if all those ascribed to him are really his, are mere souvenirs of a coarse age. On measuring these against Addison's erotic translations of the *Metamorphoses*, one wonders why Pope should be censured and Addison escape.

Time and honest critics have tended to abolish most of the pictures of Pope's moral weakness, but one accusation has lingered on, gathering force with the years since Pope's death. It concerns his deism. The factual proof of the assertion that he was a deist rests mainly on two things: the evidence of Elwin in the notes to the *Essay on Man*, and Pope's close relationship with Bolingbroke.

Upon careful analysis, the evidence of Elwin—in the introduction to the *Essay on Man*—is seen to be trifling and malicious:

> Mrs. Mallet told General Grimouard that Pope, Bolingbroke, and their friends, who frequented her house, were "a society of pure deists." Bolingbroke was more of an infidel than Pope, for though he admitted that a future state could not be disproved, he laboured passionately to discredit the arguments in its favour. Pope held to the immortality of the soul. "He was a deist," says Lord Chesterfield, "believing in a future state; this he has often owned himself to me." He frequently avowed his deism to Lyttelton, and acquiesced in the deistical interpretations which the Richardsons put on the Essay on Man. Revelation he rejected entirely. Lord Chesterfield relates that he once saw a bible on his table, and adds, "As I knew his way of thinking upon that book, I asked him jocosely if he was going to write an answer to it?" The evidence that he had renounced christianity comes to us from various independent sources, and some of the witnesses are above the suspicion of misunderstanding or misrepresenting him.[3]

General Grimouard was told his facts by Mrs. Mallet, whose husband was the chief of the Bolingbroke coterie which tried to blacken Pope's reputation after his death. Pope is said to have been less an infidel than Bolingbroke. We are assured that Pope believed in the immortality of the soul but not in revelation. This cannot be the man who told Spence, "Some of Plato's and Cicero's reasonings on the immortality of the soul are very foolish; but the latter's less so than the former's —without revelation, it certainly is a grand *peut-être*."[4]

The testimony of Lyttelton and the Richardsons is undocumented, as Elwin presents it. Lord Chesterfield was never an intimate of Pope's, and his comment on Pope's attitude toward the Bible is all Chesterfield and no Pope. It is this type of evidence which brought forth Pattison's scathing denunciation of the work of Elwin.[5] Pope had been convicted of deism and unbelief before he had set foot in court.

In his actions and words there is everything to show that Pope remained a Catholic and died a Catholic. Yet it is alleged by his enemies that he was only a formal Catholic and that he propagated deism in the *Essay on Man*.

Those who are determined to keep Pope a deist make much of the fact that the first publication of the *Essay* was anonymous—Pope concealed his authorship from all, including his good friend Caryll, to whom he often revealed his projects in advance. Such reasoning seems to ignore the fact that Pope had first published the *Dunciad* without his name on the title page, and had found its acceptance and sale augmented by that subterfuge. If he were to turn philosopher, a new departure for him, the number of his enemies alone would suggest caution and something of the same method he had already employed.

When first issued, the *Dunciad* had been without its dedication to Swift, which might have exposed Pope's authorship and shown his hand. In the initial edition of the *Essay on Man*, Bolingbroke's name may have been withheld for the same reason.

The *Essay* caught on at once, and Pope, certain of success—and pleased, we may be sure—acknowledged it as his own work. No one suspected its so-called "deistic implications." In France, where the *Essay* sprang into instant popularity, the Jesuit critic P. Tournemine spoke well of it, and detected in the poem much the same trend of thought found in Pascal's *Pensées*.[6] The poem was translated into French by both Silhouette and the more famous M. de Resnel. It seemed assured of unlimited fame. At this juncture, in 1737, the *Essay* in de Resnel's translation fell into the hands of Crousaz, a Swiss professor and archdogmatist. Crousaz was reading a bungling translation. It garbled Pope's doctrine hideously. Yet this pedant, without a more thorough investigation, wrote a pamphlet accusing Pope of all sorts of philosophical slights which were quite beyond him. To the unamiable Crousaz the *Essay* was no more than an olla podrida of warmed-over Leibnitz and Spinoza.[7]

"The comments of Crousaz, often founded upon mistranslations and misconceptions,"[8] to use the words of Elwin, brought the whole organized world in cry on the heels of Pope. His enemies had at last found a solid club with which he could be beaten. They were not slow to use it. Pope, who was terrified at the outcry and, it may be, too unlearned in dialectic and philosophical subtlety to defend himself, or unwilling to acknowledge the true sources of the *Essay*, welcomed Warburton's unexpected defense—and the defender—with a naïve gratitude which is a confession of his inability to understand where in the *Essay* he had sinned. It is not without significance or importance that Rome made no attempt to put Pope's work on the *Index*, as she did the works of literary men and philosophers whose books had occasioned far less public outcry than Pope's *Essay*.[9]

Those who envied or hated Pope showed nothing of the tenderness of the dreaded Holy Office. The ineptitudes of Crousaz opened the way now for a spate of proofs in support of the long-iterated cry that Pope was irreligious. Pope's detractors tore into him like hyenas, using the accusations of Crousaz, lines wrenched from their context in the *Essay*, and their own former statements, as proofs of something which had no existence.

The ghoulish feast was not to end there. Accepting the uncertain certainties of Pope's enemies as a foundation of fact, serious scholars pawed about the bones of Pope's life and works in the nineteenth century. They prepared to embalm him definitively in spiderwebs of footnotes spun out of gossip, noble impudence, and malicious chit-chat.

All these ponderous misconceptions and illogical proofs were set down for posterity in the Elwin-Courthope edition of Pope's works, which still remains "a respected treasury of fact" for Pope's life and labors. Yet, where Pope's religion and the doctrines of the *Essay on Man* are concerned, the Elwin-Courthope edition of Pope's works is a tissue of inconsistencies. So snarled, confused, and often biased is the evidence there, that it requires the most pitiless scrutiny and minute sifting before it is possible to see either truth or order—and, what is much more important, the soul and intent of Pope in making the work.

It is of some moment to answer the question: Was Pope a deist? Elwin was convinced that he was. This gave him an ax to grind, and he ground it well enough to hack at Pope through his entire commentary on the *Essay on Man*. In addition to this intemperateness, Elwin insisted—in the introduction to the *Essay*—that Pope had gone over to Bolingbroke's deism, or had at least acquiesced in it and *secretly* propagated it in his *Essay on Man*.[10]

The more balanced Courthope, who finished the task of editing Pope's works, was convinced that Elwin had done Pope some considerable injustice. In keeping with this conviction, Courthope adopted the charitable assumption of Warburton and Johnson, which maintained that Pope had been deceived by Bolingbroke, and had, without intending to do so, propagated the deism of the Petronian lord.[11]

This idea, however amiably assumed, went to the opposite extreme from Elwin's explanation. Of course it could not be supported or proved, because in its own fashion it was as little suited to the facts as Elwin's assumption had been. That Courthope intuited this only too well is proved by two other statements he made in a sort of zigzag retreat from Moscow.

The first of these statements was blunt and unequivocal. It seemed to support the thesis which maintained Pope had been deceived by Bolingbroke:

> The poet [said Courthope] no doubt liked to think himself as superior to sect in religion and to faction in politics. But in respect of *esprit de corps*, he was a staunch adherent both of his church and his party. He made no response to the endeavours of Atterbury for his conversion. On the contrary, his hostility to the Church of England became more active as he grew older, and he rarely neglected the opportunity of a stroke at a bishop or a church dignitary, particularly if these happened to be Whigs.[12]

Had Courthope allowed this statement to stand, it would at least have given evidence of his logic and consistency. But, being a genuine scholar, Courthope still had his doubts concerning the deception practiced on Pope and he weaseled them into a statement which maintains that although Pope remained a formal Catholic, "the governing principle in his idea of Nature may therefore be described as Catholic Deism, but of this metaphysical element there is no trace in his poetry, he deals only with the *effects* of Religion, which he holds to be Virtue, or the want of it, which he pronounces to be Vice."[13]

This statement nullifies everything else Courthope said. It gives logic a black eye and kicks philosophy and fact down the back stairs. It requires none of the antics of semantics to demonstrate the fatuity of Courthope.

Catholic deism! Where is it to be found, if one believes, as one must, in the law of contradiction? Find me a Catholic deist! It is like the search for the unicorn.

And, it may be queried—not without archness—if "this metaphysical element" is not to be traced in Pope's poetry, where shall we find it? It cannot be discovered in Pope's letters, which reiterate and emphasize Pope's Catholicism, and there is nothing in his life as a *confirmed recusant* which would lead us to suspect that his idea of nature is "Catholic deism," if there were such a thing as Catholic deism.

There is not a shred of genuine proof that Pope was ever a deist, or looked upon the movement with anything but alarm and disgust. Must we then presume that Bolingbroke deceived Pope and palmed off on him a system which Pope turned into memorable verse, innocently of course? Such a presumption would have us believe that Pope versified something he did not understand—a presumption fantastic enough to demand its instant rejection.

Did the deception consist in the exercise of Bolingbroke's considerable charm and persuasive powers in such a subtle fashion that Pope became in his hands a puppet, and no longer a free agent to think or write what he wanted?

Pope was very much a free agent; he was entirely capable of thinking for himself. His actions show this, in a manner which brooks no doubt.

[185]

Pope believed in the immortality of the soul and said so,[14] Bolingbroke doubted it;[15] Bolingbroke tried to argue away the moral attributes of God, and Pope, who believed them, was alarmed and forced Bolingbroke to a verbal evasion;[16] Pope made Warburton a close friend and his editor, although Bolingbroke loathed him.[17]

These instances alone are overwhelming evidence, but if it could still be doubted that Pope was free to think and act for himself, we have only to recall Pope's independence in secretly printing fifteen hundred copies of Bolingbroke's *Patriot King* without telling Bolingbroke. The poet added insult to injury by changing some few words and expressions in the treatise to suit his own pleasure.[18] These are the acts of an untrustworthy friend, if you will, but certainly not the hypnotized conduct of a man dominated by Bolingbroke and without mind or ability to think for himself. It would be more nearly correct to believe Pope had deceived Bolingbroke in allowing him to think the poet was so lost in admiration of his Lordship that he could no longer tell a hawk from a handsaw.

Pope admired and loved Bolingbroke in his own way, but if there was a game of deception played, Bolingbroke was playing it with a man who had no master in his own day, and who, it seems, played on occasion for the fun of matching wits with those who had a tendency to ignore or despise him as an adversary. It may very well have been Bolingbroke's discovery of Pope's deception and his chagrin at being outwitted which turned him so violently against Pope after the little poet was dead.[19]

Bolingbroke was a man determined to rule in great or small. He fancied himself the Petronius of the age, and it would have touched him in his tenderest part to discover he had been as great a failure in ruling a poet as he had been in trying to rule a kingdom. Yet, if Pope allowed Bolingbroke to fancy that the poet had played the bird to my lord's serpent, no real injustice was done—the deception was slight and rather humorously conceived.

Bolingbroke had turned Pope's muse from "things of fancy to the heart"—the poet admitted it; he spoke his gratitude in immortal lines. In his daily intercourse with Pope at Dawley and Twickenham, Bolingbroke had warmed the poet's mind with conversation about philosophy, and flattered his intellect by putting Pope on the same philosophical level with himself.[20] But to presume that Pope was not free to select the elements of the curious philosophy he enunciated in the *Essay on Man* is to deny that Pope was a man who detested any form of dictation,[21] that Pope had received his early education as a Roman pietist,[22] that his own independent and desultory manner of reading had prepared him to write, even without Bolingbroke, the type of philosophical poem which the *Essay on Man* is.[23] It would seem fair to say, in consideration of all these facts and drifts of personality, that Bolingbroke was, in an inspirational sense, the animator of the *Essay on Man*; that Bolingbroke not only kept the subject warm in Pope's mind by almost daily discussion, but suggested the general technical method to be employed in the poem, when he observed:

He [the poet] may write as you have begun to do on philosophical subjects, but he must write in his own character. He must contrast, he may shadow, he has a right to omit whatever will not be cast into the poetic mold, and when he cannot instruct he may hope to please . . . In short it seems to me that the business of the philosopher is to dilate, if I may borrow the word from Tully, to press, to prove, to convince; and that of the poet to hint, to touch his subject with short and spirited strokes, to warm the affections and speak to the heart.[24]

If Pope had out-Heroded Herod; if he was successful in outwitting his guide, philosopher, and friend, what then becomes of the pretty story told by Bolingbroke, *after Pope's death*, in which my lord claimed Pope had versified his deistical *Minutes of Essays*—had in fact done no thinking of his own?

What, precisely, had Bolingbroke given Pope? Spence tells us that Pope

> "mentioned then, and at several other times how much (or rather how wholly) he himself was obliged to him for the thoughts and reasonings in his moral work, and once in particular said that beside their frequent talking over that subject together, he had received, I think, seven or eight sheets from Lord Bolingbroke, in relation to it, as I apprehend by way of letters; both to direct the plan in general, and to supply the matter for the particular epistles."[25]

It is plain that Pope was in no way attempting to evade either his debt to Bolingbroke, or his gratitude to the man for his aid. Through Mallet and Bathurst, Bolingbroke insisted it was not "seven or eight sheets" but the entire *Fragments* or *Minutes of Essays* "which were communicated to Pope as they were occasionally writ."

Are we supposed to believe that they were communicated to Pope in readings, discussed by the two friends, and then summed up in the seven or eight sheets which Pope says he received? That would clear up many things, but from Bolingbroke's statement and that of Bathurst, one is convinced Bolingbroke intended to convey to the world that Pope had merely versified the *Fragments*. Bathurst had got his story from my lord himself, and since the tale came into being at a time when Bolingbroke had become Pope's enemy, and the poet was no longer alive to defend himself, one is at liberty to suggest that the whole affair smells suspicious. We know that Pope was sometimes given to deception, but how is one to trust his flattering statement about Bolingbroke's influence less than the word of a man whose father said of him on his being made a lord, "Ah, Harry, I ever said you would be hanged, but now I find you will be beheaded."[26] A scrupulous weighing of the evidence becomes particularly pertinent if we recall that Bolingbroke, who made the wider claim, was at the time he made it Pope's enemy. Bolingbroke realized only too well that the worst disservice he could do his former friend was to claim not only the inspiration of the *Essay* in a general way, as is consonant with Pope's dictum to Spence, but actual control of both the poet and the *Essay* in every phase of composition, and to further claim that Pope had versified Bolingbroke's system.[27]

The affair has a still more sinister implication when we remember that Bolingbroke, who made these sweeping claims, was the guardian and sole disposer of the papers Pope left behind him. He was perfectly free to augment or lessen those "seven or eight sheets" as his caprice and honesty dictated.[28] The "seven or eight sheets" were never seen, even had they remained among Pope's papers, and it is a small wonder, under such circumstances, that Pattison says, in summing up the matter: "But even if the communication of the fragments preceded the composition of the *Essay on Man*, they are far from containing the whole scheme of the poem."[29]

What did Bolingbroke find among Pope's papers? We shall never know, because Bolingbroke burned them. But isn't it strange that Bolingbroke, if he designed to prove Pope's dependence upon his philosophy, found no factual proofs among Pope's most personal papers; factual evidence which might have been brought forward to prove the statements he later made to Mallet and Bathurst? There is a strong indication that

Bolingbroke discovered, among Pope's papers, the opposite of what he had expected to find. By destroying all the evidence, he prepared the way to claim what he wished, without fear of detection.

It is clear that Bolingbroke played a prime part in turning Pope toward a philosophical subject. He encouraged the poet through the composition of the four epistles; he may even have communicated his whole scheme of ideas to Pope in their long conversations while the work was in progress.[30] This agrees with Spence, but if Bolingbroke did these things, he necessarily left Pope free to choose the elements of his poem, and the poet chose those things with which his education, religion, and haphazard thinking on philosophical subjects had made him familiar. These things have proofs and they are in keeping with both Spence's words and the general influence of Bolingbroke, whose so-called philosophy, apart from two points, cannot be called original or new.[31]

The impudent deism of Bolingbroke, who charged a "blunderbuss against religion,"[32] is not found in the *Essay on Man*. In the main it may be said, and will be proved later, that with few exceptions the doctrine Pope is supposed to have taken from Bolingbroke might have been derived elsewhere. Bolingbroke's influence was general, and in no way was it destructive of Pope's Catholicism. Such a theory is the only one which fits the man and the evidence, and gives point to Pope's statement, "If I could flatter myself that this Essay has any merit, it is in steering betwixt the extremes of doctrines seemingly opposite, in passing over terms utterly unintelligible, and in forming a temperate, yet not inconsistent, and a short, yet not imperfect system of ethics."[33]

If Pope had intended the *Essay on Man* to be no more than a brief outline of Bolingbroke's philosophy, one should, at the very least, expect to find in the *Essay* the most important doctrines of Bolingbroke's system. "Bolingbroke's system"—the term is something of a misnomer, for, as Leslie Stephen says:

> Bolingbroke is monstrously diffuse; he is rhetorical where he ought to be logical; he repeats himself incessantly and contradicts himself as often; no solid ground of thought can be found in this shifting quagmire of speculation, where the one genuine ingredient seems to be a hatred of all philosophers and divines. . . . Indeed he contradicts himself almost as often as he contradicts Leibnitz. . . . It would be hopeless to give any coherent account of the 'first philosophy' of which he professed to be a teacher . . . Bolingbroke was in the first place a theist . . . but a theist on a plan of his own . . . His favourite assertion is the existence of a tacit confederacy between atheists and divines. It is connected with a peculiar doctrine as to evidences of a divine ruler, which though it shifts into varying shapes, has undoubtedly a certain meaning at bottom. His theory is that we can demonstrate the 'natural' but not the 'moral' attributes of God. We can recognize, that is, the power and wisdom but not the goodness or justice of the Deity. We should receive ideas of wisdom and power from God's works, even if 'human actions gave us none,' but we derive our first and strongest impressions of benevolence, justice, and other moral virtues, exclusively from reflexions on ourselves and our neighbors.[34]

This is the judgment of a man competent to speak of Bolingbroke's philosophy. If Pope simply versified the *Fragments*, one would expect him to have given a large amount of space to the two principal and often-stressed doctrines of Bolingbroke. Elwin wanted us to believe that Bolingbroke only implied a doubt of God's moral attributes, and he insisted that Pope acquiesced in Bolingbroke's opinion. In the long and confused account of this affair which precedes the *Essay on Man* in the Elwin-Courthope edition of Pope's works, Elwin was not only content to present his evidence, he hid in the grass of words and sniped at Pope and Warburton between the points of the argument.

To sum up the evidence given there, Pope's uneasiness when Hooke told him that Bolingbroke denied the moral attributes resulted in a discussion between Bolingbroke and Warburton. Pope was present at the discussion. Bolingbroke protested to Pope, what he had protested all along, that he did not deny the moral attributes of God, and he maintained against Warburton in Pope's presence, what he had all along avowed, that "they were not the same as in our ideas."[35]

Anyone who reads the *Fragments*, especially page 63, will be convinced that one may accuse Bolingbroke of radical inconsistency. As Leslie Stephen says, "Bolingbroke tried to take both lines at once; and therefore half asserts and half denies the goodness of God, and declares the perfection of the universe, whilst denying the legitimate inference from his assertion."[36]

The very fact that Pope took alarm that Bolingbroke should have denied the existence of the moral attributes is a fair indication that he himself believed in them. Though the events noted above took place some time after the writing of the *Essay on Man* and its publication, it is well to note that since Bolingbroke leaves no doubt of his practical denial of the moral attributes in his *Fragments*, and holds that his opinion is one which it is "impious to alter,"[37] it would seem that either Pope had not seen this section, or else the original version, said to have been "communicated as writ," had continued a radically watered version of Bolingbroke's ideas.

In further proof of Pope's full agreement with Bolingbroke's views of the moral attributes, we are told by Elwin that "Bolingbroke had not concealed his hypothesis from Pope." This, he says, is shown when we remember that the "philosophical papers of Bolingbroke" were "all communicated to him [Pope] in scraps as they were occasionally written," and the whole must have already passed through his hands.[38] This is not a valid argument. In the first place, Bolingbroke does not claim that *all* his philosophical papers were communicated to Pope; he says this of the *Minutes of Essays*.[39] This assertion rests solely on the word of Bolingbroke, and it cannot now be proved because the evidence which remains after the convenient destruction of Pope's papers is contradictory.

There is nothing in the *Essay* itself which implies a denial of the moral attributes. Pope had not intended any intimate comment on the nature of God. He had set out to discuss what we can know of God *without* revelation. The idea, as Pope planned it, precluded any attempt to discuss the nature of God.

Elwin tells us, in Volume two of the Elwin-Courthope edition, that the implicit denial of the moral attributes in the *Essay* lies in the statement that man could "just find a God," and consequently, man was to be the only study of man.[40] It is raddled logic to say that a man implies a denial of the moral attributes of God because he states that since it is just possible to know God by reason, he is not going to try to analyze Him, but is going to talk about something he does and can know—man. And though Pope makes no attempt to philosophize about God or His nature, he tells us in the First Epistle that Providence is all *good* and all wise;[41] that God has a care for all, both beast and man.[42]

In the Third Epistle, while developing his romantic picture of the state of nature, Pope further says that Heaven's attribute is "universal care,"[43] and that natural man owns him (God) "one great first father." But the best of all the examples of Pope's oblique tributes to one of God's moral attributes is found in the passage which follows the long description of the state of nature, or the golden age. Pope draws his fanciful picture and polishes it romantically, until he reaches the lines:

> Then, looking up from sire to sire, explored
> One great first Father, and that first adored;[44]

At this point the whole tone changes, and it is curious here that no commentator has any intelligent comment to make on the next fourteen lines, which do not conclude the section on nature and man's discovery of God, but give us an alternative to that picture. To quote the full passage, with the two lines which precede it:

> Then, looking up from sire to sire, explored
> One great first Father, and that first adored;
> *Or plain tradition*,* that all this begun,
> Conveyed unbroken faith from sire to son.
> The worker from the work distinct was known,
> And simple reason never sought but one.
> Ere wit oblique had broke that steady light,
> Man, like his Maker, saw that all was right,
> To virtue in the paths of pleasure trod,
> And owned a Father when he owned a God.
> Love all the faith, and all th' allegiance then,
> For nature knew no right divine in men,
> No ill could fear in God; and understood
> A sov'reign being, but a sov'reign good.
> True faith, true policy, united ran,
> That was but love of God, and this of man.[45]

Here Pope gives the other side of the picture. He tells us that man may have developed and gradually built up an idea of God, or, as "plain tradition" has it, that the pure faith was passed down from sire to son. By "plain tradition," Bolingbroke's term for the Scriptures, Pope certainly refers to the

* Emphasis the author's.

[194]

biblical account, and the orthodox explanation that man was from the first given the pure idea of God; and that he lost or obscured it, and the simple outlook on goodness of God's providence, through his own perverted acting and thinking. The passages cited alone are solid proof that though Pope in no wise intended to discuss the moral attributes in the *Essay*, a thing which the very limits he had set himself forbade, he actually referred to one of them in passing.

Of the "first idea" in Bolingbroke's philosophy, which maintains there is a "confederacy between atheist and divines," Pope's *Essay* shows no trace; nor is there any hint that Pope disbelieved in the immortality of the soul, or the system of rewards and punishments favored by orthodox Christian belief. Once these things are clearly seen and admitted, a point is reached which makes it possible to see with some certainty what Pope did get from Bolingbroke.

That he did not versify Bolingbroke's prose in the *Fragments* is evident. Since Pope failed to use Bolingbroke's two chief ideas concerning the confederacy of the atheists and divines, and the practical denial of the moral attributes of God, one may conclude that the *Essay* cannot be expected to show Bolingbroke's peculiar stamp or deistic thought, whatever Pope may have received from the man in conversations and the "seven or eight sheets" he had received to guide him in the work.

By encouragement and conversation, by some written material and a great deal of flattery, Bolingbroke kept Pope at his task until the poet had finished it. Normally Pope was a pedestrian worker, but there is every sign in the *Essay on Man* that he composed swiftly and in a mood of exaltation. Of course he was grateful to Bolingbroke, and at the beginning and close of the *Essay* the poet expressed that gratitude and the admiring affection he felt. On the other hand, there is every evidence from Pope's letters, amended or unamended, rephrased or in their original state, that Pope fancied himself a philosopher and loved to play with philosophical idea within his superficial and limited sphere.

Distaste for the wrangling of the schools and schoolmen was one of the marks of Pope's mind. It was likewise one of the characteristics of the eighteenth century, along with a coffeehouse appreciation of philosophy such as that often found in the pages of the *Tatler*, *Spectator*, and *Guardian*. Measured against genuine philosophy, such effusions are like a teaspoon of water compared with the sea. Water is, however, a relative thing; to Dives in hell a teaspoon of water is of heavenly consequence. Coffeehouse philosophy in its own shallow sphere is capable of great good and provides genuine mental refreshment.

Pope's *Essay on Man* is a philosophy of this kind. It is not a thing of patchwork, as Pattison maintained, but a skimming off from philosophy of the broths and juices most easily ingested by those who find metaphysics too abstruse or too wearisome.

The *Essay* is also, in a primary sense, a popular natural theology. It points up significant ideas of God, man, and the universe, and what can be known of them by reason's light alone, without revelation. It should be pointed out that Pope's method is much the same as that his Church employs. In the course of studies designed for all clerics natural theology is the proper introduction to dogmatic theology and revelation. This procedure grounds theological studies in their natural soil, in reason and reasonableness. It is equally interesting that a tract *De Homine* is one of the divisions of theology. Did Pope derive his title of the *Essay* from this source? It seems more likely he took the title of his poem from a saying of Pascal's in the *Pensées*.

[196]

In much the same manner he had pursued in writing his *Essay on Criticism*, Pope in the *Essay on Man* took his stand as one placed between an age which had turned its back on the old philosophies, but had not yet formulated one of sufficient intensity to catch the fancy of the times. Pope, within the limits he set himself (the limits of his own natural theology and common sense) constructed a popular theodicy which was designed to guard the old things of genuine value, censure the anthropomorphic drift of religion, and turn toward happiness and that millenium which will come into being when reverence for God and integrity of self shall remake the world into something worthy of both God and his creatures. This design of Pope's seems to have eluded his commentators. Their determination to make him a deist has persisted in spite of everything in the poem itself and its surrounding circumstances.

Since the facts brought forward by Bolingbroke and Pope's enemies are seen, upon examination, to be of slight importance in comprehending the actual composition of the *Essay*, it will be of some justice and moment to determine where Pope got the ideas which he juggled so deftly in the *Essay*, joining them together, with the living beauty of the poor Indian or the exquisite spider, in a doctrine of superficial natural theology, general, consoling, uplifting, and Christian.

Certainly Pope and Bolingbroke talked much of philosophy in the days when the *Essay* was in the making. In Bolingbroke's oak parlor they chatted and argued, the light of the fire shining on their animated faces: Pope quick and creatively stimulating, Bolingbroke exuding the fatal charm of gesture and play of feature, the burning sentences which made him the most loved and hated noble figure of his time in England.

The poetic result of those endless conversations by the fire in the shining room redolent of wax and wood smoke, or under the June sky of England with its rolling clouds and soft lights, was not the deism of Bolingbroke, since it does not contain the chief clauses of the doctrine he himself professed, and attempted to propagate in the *Minutes of Essays*. In talking philosophy with Bolingbroke, Pope was at some disadvantage. He was not well read in the works of the ancient philosophers, and his knowledge and opinions of the great Schoolmen were shallow. But behind these deficiencies the core of his spirit burned white hot with the piety he had learned in his youth. It was not knowledge of philosophies that made the *Essay on Man*, but the love of God and the optimistic heart of a Christian.

9

Shadows of the Absolute

All are but parts of one stupendous Whole,
Whose body Nature is, and God the soul;
That changed thro' all, and yet in all the same,
Great in the earth as in th' ethereal frame,
Warms in the sun, refreshes in the breeze,
Glows in the stars, and blossoms in the trees.

Essay on Man

THE old story of Pope's complete dependence upon Boling-broke and the tale of Pope's supposed deism are without foundation. Yet, in all probability, these things will continue to be taught as truths for generations to come. So hard it is to kill a legend once warmed into a life of its own. It is passed down in footnotes and scholarly scribblings. These serve to build up a façade of truth for things which have no more verity than a milkmaid's dream.

It has been easy for scholars to presume Pope was without philosophical training. It has been easy, but is it true?

Pope was at ease with Swift, Atterbury, Arbuthnot, Hooke, Warburton, Spence, Parnell; he found himself at home in "the High" at Oxford and in the company of "two-bottle" dons who staged philosophical battles "in hall." Are we to presume that Pope sat silent among them, or must we believe they never talked philosophy?

To be certain that Pope knew nothing of philosophy is to ignore his early training, to forget his Catechism, and to slip blithely over De Sales, Pascal, and Fénelon. Such certainty must ignore the letters to Caryll, the *Essay on Criticism*, and turn a blear, blind eye on the *Tatler*, *Spectator*, and *Guardian*.

Pope knew considerable philosophy. He would not have been at home in the eighteenth century had he ignored it.

If Pope was shrewd enough and skilled enough to pick his way among philosophical authorities; if the Bolingbroke legend is mostly eyewash—aristocratic eyewash it is true—where then, did Pope derive the doctrines he used with impressionistic verve in the *Essay?*

It seems probable that Pope read and digested his chief doctrine from four principal sources. The first of these was Bishop Ralph Cudworth's *Intellectual System of the Universe*, published in 1678. Pope's copy of this book remains in the library at Hartlebury Castle, which Bishop Hurd raised as a sort of a shrine to Bishop Warburton and eighteenth-century learning. The volume is signed in the poet's beautiful print hand.

Cudworth might be called, without exaggeration, one of Bolingbroke's most intense and purple hatreds. My lord in the *Minutes of Essays* went to great lengths to abuse Cudworth, linking him with those divines who were confederates of the atheists. Pope did not show his "guide's" distaste for the eminent Bishop, whose book is, in many ways, a monument of seventeenth-century learning. It is salted with Cudworth's superb translations of Greek, Latin, and Hebrew—translations of great passages from Plato, Aristotle, Plotinus, and the *Orphic Fragments*, which many Pope commentators have doubted that the poet knew. This book must have seemed a compendium of extreme interest to a man of Pope's limited background in the Greek language and philosophy. It opens

a door for him into the wisdom of the ancients. To read Cudworth's book, comparing it with the thought in the *Essay on
Man,* is to see how thoroughly Pope made use of the *Intellectual System.*

This is not to assert that Pope versified Cudworth's *System.*
Such a hypothesis does not fit into Pope's manner of working.
The value of Cudworth to Pope was in the wealth of beautiful quotations from ancient authors and philosophies made
available to the poet's poetical and selective intuition. Pope's
use of Cudworth means that Pope used Plotinus, Aristotle,
Origen, and the other mystical passages found in abundance
in Cudworth's book.

The main caution to be observed in arriving at an objective
view of the written inspiration of the *Essay on Man* is one
against the premise that Pope employed any author or his
work without straining such contributions through his own
consciousness; without, in a sense, redirecting them through
the sharp focus of his own intelligence. It may have been a
limited intelligence in regard to scholarship and philosophy,
but in respect to poetry it was one of the finest in our literary
history. It was particularly adept in transforming the basest
ores into something rich and beautiful.

There is every reason to believe Pope made frequent use
of Cudworth's book. He used it like the superb poet he was—
in a creative way—and not like the student or professor who
can only say what the book says.

Something of Cudworth's prime importance to Pope will be
appreciated by selecting two points on which both authors
move among the same ideas.

The first of these two parallels concerns itself with the idea
of the "best universe," which Pope propagated in his First
Epistle of the *Essay.* This was one of Pope's doctrines most
censured by Crousaz, who maintained with mulish obstinacy

that Pope had taken the idea from Leibnitz. Most commentators since Crousaz have clung to the same assertion. They have slanted it now to indicate that Pope probably got the idea from Leibnitz (knowingly or not) through the philosophy of Bolingbroke.

It cannot be proved that Pope knew the philosophy of Leibnitz. Even if he did know it and had read the account of the "best universe" in Bolingbroke's *Fragments*, the materials on the same subject to be found in Cudworth are more complete and, what is far more important, are more poetically inspiring than anything to be found in Leibnitz, or in Leibnitz via Bolingbroke.

Cudworth went to great lengths to illustrate his idea that our universe is the best possible one. To substantiate it he ransacked both the pagan and Christian philosophers. Cudworth first appealed to Aristotle and the ancients in support of his assertion.[1] He proceeded to build up his theory of the goodness of the universe by translating a passage from Origen,[2] one of the Greek Fathers, but it was on Plotinus that he chiefly relied for his most telling arguments.

It is easy to understand why the selections taken from Plotinus would appeal to a poet like Pope. One, in particular, is almost a poem:

> *God made the Whole most Beautiful, Entire, Compleat, and Sufficient; all agreeing, friendly with it self and its parts; both the Nobler and the meaner of them being alike Congruous thereunto. Whosoever therefore, from the Parts thereof will blame the whole, is an Absurd and Unjust Censurer. For we ought to Consider the Parts, not alone by themselves, but in reference to the whole, whether they be Harmonious and Agreeable to the same. Otherwise we shall not blame the Universe, but some of its Parts only, taken by themselves; as if one should blame the Hair or Toes of a man,*

*taking no notice at all of his Divine Visage and Countenance;
or omitting all other Animals, one should attend only to the
most contemptible of them: or lastly overlooking all other
men, consider only the most Deformed Thersites. But that
which God made was the Whole as one thing; which he that
attends to, may hear it speaking to him after this manner.
God almighty hath made me, and from thence came I, Perfect and Compleat, and standing in need of nothing, because
in me are contained all things; Plants and Animals, and Good
Souls, and Men happy with Virtue; and innumerable Demons,
and many Gods. Nor is the Earth alone in me adorned, with
all manner of Plants, and Variety of Animals; or does the
Power of Soul extend at most no further than the Seas; as
if the Whole Air and Æther and heaven, in the mean time,
were quite devoid of Soul, and altogether unadorned with
Living Inhabitants. Moreover all things in me desire Good,
and every thing reaches to it, according to its Power and Nature. For the whole World depends upon that First and
Highest Good, the Gods themselves who reign in my several
parts, and all Animals and Plants, and whatsoever seems to be
Inanimate in me.*[3]

This passage does worlds more than explain the perfection
of the universe in a fashion which would appeal to a logical
man. It is poetic; it sings. It cries aloud on the kickers against
the goad; against all those who mewl and whine and complain
against the creation of God from the depths of their thronging
sorrows and self-pity.

Here was God's plenty for Pope in constructing his idea of
the goodness of our universe. The material was more than
suitable because Plotinus, in proving his point, used the doctrine of "whole and parts" in exactly the same way that Pope
employed it in his First Epistle.

Against such evidence, it is trifling to maintain that Pope
took his doctrine of the "best universe" from Leibnitz or

Bolingbroke. Continuing to maintain it in the face of this proof and the further proof to be found in the works of Pascal, Fénelon, and King, which without a doubt were known to Pope, can only spring from a determination to keep Pope a deist in spite of every contrary indication.

The second example selected from the many in which Pope clearly used Cudworth's book is still more extraordinary than the one already cited. It is concerned with the similarity of thought in the panegyric to nature, with which Pope concludes his First Epistle, and with the abundant materials from which he drew in Cudworth's work.

Pope's superb poem in praise of nature has always been used as one of the decisive proofs of his deism or pantheism. Here, once again, the enemies of Pope, and his no less determined commentators, tried to show in every possible way a positive connection between the thoughts in Pope's lyrical apostrophe to nature and the ideas to be found in Shaftesbury's *Characteristics*. Link Pope with the known deists! Connect him with them by every possible means, however irrational!

What is the evidence of any connection between the deist Shaftesbury and the poet Pope? It is improbable that Pope knew Shaftesbury personally. Shaftesbury's ill health and the "smoak" of London made him more or less a recluse, and forced him to leave for a sunnier climate in 1711.[4] The Shaftesbury of the *Characteristics*, aligned with Toland as he was, would be an object of suspicion to Pope because of his deism, for Courthope, himself, for all his confused talk of Pope's "Catholic deism," says of Pope: "His opinions may have been influenced by isolated speculations in Shaftesbury, Mandeville, and the Deists, but he always manifested abhorrence of their principles as enemies of the established faith."[5]

Yet, in spite of these obvious difficulties, commentators

have continued to insist that Pope took his hymn to nature from deistic sources. Had they examined Cudworth's *Intellectual System* with the attention it deserves, they would have found in it the complete elucidation of many mysteries which still plagued their minds in regard to Pope's exalted conclusion to the First Epistle.

Did Pope know the *Orphic Fragments*, they wondered? Had he seen into the Egyptian mystical doctrines? How could he? They were hidden away in the characters of Greek, and Pope knew little Greek.

In the *Intellectual System of the Universe*, which was beside Pope on the shelf, were to be found the answers to these things. Cudworth had made a beautiful translation of the *Orphic Fragments*, with their profound emphasis on monotheism and the antique doctrine which detected Jove in the core of all being: the animator and source of life.[6]

The great seventeenth-century bishop had done far more. He took the doctrine of the *Orphic Fragments* and traced it down in Virgil's great epic;[7] he found the same doctrine in the sacred writings of Egypt.[8]

These splendid quotations were enough in themselves to convince a poet or a mystic, but Cudworth was rich beyond this mere demonstration. He quoted the words of Eusebius, in which a father of the Church did justice to the monotheistic core of the ancient world:

> *That they did not Deifie those visible Bodies of the Sun, and Moon and Stars, nor the other Sensible Parts of the World themselves, but those Invisible Powers of the God over all, that were displayed in them. For they affirm, that God who is but One, but yet Filleth all things with His various Powers, and passes through all things, forasmuch as He is Invisibly and Incorporeally present in all, is reasonably to be worshipped in and by those Visible things.*[9]

From the mystic wealth Cudworth had brought alive for the poet, Pope fashioned the magnificent conclusion of his First Epistle in the *Essay on Man*. The universe was not simply the best because it was just to man when seen as a whole, or in its final implications. It was the best possible universe because God was in every part of it: He glittered in the sun-warm air, He informed the clod and the lucid flesh of the lily. "By Him and with Him and in Him were all things," which Pope knew only too well from the "little elevation" and the words of the Canon of the Mass.

From frequent Masses, from his knowledge of the mystical saints of his Church, Pope was prepared in soul for the chord struck in him by the translations found in Cudworth. He was at home with the idea of a world in which the heavens declared the glory of God and showed his handiwork.

In making the *Essay on Man*, Pope owed a great debt to Cudworth. He was also indebted to another English bishop for some excellent things. This churchman, Archbishop King, had published, first in Latin and later in English, a treatise called the *Origin of Evil*. The English translation of the book appeared in 1731 at the very time Pope and his mentor were busied with the study of philosophy. It is plain that Pope and Bolingbroke read and discussed Archbishop King's book before Pope completed his *Essay*.

King treated *in extenso* many of the universal problems in which Pope and his "master" took a keen interest. The book was timely. Men were talking about God and the universe over the tables of inns and coffeehouses. Here was a book which advertised itself as "A sort of *Compendium of Metaphysics or Speculative Divinity*."[10] It was bound to be popular.

Articles in the *Spectator* had prepared people for this kind of book. On foggy mornings, which there were in plenty, my lord probably tumbled it about in his mulberry satin bed while he sipped his morning coffee. Bluestocking ladies peeped into its pages propped up against the silver of their mirrors while they were lazily curled and powdered, and donned their patches for the battle of the day. It was a work Pope and his guide could not afford to neglect.

Bolingbroke, the *Fragments* declare, was particularly pleased with King because he had given up the old point of view which maintained that all things in the universe were created for man alone. Bolingbroke's cordial approval of the book must have given it an added value in Pope's eyes. There were few clerics or their "works and pomps" of which Bolingbroke did approve.

Bishop King, like Cudworth, spoke of our universe as the best possible universe. He tried to show that the evil we seem to detect in it arises from the imperfection of things, our limited view of them, and our imperfect knowledge of the perfection of God himself.[11]

The book abounds in striking passages on the "ranks of being," and contains, at length, the inevitable argument concerning the "whole and parts" which so fascinated seventeenth- and eighteenth-century philosophers, and which Pope himself had used in the *Essay on Criticism* in 1713.

Though the discernible influence of King is much less evident than that of Cudworth, Pope probably used King's book for his poetical explanation of the purpose of the passions. They are the "seeds and principles of social life," and are to be found in two appetites: "*Self-Preservation*, and the *Propagation* of our species." Pope may well have used King, also, in evolving his theories of happiness in the Fourth Epistle of the *Essay*.

If Pope owed a profound debt to Anglican divines and scholars, he was still more indebted to the thinkers of his own Church. The story is an interesting one which may be traced back to Pope's very childhood. It grows out of his habits of mind and early Catholic training: it flowers in his sermons to Caryll and Martha Blount. A complicated wealth of detail indicates Pope's long preparation in mind and heart for the exact collation and expression of the ideas he versified in the *Essay on Man*.

When in 1730 Pope first informed Caryll of his design to write "on life and manners not exclusive of religious regards," his Sussex friend at once demonstrated an active interest and offered advice in a letter which recommended Pascal's *Thoughts* to the poet.

In reply to Caryll's suggestion, Pope observed with careless omniscience: "I have been before-hand with you in it (the reading of the *Thoughts*) but he will be of little use to my design, which is rather to ridicule ill men than to preach to them. I fear our age is past all other convictions."

This may sound like a dismissal of all possible Pascalian color in the *Essay*. It is actually not that, but the assumption of a mask by which Pope hoped to conceal the sources of his inspiration.

Contrary to his words, Pope *had* employed Pascal in making the *Essay* and he had used a work of Fénelon's as well. After the attack of Crousaz, when Pope was both confused and terrified at the determined outcry against him, he wrote a note to Louis Racine, the younger, which was forwarded to Racine by Chevalier Ramsay. The letter admits the influence of Pascal and Fénelon, and offers a remarkable testimony of Pope's faith at the time it was said to be suspect. Pope's letter to Racine, which was mentioned by both Johnson and Warton, was considered of doubtful authenticity. The original copy was discovered by Emile Audra in the Bibliothèque Nationale in Paris. It is worth quoting in its entirety:

Sir:

Nothing has delayed my Acknowledgement for your most obliging letter, but the Expectation of that agreeable Present with which you have honoured me, the Book itself. The only Allay to the pleasure it gave me, in reading it was to find that you imputed to me Principles I was never guilty of. But then again your Declaration at the end of it, that you did not understand the Original, that you could not be certain whether it really contained those Principles or not, and that you had done this only because Others had thought they found them there: this Sir, I must look upon as a great and extraordinary proof of your Candor, your Temper, & yr. Charity.

But I assure you Sir, a total Ignorance of our Language has not been so fatal to me, as an Imperfect Knowledge of it. And all the Beauties of Mons. de Resnel's versification have given less advantage to my Essay, than his continued Mistakes of my Doctrine and Reasoning have injured it. You will see them sufficiently exposed in the Work I send you (written by the Learned Author of the Divine Legation of Moses), and I flatter myself, that the Chevalier Ramsay, who has so warm a Zeal for Truth will take the trouble of explaining it to your full Satisfaction: after which I may trust to Your own Justice.

Upon the whole I have the pleasure to answer You in the manner you most desire, a Sincere Avowal that my Opinions are intirely different from those of Spinoza, or even of Leibnitz; but on the contrary conformable to those of Mons: Pascal & Mon: Fénelon; the latter of whom I would most readily imitate, in submitting all my Opinions to the Decision of the Church.

I have the honour to be, with just regard,

> Sir,
> > Your most humble &
> > > most obedient Servant,
> > > > A. Pope.[12]

Had Pope never written this letter to Racine, it would still be possible to establish the influence of both Pascal and Fénelon on the making of the *Essay*. Pope was well acquainted with Pascal's *Pensées* from his childhood. The year of his birth saw the first English translation of the *Thoughts* by Thomas Walker. Their vogue was sufficient to impel Bishop Kennet to translate them again in 1704, much more beautifully than Walker had done. It may be presumed that the *Thoughts* had become a part of Pope's mentality. It may even be inferred, with some degree of accuracy, that Pope used Pascal as a norm by which he judged the orthodoxy of materials incorporated in his poem. There is, moreover, a strong possibility that Pope obtained his first complete idea of writing the *Essay* from Pascal.

After Crousaz had attacked the *Essay*, many narrow-minded people took some scandal from Pope's couplet at the opening of the Second Epistle:

> Know then thyself, presume not God to scan,
> The proper study of mankind is man

Perhaps such critics had meditated too little on Christ's dictum, "The Kingdom of heaven is within you," but they obviously did not know Pascal's *Thoughts*. Speaking of man, Pascal observed: "I had hoped at least to have found Companions enough in the study of Man, because that is what is proper to him."[13] Following his "reasons of the heart," Pascal elsewhere re-emphasized the same idea: "Our instinct makes us find, we must seek our Happiness in ourselves."[14]

Close comparison of the *Thoughts* and the *Essay on Man* makes it obvious that Pope used Pascal for the opening lines of his Second Epistle and it is likely that Pascal furnished the inspiration for forty-nine lines of the same Epistle, and for

SHADOWS OF THE ABSOLUTE

the scattered thoughts in the treatise concerning the passions and reason.

"The *proper* study of mankind is man," said Pope in the accents of Pascal. In Epistle II Pope proceeded with that necessary study. He used the same method Pascal had employed in the *Thoughts*. Man is "a little less than the angels." He occupies a middle state between Pascal's "two Abysses of Infinite and Nothing."[15] Man's very mind and understanding keep this middle station;[16] it is observable in all our faculties,[17] our passions and desires.[18]

Under these circumstances, it is not surprising that Pascal remarked that man does not know whether to think himself a beast or a god.

> What a Chimera then is Man? What a Novelty? What a Chaos? What subject of Contradiction? Judge all things, weak Worm of the Earth, Depositary of Truth; Receptacle of Uncertainty; the Glory and the Refuse of the Universe. If he boasts, I'll humble him; if he is humble, I'll praise him and will contradict him always, until he comprehends that he is a Monster incomprehensible.[19]

Pope employed all this Pascalian thought in the *Essay*. It is not found in Bolingbroke's *Fragments*. It is possible that Pope, being what he was, a Christian and a Catholic, employed the greatness and misery of man because this contrast drove home another shrewd observation Pascal had made: "No other Religion whatsoever besides the Christian Religion, has understood that Man is the most Excellent, and also the most Miserable Creature."[20]

Pope founded his Second Epistle on the *Thoughts* of Pascal. If it could be doubted that he did, such doubts would be dispelled by two passages in the *Essay on Man* which remain shrouded in mystery without reference to the superb French thinker. Speaking of vice, in Epistle II, Pope remarks:

> But where th' extremes of vice was ne'er agreed:
> Ask where's the North? at York, 'tis on the Tweed;
> In Scotland, at the Orcades; and there,
> At Greenland, Zembla, or the Lord knows where.
> No creature owns it in the first degree,
> But thinks his neighbor farther gone than he;
> Ev'n those who dwell beneath its very zone,
> Or never feel the rage, or never own;
> What happier natures shrink at with affright,
> The hard inhabitant contends is right.[21]

How the poet was abused and persecuted for this passage! Because of it, he was called unbeliever, rogue, and deist. Yet Pascal, and he alone, had given Pope his clue in a quiet passage: "One scarce sees anything, just or unjust, but changes Quality, in changing Clymate. Three degrees of Elevation of the Pole, overturn the Laws: A Meridian decides all Controversie, or a few years the Possession: Fundamental Laws do change; Law has its bounds: Pleasant Justice, that a River or Mountain does limit; Truth on this side of the *Pyrenean* Hills, Error on the other side."[22]

The second illuminating instance of Pope's close reliance upon Pascal is found at the end of Epistle II. It is the peroration of Pope's sermon on man and his middle state:

> Mean while *opinion* gilds with varying rays
> Those painted clouds that beautify our days,
> Each want of happiness by hope supplied,
> And each vacuity of sense by pride:
> These build as fast as knowledge can destroy;
> In folly's cup still laughs the bubble, joy;
> One prospect lost, another still we gain;
> And not a vanity is giv'n in vain;
> Ev'n mean self-love becomes, by force divine,
> The scale to measure others' want by thine.

See, and confess, one comfort still must rise;
'Tis this, though man's a fool, yet God is wise![23]

Again, in this passage, Pope was accused of writing non-sense or of encouraging unbelief. Had any of his learned commentators cared to look in Pascal's *Thoughts* they would have found a long passage which explains Pope's doctrine in the *Essay*.

Opinion has set up a second nature in man contrary to that of reason. It measures things by outer circumstances.

> It cannot make fools wise, it makes them content. . . . Who gives reputation? Who gives respect and Venerations to Persons, to Works, to great Folks, but Opinion? How empty are all the Riches of the World without its Applause? Opinion governs all things: It determines Beauty, Justice, and Happiness, which is all the world can afford. I would willingly see the *Italian* Book, whose Title I only know, which its self alone is worth many Books: *Della Opinione Regina del Mondo*.[24]

That Pope used Pascal is crystal clear: there are certain doctrines in the *Essay* which are otherwise unexplainable: the doctrine of the greatness and misery of man, the parts concerning Pope's meaning of "Opinion," the opening lines of the Fourth Epistle, and Pope's honest man, "the noblest work of God." Bolingbroke has none of these, and they appear to be found only in Pascal.

Pope was also indebted to Fénelon. *Telemachus* may have been one of his boyhood books. It was written as a guide to a king's son; it recommended itself to the nobility because of its ripe wisdom, exuberant fancy, and moderate tone, making it for the times a sort of boys' guide to good conduct. A childhood acquaintance with Fénelon would have predisposed Pope in favor of the French bishop.

Pope had a more intimate link with Fénelon than anything found in his excellent book for boys; a link, extremely close and personal, in Hooke, who had been one of Fénelon's secretaries. Hooke was a historical writer of some promise. He was Pope's close friend at the period in which the *Essay on Man* was written. Pope recommended him to the great Duchess of Marlborough for the writing of her apology and history. That Pope and Hooke were close to each other is particularly evident, for it was Hooke who boldly came forward to suggest that a priest be called in Pope's final hours of life.

If Pope found many things in Pascal which encouraged him to study man and the ideas of God and the universe which can be known by reason alone, he found in Fénelon's book, *A Demonstration of the Existence of God*, still wider suggestions for his verse. The poet employed, in almost identical fashion, the method used in Fénelon's book in exposing the ideas enunciated in the *Essay on Man*. There was both a likeness of method and a correspondence of ideas between the *Essay* and Fénelon's work.

Fénelon's volume on the existence of God, translated into English in 1713, was popular. Within two years it went into four editions. Such a wide dissemination of the book makes it impossible that Pope should not have read it.

The advertisement of Fénelon's *Demonstration* informs us that of all the proofs for the existence of God, "*The most evident is that which is drawn from the Knowledge of the Universe and Man in Particular.*"[25] It is this sort of opinion, given by a bishop of Pope's own Church, which explains the attitude that the "proper study of mankind is man," and why Pope and Pascal[26] held that opinion. Fénelon was very precise on the subject. His treatise, with its fine Greek clarity of style, covered in a general way the same ground Pope traversed in the *Essay*.

Fénelon spoke of the complexity of the universe: he explained it in detail, painting vivid pictures of the earth—plants, water, fire, the heavens, stars, animals, and insects—its vastness[27] and smallness.[28] The intricate, meshing order of all things is described in memorable language.

Fénelon also provided Pope with his figure of the universe as a great house, which Pope had already used to advantage in the introduction to his edition of Shakespeare.[29]

It is a reasonable universe that Fénelon exposed with shining brush strokes—the same "best universe" Pope melodized in verse—and it is shown to be reasonable if we look at its whole organization and not merely at its parts.[30]

Understood properly, God may be thought to be the "soul of the Universe":

> With them [the pagans] great Rivers were Gods, and Springs, Naiads. Woods, and Mountains had their particular Deities; Flowers had their *Flora;* and Fruit *Pomona.* After all, the more a man contemplates Nature, the more he discovers in it an inexhaustible Stock of Wisdom, which is, as it were the Soul of the Universe.[31]

In Fénelon's book on natural religion, there are passages which are seen to be of utmost importance in any truthful or enlightened discussion of Pope's Second Epistle of the *Essay*. Like Pascal, or perhaps it would be better to say, following Pascal, Fénelon commented at length on the two aspects of man: his greatness and his folly.[32]

Fénelon's view of moral evil and the passions coincides in general with that expressed by Pope. Even more precise is the likeness between Fénelon's appreciation of the infallibility of animal instinct and the explanation of it which leaps out from the symbols of Pope's lucid couplets. His "hound sagacious on the tainted green" is the same wise creature moving

[215]

through Fénelon's exposition of the difference between instinct and reason, and the illustrations employed by Fénelon are the same birds, insects, and animals used in Pope's poem.[33]

The idea that "mutual want built mutual happiness" is likewise expressed in Fénelon,[34] who also suggests—as Pope docs—that man learned the art of government from animals,[35] a theory directly contrary to Bolingbroke's reasoning in his *Fragments*, at least.

For the Fourth Epistle of the *Essay*, there would seem to be little in Fénelon's book which could be of use to Pope in writing his sermon on happiness. Fénelon did believe that virtue is largely its own reward, but in his *Demonstration of the Existence of God*, Fénelon maintained what he said elsewhere, that "the step from Power, to a Virtuous Act, is the greatest Perfection in Man. Power is only a Ballance, or Poise between Virtue and Vice, or a suspension between God and Evil."[36]

A close study of Fénelon's book is important in the proper orientation and integration of thought in the *Essay on Man*. It and Pascal's *Thoughts* are of still greater moment in understanding how Pope came to write his *Essay on Man* and why he enunciated the ideas in it.

Pope's reading of both Pascal and Fénelon early in life dropped into his mind and unconscious those seeds of ideas which produced, in time, the glowing fruit of the *Essay*. Seen in this fashion the whole process becomes a human thing, with its period of gestation in which congeries of clustering roots sprouted from the original seed dropped in the earth of the poet's mind. It makes the whole story of the *Fragments* and the superficial excursion into philosophy under the compelling energy of Bolingbroke as a prelude to the composition of the *Essay* a complete tissue of nonsense.

A thorough study of Cudworth, King, Fénelon, and Pascal

offers indubitable evidence that Pope knew from their works the chief ideas he used in his poems, without recourse to Bolingbroke or the *Fragments*. In such authors Pope found expressed in a glowing genius of language, so stimulating to the poetic imagination, the very ideas Bolingbroke is said to have given the poet in his labored *Fragments*.

It is also of importance to reiterate that the supposed deism ascribed to Pope's doctrine in the *Essay* has never suffered the condemnation of the Church. There are reasons for this Roman kindness. The poem is well integrated, according to its own creation, and orthodox as well. There are, it is to be expected, points where Pope made small mistakes. He followed the thread of his argument like a poet, in a series of glittering impressionistic pictures and not like a philosopher reasoning with care from conclusion to conclusion.

Failure to understand this elementary fact has engendered most of the laughable footnotes of Warton, Wakefield, and Elwin, and the mistaken appreciation of Dr. Johnson, who, in the good things he alleged of the *Essay*, came within an eyelash of seeing its real drift and importance.

Pope had set out with an ambitious plan[37] (probably Bolingbroke's grandiose elaboration) which he later, with good taste, abandoned. His idea, Griffith maintains, was to place man "in large structural frames of things" for the purpose of tracing the relations between Man and his absolutes. In outline, it had the following structure:

I Man's relation to God
II Man's relation to Self
III Man's relation to Society
IV Man's relation to Happiness[38]

In following this plan, Pope escaped from the pure logic of the philosopher to the intuitive method of the poet. The *Es-*

say on Man is more than a "poem to nature." It is a tribute to God which, coupled with the portraits of the *Moral Essays* meant to illustrate its reasoning, is a vast affirmation of both God and man.

That it should be necessary to descend to the ungrateful task of defending the *Essay* against the charge of deism is the unfortunate result of generations of detractors who have almost obscured the poem's reasoning and beauty. Yet, in a sense, the task is a welcome one, for in the same way in which the accusations of immorality, envy, spite, and dishonesty disappear when exposed to the pitiless light of truth, so too this last accusation against Pope, the deism of the *Essay*, evaporates in the light of facts.

The task of defending Pope is disagreeable because it should be unnecessary to defend a man who, his whole life long, followed the religion of his father and mother and died in that faith with the full rites and consolations of his Church. This is the man who refused the blandishments of Atterbury, Warburton, and the Oxford dons, who urged him to conform to the Establishment; this is the cripple who refused the oaths and suffered the fines and disabilities of his religion, not once but continuously to the end of his life; this is the patron who pensioned Deane, found Southcote an abbey, and interposed his influence between his friends and the penal laws. This is the friend commended by Swift for his orthodoxy, who swinged Settle and Philips, Oldmixon, Cibber, and all the bigots of his age; who professed in his letters, redirected to the greatest men of his time, his adherence to Catholicism; the man who tried to convert others to his faith, by being in fact what he more than seemed to be—a Christian and a Catholic.

That Pope's theodicy is as orthodox as Fénelon's, any unbiased examination will prove. In Epistle I, Pope looks about him for the footprints of God in the world and the universe. He first finds a complicated universe, yet in spite of its complexity he finds it *reasonable*.

Bolingbroke's beliefs in the *Fragments* cannot elucidate the doctrine of Pope's First Epistle. My lord's universe is mechanical. God, in Bolingbroke's estimation, has only the cold wisdom of the watchmaker who from the arctic distance watches the wheels go round, without caring to know what is the time of day. Pope's universe, on the contrary, is that of the Greek and Christian mystics: bursting with life and divine beauty. It is not a universe wound up, but a divine comedy whose chords of good and evil are to be lifted in the final act into heavenly harmony.

Having established what we can know by reason of God and the universe, Pope proceeds with his analysis of man in Epistle II. He finds man both great and miserable. Self-love is his pole-star. Under its light the passions move blindly toward the things which seem to promise happiness. Reason restrains the passions, and Providence grafts on them the stock of ultimate good. Whatever our condition of good or evil, pride gives us a good opinion of ourselves and makes us serve the *whole* economy of God and nature.

Pope would have known all this, perhaps not "from his nurse," as Dr. Johnson suggested, but at least from his Catechism, Pascal, Fénelon, and books of piety. Self-love is our greatest failing, and pride, avarice, lust, wrath, gluttony, envy, and sloth are the capital sins and the heads of self-love in each person. Yet, the masters of the spiritual life maintain, the opposites of these sins can be cultivated to turn the capital sins toward good ends. Love of women can become love of humanity, as it did in Shelley; avarice can be turned into the honest administration of other's goods, or the magnificent benefactions of the financier. The whole Second Epistle is orthodox: it fits Pope's life and thought, and illustrates his Christian and pietistic training.

The Second Epistle has a strong Pascalian coloring, but to imagine that Pope versified Pascal is to misunderstand creative artists in general, and Pope in particular. It is like the shallow assertion that Dante is St. Thomas in verse. Whatever the source of Pope's inspirations, he strained them through his own mind, and his ultimate doctrine took the complexion of his habitual mode of thinking in reference to those permanent bases of his orientation. These were Christian and Catholic.

In Epistle III, Pope turns from the study of man himself to man in his social sphere. God acts to one end by various causes and agents. All the beings in creation are linked in a set order which serves the whole. Whatever serves men best ("is best administered") is best. Narrow-minded people may fight in public over the forms of their faith and belief, but the man of good life refrains from such bickerings because, though faith and hope disagree, charity is mankind's great concern. Man lives by what he gives. The earth has two motions, one on its own axis, the other about the sun. The soul also has two inclinations, one toward itself, one toward the other creatures in the universe. True self-love and true social love are seen to be the same.

In this Epistle, Pope again shows no trace of unorthodoxy. He pursues an imaginative orthodoxy, it is true, in giving two pictures of the rise of civilization and culture. One is the picture of scientific historians, the other of the Bible account (from line 227 to line 240). It cannot be doubted that by *plain tradition* Pope meant the Bible account which his Church believed and propagated. For the remainder of his argument, who can see any particular deistic implication in the belief that self-love and social love are one and the same thing? Charity does constrain us all to God's intent, if we are to achieve our ends and His.

Pope's conclusions in his fourth and final Epistle are Christian; they are almost mystical, in fact. Happiness implies honesty and virtue; honesty and virtue imply the charity which looks "through nature up to nature's God," beholding there His benevolence which shines down from unity and is refracted back to Him in the multiple loves of creation. The reward of virtue is love, and God is love.

Pope concludes this Epistle with his glittering series of compliments to Bolingbroke, humbly giving himself a minor fame to that of his "philosopher and friend." Already in this Epistle, Pope proceeds toward the method of his *Moral Essays*, with Goyalike sketches of Umbra, Sir Billy, Gripus, and many others.

The crop-haired boy in *Windsor Forest*, poring over the lives of the Saints, has come to the fruitage of those hours in the *Essay on Man*. The heavens declare God's glory and the earth shows His handiwork. The crippled poet has joined the music of his numbers to the chorus of creation and the wisest men of all times and nations. At a period of time in which men were divided and confused, he restated many of the fundamental doctrines of Christianity and he made a magnificent affirmation of his faith and love. Bolingbroke's *Fragments* are consumed in the conflagration. The measure of Bolingbroke's greatness sinks to something ashen, confused, and malicious by comparison. Not the great, glittering lord, but the crippled poet, has walked into the eternity of those, like Shakespeare, who turned their backs on negation the more they intuit the deeps of the human heart, seen against the serene background of the eternal stars and God.

10

Baucis and Philemon

I loved where I was loved, and set no bound
To love, in six scant feet of heavy ground.

THE intimate affairs and circumstances of Alexander
Pope's life are often ignored in arriving at a complete and just
estimation of the poet's character. Pope was one of the principal actors on the stage of his time. He is judged by his appearances under the proscenium where the pitiless glare of the
lights often indicated some discrepancy between the magnificent flow of his rhetoric and the humanity of the actor.

No man, particularly a poet of the first order, who must
live by his fleeting intuitions even more than he lives by logic
or the articles of the creed, will bear without some lessening
of reputation a comparison of his best works with his life. He
may be one thing as a poet and another as a human being.

Like other writers, Pope is sometimes judged harshly because his language and sentiments fail to correspond with his
nature. So much of his career was spent in the pitiless glitter
of the public stage that biographers have a tendency to underestimate or underpublicize the quieter things and moments of
his life: days and hours in which his humanity shone out "like
a good deed in a naughty world." When the grease paint was

removed and the lights in the theater were dimmed, how did he seem to act? What did he do? The record is creditable to any man.

It is customary to judge Pope by his friendship with the notable personalities of his period: Lady Mary Wortley Montagu, the Duchess of Marlborough, Addison. . . . Yet in these appearances Pope was acting, for the most part. In attempting to influence the reactions of his audience in his own time he acted to steal the scene and rivet attention to himself, fulfilling the nature of a true actor. There is another side of his character—sentimental, tender, admirable—which flashes out of his most intimate friendships and his family life; times and occasions not governed by the thirst of applause or fame, times in which there was nothing to be gained by acting something he was not.

Of the close friends of his heart, such as Swift, Arbuthnot, Atterbury, and Hooke, John Gay stands out as perhaps the most intimate companion Pope ever had. Their friendship began early, with Pope's appearance at Will's and Button's. It grew and prospered with every year of their lives until the death of Gay, much lamented by Pope. It may be said with some justice that in his friendship with Gay there was none of the false glitter apparent in Pope's dealings with Bolingbroke or even Swift at times. In his converse with Gay, Pope was one simple human being speaking to another. In consequence, the human side of his character in this instance gives us a clear, unsullied light.

There was little physical likeness between Gay and Pope. Pope was tiny, like a crippled wren: the twisted cords of his face were knotted with the pain of migraine. Gay was a giant, ruddy, corpulent; he exuded good humor. He would have made two of Pope, the poet ruefully exclaimed. It was their minds which made it possible for them to be so much at home with each other. In this circumstance, nature marks the first condition of our humanity, by making mental rapport a primary condition of intimacy.

In their mental weather Pope and Gay were much alike. They were both quick in their humor; it arose spontaneously in them from circumstances and things and the refractions and relations of experience: it was truly *occasional*. This quality kept Pope and Gay in perpetual demand by the people whose consciousness had little or nothing of their quick perception and intelligent hilarity. In both men this occasional humor was tinged with cynicism: the wry truth of Gay's epitaph which he sent to Pope before his death, seen from any point of view, pagan or Christian:

> Life is a jest and all things show it
> I thought so once and now I know it

has something of the coarse raillery on life found in the *Beggar's Opera* and *Polly*. Pope, in his vulgar poetry, and in many portraits of the *Moral Essays*, exhibited something of this shrill protest against the rules of life. The ultimate purpose of every critic is moral; Pope, unlike Gay, had time to mature and see his criticism grow into something remotely religious; Gay was cut off before the implications of his attitude could declare themselves to him.

Pope and Gay spent many happy hours in each other's company: they often composed together, suggesting, emending, and joking; fought their mutual enemies; wrote plays and poems, skits and verse; and amused a whole circle with the sparks of wit which were struck from each other when they met in company. Their obvious joy of life was one of the few things which could take Swift out of himself into the atmosphere of jest and gaiety he loved. In the company of Gay and Pope, the vultures brooding in Swift's mind took flight; for his tragedy was not disappointed ambition or pride, but the misery of being condemned to move in a society whose best efforts were light-years removed from the sharp lightnings of his intellect and fancy. He was the Erasmus of an age not large enough to appreciate an Erasmus.

The friendship of Gay and Swift deepened as the years went on, with a thousand overt signs of their affection expressed in their defense of each other, in their letters and conversations, and in a light, teasing note which is the surest exterior indication of genuine admiration. When Gay failed to obtain a place at court Pope's words to Gay brimmed with witty consolation. "Blessed is he who expects nothing, for he shall never be disappointed."

During Gay's alarming illness at Hampstead, in 1729, Pope was confined at Twickenham by the serious condition of his mother's health. Her life was despaired of from day to day. Pope waited on her every hour, though he was torn between his duty and a strong desire to assist Gay in his sickness. The letter Pope sent Gay at the time is one of the most unaffected he ever wrote. It gives a fine insight into his sympathetic nature, generosity, and faithfulness to friends:

Dear Gay,—
No words can tell you the great concern I feel for you. I assure you, it was not, and is not lessened by the immediate apprehension I have now every day lain under of losing my mother. Be assured, no duty less than that should have kept me one day from attending your condition. I would come and take a room by you at Hampstead, to be with you daily, were she not still in danger of death. I have constantly had particular accounts of you from the doctor, which have not ceased to alarm me yet. God preserve your life, and restore your health! I really beg it for my own sake, for I feel I love you more than I thought in health, though I always

loved you a great deal. If I am so unfortunate as to bury my poor mother, and yet have the good fortune to have my prayers heard for you, I hope we may live most of our remaining days together. If, as I believe, the air of a better clime, as the southern part of France, may be thought useful for your recovery, thither I would go with you infallibly; and it is very probable we might get the Dean with us, who is in that abandoned state already in which I shall shortly be, as to other cares and duties. Dear Gay, be as cheerful as your sufferings will permit: God is a better friend than a court: even any honest man is a better. I promise you my entire friendship in all events, heartily praying for your recovery.

Do not write, if you are ever so able. The doctor tells me all![1]

That Pope meant what he said is indicated by a letter written to Lord Oxford at the same time:

Indeed my poor mother continues in a most uncertain, dangerous way. . . . There is no possibility of quitting her for a day, or else I had been with my poor friend Gay. God preserve him; if he dies, he will not leave an honester heart behind him in this kingdom.[2]

Such sentiments are a fine, unvarnished tribute to Gay's friendship and admirable qualities. They are a far greater tribute to Pope's genuineness, humanity, and tenderness. With so many friends and acquaintances he had to exert himself to act the great poet or wit; with Gay he was at ease, and he found in the man none of that hatred of his faith which curdled so many of his fine friendships. There was no danger of being considered a "little false dog," or a "crooked papist," or having his motives misinterpreted because of some spurious idea of his faith or its demands upon him.

From our vantage point of distance these things may not seem to be important. A careful reading of Pope's collected correspondence and all the passages in diaries and letters which refer to himself and his affairs will help us to understand just how much Gay's understanding and freedom from all bias meant to Pope. Those of Addison's circle, even when they expressed admiration of Pope's talents, seasoned their praise with doubt of him as a man. In most cases this doubt arose because of Pope's religious background. Many of his noble friends had essentially the same mentality, and though Pope's friendships with Parnell and Swift were cordial in the extreme, there never was that complete relaxation in their company which Pope appreciated in his familiar intercourse with Gay. This sensitiveness of Pope's toward those who disliked his religion is shown at every step of his life. It explains his friendship with men like Garth, Arbuthnot, and the Richardsons: men of no particular religion whatever. Since they had no faith to defend, relations with them were good-natured and even amusing. It was possible to demonstrate one's excellences *as a man* in company where religious suspicions did not intrude, where old Reformation quarrels need not color every fact of life and every fancy of wit and literature.

To understand how much these things meant to Pope it is necessary to be a Catholic. In books, in words, in law and taxes, in literature, in every single aspect of living, the bias declared itself. It was the atmosphere in which Pope lived and moved. The sneers at Button's, the mob that broke the windows in his villa at Twickenham while he was dining with his friends, the pasquinades, poems, and abusive letters that followed every work of Pope's, the refusal of Crown and University to pay him the honors they conferred on literary men without one farthing of his talent, are all part of the story. They make us see into Pope's distaste for the Buttonians, Settle, Philips, and Cibber. It is always alleged that Pope was jealous of Cibber's success in playwriting, but it is significant that Pope's real dislike of Cibber dated from the success of the *Non Juror*, in which the men of Pope's religious persuasion were vulgarly exposed as fools and knaves.

Consideration of these things explains Pope's sensitiveness, suspicion, and deceit, in a partial sense at least. It indicates why his own sweet and merry nature built a tough carapace about itself. On this tough defense the darts and burning envies of the world were blunted and quenched. In Pope's friendship with Gay the cover is withdrawn for a moment—we catch a glimpse of the real man.

The true nature of Pope is shown with greater clarity in Pope's relations with his parents, to which his friendship with "honest John Gay" is a graceful introduction. In an age and time not noted for filial consideration, Pope's love of his father and mother was charming and exemplary. It was unmarred by deceit or suspicion; on the contrary, it breathed a perfume of antique piety and Christian tenderness.

There is nothing in the background of his family which would seem to account for the brilliance of Alexander Pope. His father's family seems to have been remarkable for commonplace clergymen and men of affairs. They were gentry, but insignificant. Pope's father inherited the business competence of his ancestors. In his linen business with the Colonies he made a fortune, perhaps not great, but sufficient for his needs. Pope has given us a radiant picture of his father in the *Epistle to Arbuthnot*. The portrait which emerges is more admirable for its integrity than for any fancy touches Pope might have intended in praise of his lineage. From the testimony of those who knew the family, Pope's portrait of his father was both real and accurate.

So gentle was the elder Pope that he thought it a sin to call anyone a fool; he observed St. Paul's caution against civil disputes with his neighbors and coreligionists, and was a model of serious probity. Unlike some of his Catholic neighbors, he refused the oaths of allegiance and supremacy. Year after year he paid his fines for recusancy. He was a truthful, plainspoken, healthy, common-sense man; a happy husband and a Christian in the width of his charity.

It was he who first encouraged his son to write "verses"—no doubt on pious subjects, for he loved prayer, the lives of the saints, and the liturgy. As he watched his Alexander grow in literary excellence, something of the amazement of the ugly duckling's parents must have risen in the older man's mind. His homespun character could in no wise account for this extraordinary son. The great, the noble, and the witty came in their glittering coaches. They sat with the family at Binfield, and all who came there went away with a healthy admiration of Mr. Pope and his kindness.

The poet himself always treated his father with the most profound respect. His own life widened out into influence and brilliance, but no shadow was ever detectable of diminution of this respect; never once the faintest sign of being ashamed of his father's bluntness and lack of polite polish. The letters Pope wrote his father are saturated with the most profound regard. These epistles are written in Pope's best business style, terse and direct, without compliment or excessive detail. Yet Pope always signs himself "Your dutiful and affectionate son," and defers to his father's judgment. Pope asks about places where he may board his friends, he sends a recipe from Dr. Arbuthnot for his "dear mother's illness"; he writes from Oxford to tell his father he is leading the simple life; he sends advance warning of an impending visit with friends. All the gentle, obedient qualities of Pope's nature flash out to us from these scraps of paper.

There is no indication that this loving respect diminished as the years went on. Pope's letters to his friends reveal something of his great sadness at the time of his father's sudden death. He was "the best of fathers." Ever after, to the end of his life, Pope defended his father's virtue and lovable character against slander and the disagreeable suggestions that he was a bankrupt, a hatter, or any one of the malign or demeaning characters the hatred of his enemies could suggest or devise.

With his mother Pope's relations were even closer and more affectionate. She was of good family; her brother's will had also made her something of an heiress. Her only child, Alexander, was the apple of her eye. In his wanderings Pope thought of her often; he spoke of her incessantly to all his friends, never without signs of sincerest love and grateful affection.

One such casual tribute, in a pre-Christmas letter to Fortescue, gives an indication of the closeness of mother and son: "I hope all your fireside are well, and growing merrier and merrier as Christmas approaches, I shall have no rest nor joy till I get to my mum again."[3]

From Richardson's portrait of Mrs. Pope we get some appreciation of her kindly nature and solid good sense, for it was unvarnished as well. At base, hers was a provincial speech and mentality, yet among all Pope's friends she was loved and respected. These things would seem to indicate she had qualities beyond the bad grammar and incorrect spelling which appear in her letters.

In her childhood at York she was brought up with the gentry of the town, under the very shadow of the great cathedral. In spite of York's insularity, the town did not differ materially from London in its appreciation of form and good manners. Mrs. Pope was a lady in the truest sense of the word, because gentility springs, in its most inward sense, from the heart. There is evident in her character, also, something of that repose, so admired in ancient times, which even today lends an added touch of distinction to either beauty or womanliness.

Mrs. Pope admired her son's work and wished to be a part of it. In this, as in other things, Pope indulged her to the full, allowing her to copy out some of his translations of the *Iliad*. Her copy called for extensive corrections before Pope could send it off to the printer. If we glance at the letter Mrs. Pope wrote to her son in 1719 or 1720, we can see why extensive correction would be necessary:

> My Deare,
>
> A letter from your sister yust come and gone, Mr. Mannock and Charles Rackitt, to take his leve of us, but being nothin in it doe not send it. He will not.faile to cole here on Friday morning, and take ceare to cearrie it to Mr. Thomas Doncaster. He shall dine wone day with Mrs. Dune, in Ducke-street; but the day will be unsirton, soe I thinck you had better send itt to me. He will not faile to cole here, that is Mr. Mannock. Your sister is very well, but your brother is not. There's Mr. Blunt, of *mapill Durom*, is ded; the same day Mr Inglefield died. My servis to Mrs. Blunts, and all that ask of me. I hope to here from you, and that you are well, which is my dalye prayers; this and my blessing.

This letter uncovers a great deal more than Mrs. Pope's disregard for grammar and spelling. It indicates something of her deeply religious background and profound love of her son; something too of that peasant grandeur and magnificence of self-possession which made the old lady at home in the drawing rooms of the great with the same easy repose she had in her own house. Nor need her spelling be given too much emphasis as an indication of her education or breeding. English grammar was still in a fluid state in the eighteenth century. Spelling, in those days, was more a matter of caprice than correctness. Those who could write at all, whether they were duchesses or fishwives, showed an amazing disregard for it.

After the death of his father, Pope made his mother the center of his life. He was uneasy away from her, and if possible he took her with him on his journeys. She went with him to Stowe in 1718, and whenever she fell ill Pope dropped all his cares of literature and business to sit by her bedside while she underwent the brutal remedies of her day: the cuppings, severe purges, and vomitings which were the extraordinary remedies for ordinary illness.

When Pope was rich, and had set himself up in the limited magnificence of Twickenham, it was his mother who was the recognized head of the house. She made decisions and entertained at the head of the table, sitting there in her decent black silk. Her tranquil face looked out on the company from under the spotless frill of her cap, and when she raised her hand to the gold watch or the cameos she wore, a diamond sparkled on her left hand. She was proud of her son's eminence, we may be sure, but very much mistress of herself and every situation. She played cards with guests like Dr. Swift, superintended the household arrangements, and fussed over her delicate son or his guests. There is every indication that she took part in the flashing conversation and wit of the company.

Her vast independence is shown in an incident which took place during the visit of Voltaire to Twickenham. In the conversation at dinner the French wit made some indecent remarks about her religion. Mrs. Pope rebuked him and left the table, although he was a guest in her house and Lord Bolingbroke had brought him there.

Mrs. Pope lived to be ninety-three. Pope's devotion to her increased with her feebleness. He broke appointments with all his great friends, forswore the sparkling company he loved, and gave up his rambling habits, that he might guard the frail flame of her life as it flickered to extinction.

A letter of December, 1732, written to Martha Blount, expressed something of Pope's alarm and sorrow. After commenting on the recent sad death of Gay and resignation to "the will of God," Pope said:

So will the death of my mother be! which now I tremble at, now resign to, now bring close to me, now set farther off: every day alters, turns me about, and confuses my whole frame of mind. Her dangerous distemper is again returned, her fever coming onward again, though less in pain; for which last however I thank God.

I am unfeignedly tired of the world, and receive nothing to be called a pleasure in it, equivalent to countervail either the death of one I have so long lived with, or of one I have so long lived for. I have nothing left but to turn my thoughts to *one comfort; the last we usually think of, though the only one we should in wisdom depend upon, in such a disappointing place as this.** I sit in her room, and she is always present before me, but when I sleep. I wonder I am so well: I have shed many tears, but now I weep at nothing. I would above all things see you, and think it would comfort you to see me so equal-tempered and so quiet. But pray dine here; you may, and she know nothing of it, for she dozes much, and we tell her of no earthly thing, lest it run in her mind, which often trifles have done. If Mr. Bethel had time, I wish he were your companion hither. Be as much as you can with each other: be assured I love you both, and be farther assured, that friendship will increase as I live on.[4]

Half alive, the old lady lingered until June, 1733. Pope remained at her bedside, his head filled with all the knowledge of her past love and affection for him, his mind wincing under the threat of the great emptiness when she should be gone. Happy days in the Forest, or under the great trees at Stowe, warm midsummer evenings on the level lawns at Twickenham when the twilight hazes settled into a green radiance only per-

---

* Pope is certainly writing of the comfort of his religion. Author's italics.

ceptibly lightened at false dawn; candlelight, murmuring voices, the laughter of Gay, loved faces—the core of Pope's life was wasting away.

She died without a struggle as the deformed little man watched and wept. Suddenly the lines of her face settled into that repose of death which wipes from the countenance all but the light touch of tranquillity.

In the moment of her departure Pope recalled that he had nothing to remember her by: no portrait or suggestion which might remind the heart of those loved lines of her face which had filled his life with the only unalloyed tenderness he had ever known. Turning into his study, the little crippled man dipped his quill into the ink and, as the lines scratched themselves on the paper in scrawled symbols of black, the letter to his friend Richardson the painter was completed:

> . . . my poor mother is dead. I thank God, her [end] was as easy, as her life was innocent; and as it cost her not a groan, or even a sigh, there is yet upon her countenance such an expression of tranquillity, nay, almost of pleasure, that [that it is so far from horrid] it is even amiable to behold it. It would afford the finest image of a saint expired, that ever painter drew: and it would be the greatest obligation which even that obliging art could ever bestow on a friend, if you could come and sketch it for me. I am sure, if there be no very prevalent obstacle, you will leave any common business to do this; and I hope to see you this evening as late as you will, or to-morrow morning as early, before this winter flower is faded. I will defer her interment till to-morrow night. I know you love me, or I could not have written thus—I could not (at this time) have written at all.—Adieu! May you die as happily![5]

Richardson obeyed the urgent appeal, dropped all business and hurried to Twickenham. The sketch he made of Pope's mother, in her old age and after death, has that wide-eyed self-assurance and amiability to which so many of Pope's friends had paid tribute. There is the same well-formed nose which distinguishes Pope, and the same confidence, without the nervous birdlike quality characteristic of the poet's face.

There is no extant account of the Catholic background of Mrs. Pope's death and burial. We can be sure there was one to be written, had the temper of the time permitted. A dutiful son like Pope would have seen that a swift messenger was sent to the nearest priest. Perhaps honest John Searle set out in a little curricle, like the one Pope had given over to the injured woman the day he walked down Boar's Hill in the heat of the Oxfordshire summer.

The priest would have hurried back with the oils for the final anointing of the senses, already shutting against the blandishments of the world. The litany of the dying would have resounded: the names of the martyrs and confessors, of virgins and doctors pleading for the soul of this mother as it went before the judgment seat of God. Then the final farewells of the family and friends would have been said about the open coffin, followed by the secret Mass or Masses for the repose of the soul. The priest would have stolen away when the funeral moved into its last, public phase.

Six poor men, dressed in new suits of dark gray, bore the coffin on their shoulders to the church at Twickenham. They were followed by the bent little poet and his friends. The bell tolled in the tower. The beloved Editha was shut away from sight of the son, who watched her going in a torrent of tears.

When he went back to his villa his mother's presence haunted him. He avoided her room. To pass it chilled his heart and filled him with a vague restlessness. His mother was gone and the center of Pope's life was lacking. He became more than ever a man in flight, moving about from one corner of England to another, from Bath to Oxford to London, while his fame grew and his body wasted.

Yet even in his restlessness he did not forget. In the church at Twickenham he showed something of his true mind by erecting a tablet to the memory of his parents, on which was the following inscription:

> To God the Great Creator, and the best of Beings
> To Alexander Pope, a Gentleman of Honesty
> Probity and Piety, who liv'd
> LXXV Years died MDCCXVII
> And to Editha, his excellent and truly pious wife
> Who liv'd XCIII Years, died MDCCXXXIII
> To His Well-deserving Parents, the son erected this.

He also made his own plans to be buried beside the mother who had been nearest to him of all he had known or loved, and when, in 1725, Lady Kneller tried to use her influence to have the monument removed to make place for the memorial she had designed for Sir Godfrey, Pope fought her to a standstill by every wile of his flattering pen. His letters on this subject to the Earl of Strafford are some faint indication of his love and his ability to use every psychological resource to prevent the descration of his parental shrine. He was successful in this as he was in all things to which he gave his full attention. His monument remained.

And in the *Epistle to Arbuthnot*, which appeared January 2, 1735, Pope spoke something of the praise of his mother which bubbled from the deepest wells of a loving heart. Pope allowed his final tribute to her to stand uncorrected, as he had written it in the final years of her life:

> P. Me, let the tender office long engage
>   To rock the cradle of reposing Age,
>   With lenient arts extend a Mother's breath,

Make Languor smile, and smooth the bed of Death;
Explore the thought, explain the asking eye,
And keep awhile one parent from the sky!
On cares like these if length of days attend,
May Heav'n, to bless those days, preserve my friend!
Preserve him social, cheerful, and serene,
And just as rich as when he serv'd a Queen.

A.   Whether that blessing be denied or giv'n,
     Thus far was right;—the rest belongs to Heav'n.

Such things were to be Pope's public challenges to time, imperishable as stone, or the more immortal symbols of words cunningly arranged. They were enough for the poet, but not enough for the man. There must be something for his own private reminder, something which could speak to him at home. In a secret corner of the grounds at Twickenham an obelisk arose. There in the green-shadowed seclusion of his own private oratory Pope could turn over in his mind the wealth of his memories and love for her as he gazed at the inscription on the stone:

> Ah Editha!
> Matrum Optima!
> Mulierum Amantissima
> Vale!

11

Castles in Spain

O let me be to men, at least in part,
Those things I followed in my secret heart.

THE story of Pope's published correspondence is one of
the most complex episodes in his stormy career. It has offered
the literary detectives a rich field for the exercise of their
genius. The plots and counterplots involved and the dramatis
personae of the act, could hardly be racier: a woman of the
town, Lord Oxford, the "unspeakable Curll," The House of
Lords, "P.T." a shy old gentleman much in the fear of "Squire
Pope," Lord Orrery, "R.S." (a clergyman who dressed like a
lawyer), Dr. Swift, and a tangle of cross purposes and statements, which would make the labyrinth of Crete look like a
Roman road. All this mystification has provided the literary
Sherlocks a century of beagling and sniffing and pointing
which is, today, far from being concluded.

Those who enjoy a thriller and good detective logic can
while away a most pleasant hour in the ramifications and false
turns of the plot, as the matter is examined by Dilke,[1] in the
introduction to the letters in the Elwin-Courthope edition of
Pope's works, or in Courthope's life of the poet in Volume V
of the same series. That Pope had schemed to publish his letters

no man of sound sense would deny. The case has been proved up to the hilt. It is equally obvious that in preparing his letters for publication, Pope in some, even in many cases, "cooked" his correspondence: he rephrased it, sorted it, combined letters, or suppressed them to suit his own fancy or intent. In one section, he lifted letters from his correspondence with John Caryll and redirected the letters to prominent men of the time, in a manner which implied that his speech with persons of prominence had the same forthright quality which appeared in his epistles to his Sussex correspondent. Much more interesting than the reproaches directed against the poet for the lies he acted and spoke would be some sort of intelligent surmise or proof which would survey all the possibilities and make it possible to fit the episode into Pope's life; which would make it, not something singular, but something in accord with the complex nature of the poet's character, circumstances, and outlook upon existence.

To presume that Pope schemed and plotted as he did because he was born a liar and loved equivocation and mystification too neatly fits the worst picture of the poet drawn by his enemies and acknowledged opponents. It is too pat to be true.

With the progress of the intrigue, no doubt, Pope enjoyed its tangled skeins. He loved tricks and practical jokes; he could not have been unconscious that he was perpetrating one of the "best" hoaxes in the history of letters. He may have enjoyed the game, but he must have recognized in his conscience the "pretty genteel equivocation," as his self-excusing admission once phrased it in a letter to Martha Blount.

Perhaps it would be well to state, once and for all, that there was nothing in Pope's religion which would permit or condone the deceit he practised. There seems to be at the back of the minds of some kindly and honest men a sneaking suspicion that there were "principles of casuistry" which would permit Pope a world of "mental reservations" in his dealings with those who were not Catholic or who were inimical to the Church. Such suspicions are unjustified, because the *science* of casuistry is an open study: every volume is available in public libraries for those interested in enlightenment and research. There is no arcanum, no esoteric doctrine hidden away in some secret place and handed down in whispers to a discreet circle. The science of casuistry, which is the real ancestor of psychoanalysis, attempts to establish the precise degree of responsibility, or lack of it, in any moral act. It considers the acts themselves, the background of the persons or things involved, and any circumstance which may affect the degree of guilt. It keeps its case-books, much more voluminous than those of psychoanalysis. Its principles are indispensable to the priest in his dealings with men, especially in the confessional.

In its first principles, casuistry is inflexible. In the case of lying, for example, a lie comes into being the moment we have —by word or action—given the impression that a thing is other in fact than we know to be true in our minds. A lie is a lie; but in real life one cannot always find cases in which acts are of this ideal simplicity. To take an extreme example: If I am threatened with a pistol and asked a question, and ordered to reply, and if I am certain an adverse reply will occasion the pulling of the trigger, I may not be strong enough to tell the exact truth, or any truth at all. In justice to me, it will be evident that my *culpability* will be lessened.

The most casual acquaintance with men, or their mental processes in the anguish of living, teaches us that this extreme case is, upon close examination, not extreme at all. In daily life there are extenuating circumstances which equal—if they do not surpass—the robber with his pistol or the lover with his knife. There are mental pistols which condition truth: the fear of alienating affection or appreciation, love of persons, the desire to appear in a flattering light with certain people or in certain cases. The very organization of the mind itself has a tendency to condition culpability. Casuistry aims at the practical appreciation of truth by establishing with minute exactness to what extent human culpability is lessened or increased. There are in the agents and circumstances of our acts degrees of the ideal: the near-idiot is not to be held as scrupulously responsible as the man of sound mind; the timid and defenseless are not to be blamed or held accountable for untruth in the same degree that men of balance and responsibility are.

Pope found no warrant in his Faith or in casuistry for telling lies. The belief that Pope's words and actions in publishing the letters were something exceptional, and, on the other hand, the belief that they indicate Pope's inability to tell the truth are equally fallacious.

His actions and words in this instance are part of a pattern which is not strange, or in any sense exceptional, when all the factors in the case have been analyzed and surveyed. The complete story of the long intrigue has been compressed within admirable limits by Dr. Griffith. His summary enables us to survey the case without recourse to either Dilke or Courthope. Dr. Griffith writes:

So far back as 1726 the correspondence with Henry Cromwell had been published . . . without Pope's consent. In 1729 letters to Wycherley had been included in a volume . . . that fell flat. The unsold copies had been bought in by Pope, and held (in the sheets) for further use. For a time there had been a prospect that the Wycherley letters with some additional ones would be offered again in 1733, but publication was postponed. Pope had wished the letters to be published, but had not deemed it advisable that he should himself appear responsible for publication, "P.T." and "R.S." under the guise of whom he had corresponded with Edmund Curll, the bookseller, (upon whom he had begun to practise horse-play tricks as early as 1716), offering to sell the books of the Letters in printed sheets if Curll would agree to advertise and vend them. Pope's plan had presumably been to bring to pass just about what did happen. In the spring of 1735 Curll, manœuvered into the position of a tool, published the Letters. Pope charged that the edition was surreptitious and faulty, and he could then claim with some show of grace that to protect his reputation he was forced (most unwillingly, of course) to publish an authoritative edition. To increase the grace of submission to an unpitying necessity, he postponed the publication of the "authorized" edition for two years (to 1737).[2]

As Dr. Griffith says, the whole story seems to begin with the publication of Pope's letters to Henry Cromwell. For this Pope cannot be blamed. Mrs. Thomas, Cromwell's mistress, sold the letters to Curll because she was "in need of ten guineas and he of a manuscript." The publication of the letters both pleased Pope and annoyed him. It pleased him to see some of his prose works engrossing the attention of the public, and it annoyed him to have his juvenile correspondence and labored reasoning held up to the scrutiny of men of wit.

Pope, in the period which had elapsed between the writing of these letters and their publication, had become the most touted phrasemaker of his age. He had also elevated his own critical standards in his long labors on the *Iliad*. There was honest cause for him to cry out in the preface of his edition of the letters: "If in these letters to Wycherley and those to Cromwell, which were printed without his consent, there appear too much of a juvenile ambition of Wit, or affection of Gayety, he may reasonably hope it will be considr'd *to whom* and at *what* age, he was guilty of it and how soon it was over." In a certain sense these early letters to Henry Cromwell were a genuine reproach to Pope, but it is probable they also gave him an idea for turning the reproach into something of a triumph, and they may have suggested the method which would achieve that happy result.

There is nothing which would lead us to believe that Pope had always planned to publish his letters, and in consequence had labored on them and twisted them into exercises of perfection. Pope had not one epistolary style but several: the letters, "cooked" or "uncooked," disclose this. His business style was a model of terse directness. There is not an excess word in it. His teasing letters to the Duchess of Hamilton and some of the epistles to Gay and Martha Blount are genuine "outpourings of the heart," and the entire Caryll correspondence (uncooked) is natural and probably comes nearer to the real Pope than any series of letters he ever wrote. In his letters to the great or the witty or the "fair," we observe a sense of formalism. These letters smell of the lamp. This need not have arisen from Pope's early determination to publish these letters, but may have come about from the fact that his correspondents were great, or witty, or influential. They expected Pope to reply in the grand tradition. He usually did so after some struggle with the muse of fine letter writing. The variety of styles in Pope's letters offers telling proof that Pope suited himself to circumstances and people in a fashion which makes it impossible to suspect he had always designed his letters for posterity. Curll's publication of the letters to Cromwell did make Pope realize there were possibilities in his letters which the public seemed ready to appreciate. In his war against the world and its dunces the letters also provided an instrument for a revelation of Pope's character which might silence his detractors and give the world some idea of what he was, had desired to be, or would be.

Curll's unorthodox method of acquiring the letters to Crom-

well may have suggested to Pope the trick he played on Curll.
That sneaking hound was contemptible, but he was cunning
and shrewd. It would be something of a lark to match wits
with him.

There were other considerations which made the channels
of normal publication dangerous and out of the question.
Pope's correspondents could be roughly divided into four
classes: great noblemen, ladies, intimate friends, business and
literary acquaintances. These in turn had the complexion of the
day: there were Whigs, Tories, Anglicans, unbelievers, Catholics, wits and half-wits, men in the government, and men disgruntled to be out of it, a king's mistress, an exiled bishop and
a nobleman who had been in jeopardy of the law. Publication
of any part of such a wide variety of opinions and his own remarks upon them in his replies was in Pope's day a precarious
undertaking. The dangers implicit in the delicate political balance of the period made it so. There were laws of libel and
privilege especially dangerous to one who had been a friend
to Atterbury, and who was a known papist.

I know how long it has been this Author's fate [Pope said
in the Preface to his *Letters*], whom both his *Situation* and
his *Temper* have all his life excluded in his rivalling any man,
in any pretension, (except that of pleasing by poetry) to
have been as much aspers'd and written at, as any First Minister of his time: Pamphlets and Newspapers have been full
of him, nor was it *there only* that a private man, who never
troubled either the world or common conversation with his
opinions of Religion or Government has been represented as a
dangerous member to Society, as a bigotted Papist, and an
enemy to the Establishment. The unwarrantable publication
of his letters has at least done him this service, to show he has
constantly enjoy'd the friendship of worthy men; and if a
Catalogue were to be taken of his friends and his enemies, he
needs not to blush at either.[3]

The situation was a challenge to Pope and he was, by the time it presented itself to him, well schooled in handling such ticklish matters, on which he had often had the shrewdest legal advice in the kingdom. If he could manipulate circumstances to make it appear that the letters he desired to publish had been published in spite of him, then of a certainty no one could blame him for their appearance. He would be able to avoid any reproach of bad taste in publishing private letters and—even more important—he would escape the dangers and reproaches implicit in the appearance of the opinions of such a variety of men. He could in fact, by judicious editing, build himself into something of a sage and a hero.

Had Pope from youth designed to publish his letters he might have made two copies of every letter he wrote. There is not a shred of evidence that he did so. It is fairly clear that the idea of making a collection of his letters was first suggested by Curll's bustling endeavors in publishing the Cromwell letters. There were several ways by which Pope might hope to escape all possibility of legal or government action, the annoyance of his polite friends, or the accusation of self-aggrandizement. The first of these involved Curll; the second was the pretense of a Dublin printing, which had served so well in first publishing the *Dunciad*. If Pope could manage a further pirated edition of more letters, a supposition of his innocence would be established. The way would be cleared for him to publish a reputable edition of the same work. There were other dangers to be guarded against. Careless strictures on the court, and an honest estimate of historical events in his own time still offered the hazards which had attended the publication of Buckingham's *Works*. It would be necessary to remove such pitfalls if Pope desired to protect his friends and himself.

It was in the process of such emendation and correction, obviously, that the further idea arose of revamping some of the letters to suit Pope's polite eminence as a man and a writer.

Some of Pope's friends had been reluctant to return his letters; perhaps because they valued them as a caress from fame. In any event, John Caryll, among the correspondents, hesitated. The displeasure of Pope eventually prompted him to return the letters. In order that some record of them might remain, the letters of the Caryll correspondence were all copied before being sent off to the poet in 1729.

The Caryll family had been close to Pope. He loved them, visited them, prayed with them, suffered with them. John Caryll, in particular, the nephew of Mr. Secretary Caryll, had been responsible for introducing Pope to Steele and others. He had for seventeen years been Pope's closest Catholic friend. In looking over his letters to Caryll, Pope must have noted their excellence. They are the outpourings of the pious Pope: the man his father and mother and his Catholic friends wanted him to be. They are also letters of friendly atmosphere and energy of expression. Something of the pleasure of the correspondence is revealed in its verve and width of sentiment. Yet had Pope in 1737 published these letters under Caryll's name, it would surely have been pointed out that Pope's sentiments in regard to both government and religion were dangerously free for a proscribed papist, living in the toleration of the law.

It may well be that such considerations led Pope to alter and redirect the Caryll letters. He had an affection for them. If he published them as letters to men of eminence, such as Steele, Addison, or Craggs, they would offer far more telling examples of Pope's exalted sentiments and forthright expression. The public would be in amazement at Pope's plain speech and its toleration by men high in the beau monde or in the government service. On the other hand, if Pope published these letters as part of the Caryll correspondence, the sentiments he expressed, however noble, would take the complexion of his Jacobite correspondent. To the public, such letters would indicate Pope's close connection with Lord Caryll, who had been Master of Requests to Catherine of Braganza. This would be sure to open the gates to a horde of brazen innuendoes and suspicions.

That Pope did deal most freely with Caryll's correspondence became evident in the nineteenth century with the emergence of the original copies which Caryll had made. It had been suspected earlier that Pope had revamped his correspondence. This the Caryll letters proved conclusively, perhaps too conclusively for some editors: Pope's method of protecting himself and Caryll in that section of his letters most likely to cause trouble with the government or to incite the malice of his enemies, need not incline us to believe he dealt so freely with all his correspondence.

Pope's combined irritation and pleasure in the publication of his correspondence with Cromwell received a further aggravation in 1728. In that year Lewis Theobald published some of the posthumous papers of Pope's friend, the Restoration rake and playright William Wycherley. This publication seems to have made Pope feel he had been presented in a bad light. In consequence of this conviction he retaliated in 1729 by issuing a volume of his correspondence with Wycherley. For some unexplained reason this volume found little or no sale among the public. Undeterred by the cool reception of his book, the canny poet bought up the remaining sheets from the printer.[4]

This act would seem to indicate that Pope had already formed a plan which would make it possible for him to bring out his correspondence without fear of accusation or blame. The plan would involve the disreputable Curll, and in its very boldness and compounded mystifications would stimulate the authorized edition of his letters which Pope would be "forced" to publish.

One door had been held ajar for Curll's entry. He could—without doubt—be persuaded to acquire the leftover sheets of the Wycherley correspondence. But this was a narrow door, and not inviting enough. Pope soon opened a wider entry. Some of the other letters he designed to show the world were copied by amanuenses and deposited in the library of his good friend Lord Oxford.[5] The originals and those letters Pope deemed dangerous or too intimately personal may have been destroyed—at least Pope said he burned three-fourths of them.

> He had been very disagreeably us'd, on the publication of some letters in his youth, which fell into the hands of a woman, who printed them without his or his correspondent's consent, in 1727. This treatment, and the apprehension of more of the same kind, put him upon recalling as many as he could from those he imagin'd had any. He was sorry to find the number so great but immediately lessened it by burning three parts in four of them.[6]

The copied letters Pope designed to hand down to posterity were then—or later—bound up and Lord Oxford himself made corrections on them in his own "angular hand." This happy condition of affairs soon gave Pope a chance to raise the cry that some copies of his letters had been stolen. The door was opened wide indeed, and we cannot doubt that the rodent Curll slavered in anticipation.

Against this complex backdrop the trap was set to catch Curll and make him a willing tool. Then ensued the long negotiations between Curll, "P.T.," and "R.S.," which make such amusing reading.

In the battle of wits Curll crowed his triumph over Pope, yet in the whole proceedings Curll did exactly what Pope desired.

In 1735, Curll finally published the poet's letters. The excitement of this publication, in which even the august House of Lords participated, stimulated interest in Pope's correspondence to such an extent that "no less than twenty separate editions or variant issues . . . were published between May 12 and December 31, 1735."[7] Is it any wonder the poet could now modestly pretend the necessity of giving a correct version of the correspondence?

Let it be called duplicity. It is not exactly that. Curll printed his edition from scraps and scourings furnished by "P.T." and "R.S." (Pope). Should there be found in the pirated letters anything obnoxious to government, friends, or parties, Pope could still ignore the menace. He could also ignore any accusation of bad taste in publishing his private correspondence. An edition of his supposed letters made up from pirated copy and stolen transcriptions of amanuenses would be poor evidence if it were to support any legal or government action. Such letters would have little value as evidence, especially if many of the original letters happened to be destroyed.

The biased opinion has been that Pope engineered the plot to publish his letters because of his vanity, and an ardent desire to fool the public regarding his elevation of mind and depth of virtue. It is equally valid, and much more in accord with facts, to presume that Pope planned to issue his correspondence in order to correct the impression made by the pirated Cromwell letters, and the evil character his enemies and the dunces had manufactured for him.

A Bookseller advertises his intention to publish your letters. He openly promises encouragement, or even pecuniary rewards, to those who will help him to any; and engages to insert whatever they shall send. Any scandal is sure of a reception, and any enemy is screened from discovery . . . you are therefore reduc'd, either to enter into a personal treaty with such a man, (which tho' the readiest, is the meanest of all methods) or to take such other measures to suppress them, as are contrary to your inclination, or to publish them, as are contrary to your modesty. Otherwise your fame and your property suffer, alike: you are at once expos'd and plunder'd. As an *Author*, you are depriv'd of that Power which above all others constitutes a good one, *the power of rejecting, and the right, of judging for your self, what pieces it may be most useful, entertaining or reputable to publish*, at the time and in the manner you think best. *As a Man, you are depriv'd of the right even over your own Sentiments, of the privilege of every human creature to divulge or conceal them: of the advantage of your second thoughts, and of all the benefit of your Prudence, your Candour, or your Modesty. As a Member of Society, you are yet more injur'd; your private conduct, your domestick concerns, your family secrets, your passions, your tenderness, your weaknesses, are expos'd to the Misconstruction or Resentment of some, to the Censure or Impertinence of the whole world.* The printing of private letters, in such a manner, is the worst sort of *betraying Conversation*, as it has evidently the most extensive, and most lasting ill consequences. It is the highest offence against *Society*, as it renders the most dear and intimate intercourse of friend with friend, and the most necessary commerce of man with man, *unsafe*,* and to be dreaded.[8]

Having once made his decision to publish his letters, the poet was compelled to protect himself and his friends in the publication. By confusing all the steps leading to himself as a legally responsible agent, he barred the door against all immediate recriminations and fear of persecution and displeasure.

The original hypothesis that Pope planned all the mystification because he loved lying and intrigue is not satisfactory. There are many more elements in Pope's character which show

* Author's italics.

his love of integrity and directness than there are facts which would prove the contrary. In all probability, once Pope had made his decision and had embarked on a project to publish the letters, the ensuing steps became to him something in the nature of a game with very little malice in it at bottom.[9]

A man should be free to publish his letters when he likes and how he likes. The precarious condition of the times (the Pretender was poised in France and the populace was not fond of Hanoverians), and the intimate connection between realism and treason helps us to understand Pope's actions. In the realm of pure ethics the whole affair may seem to indicate that Pope was an appalling liar. If, however, we measure Pope's lies against the hard realities involved, it is difficult to censure him. His greatest moral fault lay in the original decision to publish the correspondence. This decision fathered all the deceptions which followed; and they *were* deceptions. A nice ethical problem is posed in the circumstances of this episode.

In *Windsor Forest* the poet had first learned the method to be followed. By squinting his words he had kept himself free. In his edition of Buckingham's works he pursued the same general tactics, which he then further elaborated in the *Dunciad* and in the *Essay on Man*. In the publication of his letters Pope used everything he had learned of sleight and stratagem, from all past occasions. Our condemnation of lying must remain a total condemnation, but our understanding of Pope's situation in publishing the letters removes at least half the mystery and nine-tenths of the malice which have been attached to Pope's procedure and words.

The same kind of extenuating circumstances may be observed in Pope's edition of Swift's letters in 1741. In this instance Pope pretended he was forced to publish the letters because of a pirated Dublin edition. It was the same evasive device he had used in publishing *The Dunciad*. His pretense that

Swift had published the letters first (or that someone in Ireland had done so) was a stratagem employed to protect his witty correspondents and Pope himself.

Pope's "scurvy trick" played on the declining Dean, which nineteenth-century critics pretend to expose, becomes in effect the last practical joke of the two friends. They had played many such tricks before, and this last collaboration was a fitting climax to their Scriblerian past. Whatever the tricks employed, they were not designed to deceive any but pedants. And they did protect Pope against the malice of an age which Pope and Swift knew so well.

Dilke's pointed observations will help us to understand the case:

> . . . . let the reader as we said at starting, remember his [Pope's] antecedents—religion, country, genius of his age—remember the enforced seclusion in the forest, the confiding candour of youth silenced in fear and trembling, education stolen in secret, and the prayer of innocent childhood stammered out with the hesitation of a criminal—remember that from his birth, he and his parents and all the loving circle of his narrow home, were branded and proscribed—, lived as he himself said "in some fear" even "of a country justice,"—remember, in brief, all the degrading influences of the Penal Laws, and the result will be found general, not exceptional; and the world should learn from Pope and Pope's conduct not to condemn the individual, but the system that made him what he was.

Pope's published correspondence was a true pioneering effort. It led to a century of inspiring epistles, among them the psychological subtleties of Richardson. It was Pope who first, and not without pain, created a public for this type of literature, from which had come much consolation, profit, and artistic excellence.

In "cooking" or polishing his letters Pope, in all probability, had three objects in mind: to weed out dangerous opinions, to revise any inadequacies of style, and to give a picture of himself which could be set up for his own time and posterity in opposition to the villainous portrait the "dunces" and his enemies had etched. In so doing, the Caryll correspondence became his chief instrument. He incorporated sections of it in letters to Addison, Steele, or at any other point in his correspondence where he thought his independence of tone would do the most public good.

In his letters to Caryll Pope had been more himself than he had been to all others, except Martha Blount and Gay. In a sense, by redirecting his Caryll letters he was not altering his true visage, but rehanging it in finer frames and circumstances, where it would more readily shine down, a genuine picture of himself as a man, a Christian, and a philosopher. He should not be blamed for wishing to play tricks on time and circumstances and people who had played him so many; he should not be condemned for thinking the whole affair a "genteel equivocation," when in the abstract it deserved a darker name.

The nineteenth and twentieth centuries by exposing Pope's duplicity have brought the poet's veracity into the greatest general suspicion, which makes him seem too thoroughly "a fool to fame." But surely it is a point of wisdom to admit there was more than lies involved in his scheming. Pope had a right to that good opinion of men which his enemies seemed determined to deny him. If by clever manipulation of the letters he pictured himself plain-spoken to Addison, it was because he *was* forthright in speech to Addison when not under the threat of the laws and prison. His angry letters to Caryll regarding Catholic objections to the *Essay on Criticism* are powerful evidence of this; his business letters and the letters to Martha Blount and John Gay are equally demonstrative on the same

[253]

point. If Pope tried to show himself generous and magnificent, this was, likewise, true. That he was pious and philosophical, his letters to Caryll proved.

In his ideal of himself, Pope had built a castle in Spain. It was less than the law and the taste of the times allowed him, but in his letters he wistfully set up the shining towers and walls much as he had hoped they would be or as they seemed to be in his most secret heart.

To Pope, literature was a business which had no nonsense about it. Either you succeeded or you failed, in the degree to which you showed a genius for writing and an ability to market your wares. Moral considerations played no part in such business. You simply matched your wits against your fellows: if you were ruthless enough, you succeeded in doing exactly what you set out to do.

A world which tolerated publishers like Curll and bought their books, a fraternity which employed anonymous writing and the meanest subterfuge, was not an atmosphere into which a man might intrude with a queasy stomach or a nice scruple to use any possible weapon. Dean Swift's indictment of booksellers' practices in one of his letters to Motte is a good indication that Pope or Swift hardly looked on Pope's tricks in publishing the letters as having any moral implications whatever. This is not to confess Pope's moral obtuseness. It is, rather, a commentary on eighteenth-century ethics.

Pope's collected letters, and the replies to them, in their variety of styles and opinions, expose in many ways the best picture of the reign of Queen Anne and the early Georgian period which has come down to us. Pope was a complete man of his time: he knew the wits, politicians, architects, gardeners, printers, lords, duchesses, "the top drawer," the legal and medical world. There are in his letters unforgettable vignettes of court life, social customs, manners, sentiments, pastimes, and politics—vignettes which are an epitome of everything his age stood for or against. The multiplicity of styles and moods, sentimental, witty, self-pitying, literary, and Jovian, offer us a many-faceted approach to life in the eighteenth century, much more complete than the dreary malice of Horace Walpole, or the cool detachment of Steele and Addison in the *Tatler*, *Spectator*, and *Guardian*. Nineteenth-century critics scoffed at Pope's letters. They called them mannered and hypocritical when measured against their own voluminous correspondence. If nineteenth-century critics preferred sentiment and egoism in a dressing gown to a sword and peruke, that was their affair, but to demand of Pope a casual disregard for formality and a certain amount of balance, is to expect a Dr. Johnson to be without pose or a Sir Roger de Coverley to be shorn of pomp and circumstance. Pope's age was pompous. The neo-classic movement in architecture had its reflection in literature. Polite men were mad for the classics. They gave fortunes to Pope and others who had made Homer and Virgil available to them. The women of the time posed as goddesses and nymphs, the men tried to talk in the accents they imagined Cicero and Horace used. They perpetually quoted, many times amusingly so. Even when they travelled in some peril, like Lady Mary in traversing a Balkan war on her way to Constantinople, there was yet time and opportunity to fish out long passages from the classics with which to ornament epistles to Pope. If men talked like Cicero in his moral epistles, they seldom acted the part. An honest estimation of both Addison and Johnson, for example, shows both men to have been a complex of inconsistencies. Addison schemed and flattered the great to attain his final eminence: he did it so well in the grand style that the fact sometimes escapes us. Neither Johnson nor Addison could have possibly lived up to the morality of their writings. Johnson is supposed to be sacrosanct, but his boorishness or queasy respect for the great sometimes flashes out clearly.

Pope in his letters talks like his time. He is Cicero in a tye-wig. His exalted sentiments require now a pinch of salt, now a bushel. To expect a complete correspondence between what he said and did—Dr. Johnson himself pointed out with wry shrewdness—is to understand neither men nor the letters they write.

Pope's collected letters offer us a delightful picture of his age. They do not give us the same unvarnished view of Pope's character, nor could they express with absolute accuracy Pope's feelings toward his correspondents or political events.

Had Pope been free to say exactly what he felt and thought, had there been no penal laws hovering over his shoulders as he wrote, he would still have been conditioned by his multifarious friendships, the variety and mental drift of his correspondents, the pose of the times. What he has given us is excellent: a kaleidoscopic picture of men and manners; a full-dress portrait of a great genius in the manner of Kneller, Gainsborough or Reynolds. We still take delight in the portraits of geranium-cheeked lords and ladies, their long curved jaws and agate eyes, their satins, furbelows, bustles and bland complacency. These portraits fit the times and what the gentry claimed to be, but were not—except when they were on show. More charming, and worlds more revealing of the eighteenth century, are the letters of Pope.

12

The Complete Goya

Let the strict life of graver mortals be
A long, exact, and serious comedy;
In every scene some moral let it teach,
And, if it can, at once both please and preach.
Let mine an innocent gay farce appear,
And more diverting still than regular,
Have humor, wit, a native ease and grace,
Though not too strictly bound to time and place.

Epistle to Mrs. Blount

ON the title page of the authorized edition of Pope's letters, published in May, 1737, there is a profile sketch of the poet drawn by his friend Richardson. It is in many ways the most delightful portrait of Pope. The head is long and shapely; the strong, well-formed nose is balanced by the amiable mouth and chin. The characteristic force of the entire portrait is a feeling of brittle, sharp intelligence looking out inquiringly on the world.

It is Pope's sharp mind more than any imagined sourness of disposition or disgust with life which makes intelligible the sweeping satires of his final years. The man of discernment retains his acute awareness of things and people into middle and late life. He finds his accumulated wisdom from books and living at variance with all that can be observed or noted in the world about him. To a man who loves speculation, this contrast between wisdom and triviality deepens and enlarges itself.

Many years before asthmatical dropsy had slowed the nimble quickness of his frame and sapped his energies, Pope had begun the evolution of his satirical technique in the *Rape of the Lock*. There, in its initial emergence, his satire was light and deft, clothed with the romantic shades of youth and fancy, shimmering in a soft haze of good-natured fun and an intuitive appreciation of the mystery of personality. It had a quality much like *Romeo and Juliet:* delightfully young, yet amazing in the penetrating force of its sense and clairvoyance. It was tricked out in rainbows of language well suited to the conception of fashionable life it aimed to capture.

Pope's first satirical manner and shrewd evaluation of people hardened and deepened with the years. It acquired intellectual color and incisiveness in the portraits of Atossa and Atticus. The first drafts of these characters were published early enough to indicate something of Pope's gradual development between the first draft and their final crystallization in the *Epistle to Arbuthnot* and *The Characters of Women*. Another deepening note can be detected in the *Dunciad:* the addition of a certain coarseness which balances the pretty and holds the mirror up to nature. Life itself is compounded of conflicting notes of ugliness and beauty: a fact well known to Shakespeare and illustrated in his plays with intuitive totality.

The *Essay on Man* establishes Pope's satirical method and style: the philosophical bases of his comparisons and contrasts are evolved there in a mature fashion which indicates Pope's entire manner of working. The characters of men are compared with certain absolutes. The relative correspondence of men with these absolutes, or failure to correspond with them, focuses a blinding light in which their flaws or soundness take on an added glare of either good or evil. In the fourth epistle of the *Essay on Man*, the triumph of realism begins to be amply apparent. The critical theories enunciated in the *Essay on Criticism* have arrived at their full fruition.

In his original manner of thinking and working, Pope was a romanticist. His romanticism was both religious and sentimental. This stage of development was sharply etched in such works as the paraphrase of "Thomas Kempis," *The Prayer of Francis Xavier, Windsor Forest*, the *Rape of the Lock*, all the early letters to the Blounts and Caryll, the *Elegy to an Unfortunate Lady, Eloisa to Abelard*, and *Hadrian's Address to his Soul*. Events, disappointments, persecution, and the taste of the epoch led Pope to turn away from the romantic approach to life and literature, which, as he detected, is a flight from life into the Caerleon of fancy. A hunger for the romantic, we may be sure, lived on, deep down in his secret heart. The letter to Richardson, written the day Pope's mother died, is romantic in the extreme: his love for Martha Blount, his affection for his dog "Bownce," and the obelisk erected to his mother's memory disclose the romantic tenderness that still quickened at the roots of his consciousness.

The times were not ripe for wearing his heart on his sleeve, or his rue with a difference. The age wanted Homer, and Pope obliged. The Established Church had gone fox hunting or to Court, and in the spiritual confusion ensuing, men of manners and good will looked for something which would stay the pelting avalanche of men clamoring for gold, titles, and place. Sir Robert Walpole pulled the strings of the gilded marionettes who danced with the impulse of his fingers. The Court bought and sold men with a vulgar use of pensions and places. The times were rotten-ripe for personal and realistic satire.

Pope, with his alert fingers on the pulse of the time, detected the opportunities in the situation and made ample use of them. There were, of course, events which played a minor part in determining his ultimate direction; there were persons, too, who confirmed him in his eventual drift.

Bolingbroke was chief among those, like Swift and Arbuthnot, who impelled Pope along the paths of satire. Through the Duchess of Kendall and other powerful friends, Bolingbroke had been allowed to return to England, once it had been determined that his flirtation with the Stuarts was at an end. He was to be permitted to stay in England if he behaved himself and remained out of politics. This was impossible to one of Bolingbroke's kidney. He had been refused a seat in the House of Lords, but politics was in his blood and bones: in his own mind he was the only man capable of running the government. On that score he had not abated one iota of his heat or conviction. His past bungling at St. James's and Versailles had left him with no consciousness of failure.

Bolingbroke, upon his return from exile, settled near Pope at Dawley. It suited his humor and assumption of innocence to play at being a farmer in the mannered style of the French court at Versailles. The hall of his country place at Dawley was painted with a frieze of rakes and spades; in the field he leaned on his scythe and talked philosophy among the haymakers.

Bolingbroke was successful in carrying Pope along with him in his newly discovered love of wisdom. They studied every morning and carried on interminable discussions of life and learning. Bolingbroke had the formalized education necessary for the study of philosophy, but not the depth of mind; Pope was afire with mental brilliance, but he lacked the disci-

plines which a mastery of philosophy demanded. Yet Bolingbroke made Pope believe he might easily learn all there was to
know of philosophy. He achieved this by outrageous flattery
of Pope's moralizing nature, which had long ago shown itself
in the *Essay on Criticism*, and before that time in the letters to
John Caryll. In balanced Ciceronian periods, Bolingbroke, like
a stage philosopher, next pretended a supreme contempt for
the pushing life at court and the world of fashion. It was but
a step from this point to the further one which discovered in
Pope and himself the moral saviors of the age. Through Bolingbroke's artful manipulation, Pope, in a sense, became the
laureate of the opposition to Walpole and the Whigs. In their
rule was to be found localized—so Bolingbroke maintained—
the virus of the age.

"Twitnam" was situated at a strategic spot between the
Court and London. Pope's villa, which had become in many
ways the most famous house in England, caught every prominent visitor to Hampton Court or the city of London. Visitors
often came for dinner or a glance at the grounds and the
touted grotto: they stayed to talk and talk. In the great parlor,
over the wine, Pope caught the most secret rumors of discontent or unsavory scandal; he discovered every current of
opinion which might play a part in terminating the long rule
of the Whigs. The constant gossip Pope heard, and the endless
criticism of the party in power, gave him an atmosphere,
abundant materials, and fabulous characters for his satires.

The *Essay on Man*, the *Dunciad*, and the "forced publication" of Pope's letters had prepared the public to lend an eager
ear to his wisdom or opinions. Pope was of an optimistic nature, yet occasionally his health made him accentuate the notes
of gloom and discouragement he heard expressed on the lips
of his friends and acquaintances, and the world he heard
clamoring about him.

To fancy—and it is to fancy—that Pope hated the world and the men and women in it, after Swift's fashion; or that he earned the title "the wasp of Twickenham" by stinging all who were his enemies or disagreed with him—or any acquaintance who provided a ready target for his arrowy pen—is a sublime oversimplification. It ignores Pope's life, his merry qualities of mind, and the whole complexus of circumstances which had served to canalize the throbbing forces bubbling up within his mind. Very probably Pope had planned to include some of the so-called *Moral Epistles* in his *Essay on Man*. He found, as the *Essay* took shape and acquired a life of its own, considerable difficulty in integrating his wealth of satirical illustrations in separate epistles which would help to popularize the doctrines in the *Essay* and bring them down from a world of pure thought to the exciting plane of the characteristic and the personal.

In consequence, some of the *Moral Epistles* were published before the *Essay* itself appeared in print. The first published of the *Moral Epistles*, as such, was dedicated to Lord Burlington. It was a well-deserved dedication. Burlington had been the discerning patron and protector of Pope for many years. A community of interests had enlarged the original basis of their friendship. They were both engrossed in the Palladian revival in architecture and the new mode of "landskip" gardening. Pope had probably made numerous suggestions to Burlington when he was building and ornamenting his pseudo-Roman villa at Chiswick. Burlington belonged to the inner circles of the powerful oligarchy which really ruled England. He held the Pensioner's Staff, the Lieutenancy of Yorkshire, and the Vice-Treasuryship of Ireland, a multiplicity of benefices which suggests the venal character of the times. Burlington was everywhere admired for his taste and balanced magnificence, though he did not escape the satire of Lord Hervey,

Pope's detested "Sporus," who wrote the following epigram upon Burlington House:

> Possessed of one great hall of state
> Without a room to sleep or eat,
> How well you build let flattery tell
> And all mankind how ill you dwell.

In the beginning of his career Burlington had been deep in the confidence of Walpole, but in 1733 he found it profitable to join the opposition, which had all the glitter of names and ideals (if such they could be called).

The epistle dedicated to Burlington, in 1731, first called *On the Use of Riches* but later more aptly retitled *Of False Taste*, shows admirable organization. It is simple, too, in its reasoning. In this epistle Pope makes taste depend upon intuitive good sense, rather than on mannered and prodigal richness. In building either houses or gardens, true excellence in the builder means, in Pope's conception of it, a casual accentuation of those beauties to be found in the land itself—a principle often thought to date from Frank Lloyd Wright. Houses and gardens are not to be erected in an affront to the landscape, though many of them are, but should harmonize and blend with the surrounding beauties of nature. In giving a telling example of the opposite principles which illustrate his meaning, Pope takes his readers to the mammoth country seat of Timon. By means of the poet's descriptive catalogue we are given a review of the outer appearnce of Timon's palace and grounds, which to Pope's mind are a monstrous affront to nature. Inside the house the same disproportion appears in a library of books dearer to the master for their bindings than the sense of wisdom to be found between their covers; a dining room in which each meal is a rite, not a satisfaction of appetite; a chapel, with vacuous angels and pagan cupids painted after the manner of Versailles, which echoes to the jigging operatic music sung and played there. The prodigal display, Pope suggests, is the opposite of Burlington's exquisite taste in his book of *Palladio's Designs of the baths, arches and theatres of ancient Rome*, publication of which had occasioned Pope's epistle. Yet, Pope warns Burlington, in spite of the good examples pictured in his architectural manual, dullards will misinterpret the designs and fill the land with "imitating fools." It is to be hoped (not too fondly) that the designs Burlington had presented may at least give a stimulus to kings in the construction of parks, public works, and churches.

The *Epistle of False Taste* is perfectly executed; it is a balanced presentation of a principle and the sharp illustration of its opposite. The description of Timon's estate is in Pope's best Goya manner: all sunshine, verve, tonal vivacity, and progressive line:

> At Timon's villa, let us pass a day,
> Where all cry out, "What sums are thrown away";
> So proud, so grand; of that stupendous air,
> Soft and agreeable come never there;
> Greatness with Timon dwells in such a draught
> As brings all Brobdingnag before your thought
> To compass this, his building is a town,
> His pond an ocean, his parterre a down:
> Who but must laugh, the master when he sees,
> A puny insect shiv'ring at a breeze!
> Lo, what huge heaps of littleness around!
> The whole a labour'd quarry above ground.
> Two cupids squirt before: a lake behind
> Improves the keenness of the northern wind.[1]

Pope's enemies were quick to apply this unflattering portrait to the Duke of Chandos and his estate at Canons. There was great public indignation at Pope's satire, which the Grub-

Streeters made haste to fan into a blaze. Chandos was open-handed in his public benefactions and much admired by the common people. It was alleged by the poet's enemies that Pope had known the Duke well and had received a gift of £500 from him. Pope, with scorn, denied the gift and the close acquaintance. He maintained he had seen the Duke but once or twice in his lifetime. Still the clamor continued to grow until it forced Pope to take decisive action. In the third edition of the *Epistle of False Taste*, Pope prefaced the poem with a letter of apology and defense directed to Chandos himself:

> My Lord,
> The clamour rais'd about this Epistle could not give me so much pain as I receiv'd pleasure in feeling the general Zeal of the world in the cause of a Great Man, who is Beneficent, and the particular warmth of your Lordship in that of a private Man who is innocent.
> It was not the Poem that deserved this from you; for I had the Honour to be your Friend, and I cou'd not treat you quite like a Poet: But shure the writer deserv'd more candor even from those who knew him not, than to prompt a Report to that Noble Person which was Impertinent; in regard to me Villianous. Yet I had no great Cause to Wonder, that a Character belonging to twenty should be applied to one, since, by that means, nineteen would escape the Ridicule.

Pope's defense was manly, and probably correct and honest. The popular application of the portrait to Chandos *alone* had made the poet feel both he and the Duke were being done some injustice. The portrait was built up from many notes and many memories of flaunting magnificence in the country houses Pope had visited in his everlasting rambles.

Courthope in his comment on the *Epistle to Burlington* and its background of alarms and excursions came to an unjust conclusion:

This portrait as a whole, was an ideal one made up of a number of particular observations; but since Pope could not bring himself to say this directly, to the public, which at once perceived the likeness to Canons, thought that he was unable to deny that Timon was meant for a malicious satire on Chandos.

What a triumph of scholarship and factual criticism! Pope *had* denied that the portrait was meant for a malicious satire on Chandos. He had denied it in public in the letter quoted above from the third edition of the *Epistle;* but, like all his professions, honest or not, the letter has continued to be twisted to fit his enemies' interpretation. It is used as another example of Pope's treachery and devious nature.

The poet himself, it must be admitted, was responsible in part for the misapprehension which had arisen. In his satires he had the habit of naming some butts of his wit and not others. Had he named every character, choosing apt examples from former reigns, he could have protected himself from misunderstanding. In identifying some well-known men of his time and the period preceding it, and in making other characterizations of general application, or composing them of selected strokes taken at random from various men he knew in fact or by repute, Pope gave carte blanche to his enemies. With malicious glee they ascribed his general or composite portraits to men it would have been dishonest or mean of Pope to have satirized. Many times there was no more than a superficial resemblance to justify the ultimate identification. After Pope's death, Warburton further complicated the truth by attempting to identify many characters which Pope had never intended to apply in anything but a general sense.

Editors and commentators have swarmed over Pope's works since Warburton's death, leaving behind them a veritable ants' nest of notes which obscure the satires. A text which would shear away all this learned lumber, which would accept only those personalities identified by Pope *before* Warburton became his learned editor and Swiss guard, would be of inestimable benefit in allowing the light of the satires to shine out on our age so sadly in want of it.

Pope's disagreeable experience with the *Epistle of False Taste* taught him new caution in the use of satire, and he retrieved his reputation for objective satire in his next published letter, *On the Use of Riches*.

This epistle, dedicated to Pope's favorite titled friend, Lord Bathurst, and published in 1732, enlarged the doctrine expounded in the *Epistle of False Taste*. In elaborating its wisdom Pope relied on one of the principles he intended to enunciate in the forthcoming *Essay on Man*, which maintained that men are best understood if it is possible to detect their master passions. Pope may have derived his doctrine from the Catholic concept of the Capital Sins which mark men's souls with the individualizing features of pride, avarice, gluttony, envy, and sloth.

The *Epistle to Bathurst* is an analysis of the good and bad to be found in avarice. To have gold or not to have it was in Pope's opinion no mark of heaven's approval or disapproval. Gold in itself is nothing. It merely keeps the wheels of life moving. Wherever is found one to heap it up, there is always one to spend it. The two extremes, as in Nature, "concur to general use." Neither prodigality nor penuriousness marks the virtuous man, but a beneficent use of all his surplus goods. Pope illustrated this golden mean by a happy description of the Man of Ross and his charity. He concluded the *Epistle* with the ingenious fable of Balaam and his ruin by Satan, using the bright instrument of gold.

It is one of Pope's best satires. The general terms of his indictment of misers and prodigals give the poem a balance like some splendid gallery whose walls are hung with excellent minor portraits which with their color and contrast enhance the superb masterpieces of Cotta, the Man of Ross, Villiers, and Balaam.

> Old Cotta shamed his fortune and his birth,
> Yet was not Cotta void of wit and worth.
> What tho' (the use of barb'rous spits forgot)
> His kitchen vied in coolness with his grot?
> His court with nettles, moats with cresses stor'd,
> With soups unbought, and salads, bless'd his board;
> If Cotta lived on pulse, it was no more
> Than Brahmins, Saints, and Sages did before;
> To cram the rich was prodigal expense,
> And who would take the poor from Providence?
> Like some lone Chartreux stands the good old hall,
> Silence without, and fasts within the wall;
> No rafter'd roofs with dance and tabor sound,
> No noontide bell invites the country round;
> Tenants with sighs the smokeless towers survey,
> And turn th' unwilling steeds another way;
> Benighted wanderers, the forest o'er,
> Curse the saved candle and unopening door;
> While the gaunt mastiff, growling at the gate,
> Affrights the beggar whom he longs to eat.[2]

The satire on the abuse of riches was timely. It met the honest need of an age rocked by the South Sea scandal and the subsequent failure of the African Company, in which the Duke of Chandos himself was involved. Thousands of speculators had been pauperized, and Pope's epistle was germane, elevated, and in splendid taste. The *Epistle of False Taste* was no less timely. The greatest day of the Empire trembled to first dawn. Streams of money poured into the homeland from fabulous America and the islands of the East. The new aristocracy flaunted their riches and tried to outdo one another in the size of their houses and the elaborate splendor of their gardens. Money which might have served the public was thrown away in wretched and vain display. The common people lived in unspeakable squalor.

Pope completed the publication of the *Moral Epistles* with one on the *Characters of Men* (1733), dedicated to Lord Cobham of Stowe, and one to Martha Blount on the *Characters of Women* (1735). Cobham's epistle was divided into three parts. It speculates on the variety and contrariety of men, and the difficulty of knowing them without understanding their master passion. Once this passion is detected, Pope maintained, it is possible to observe a general direction in men by means of which we arrive at an accurate evaluation of the whole thrust of their lives. Pope speculated on some of the ruling passions, such as pride, lust, and thirst for applause, which he illustrated with good examples—not conceived, however, with the brilliance or balance which distinguished the earlier epistle to Bathurst or the later one dedicated to Martha Blount. The epistle to Cobham has a hint of stiffness and labor in it; the one to Martha Blount is fluent, sparkling, and good-humored.

Pope detected in women but two ruling passions, "love of pleasure and love of sway." He took from court society a shining series of female illustrations which culminated in the amazing picture of Atossa. It was this particular portrait which did much to give posterity an unjust idea of Pope's character. According to the story told after his death, Pope accepted a gift of £1,000 from the old Duchess of Marlborough to suppress any adverse lines about her, and then slandered her by writing this vitriolic pen-picture of Atossa. The story was first circulated by Bolingbroke. The proofs of it depend upon backstairs gossip and the contentions of those who hated or disliked Pope.

That Pope intended Atossa for a portrait of the Duchess of Marlborough lacks but one proof, the qualities of the portrait itself, which fail to fit the background, character, and events of the Duchess's life. Pope may have once intended to satirize the Duchess of Marlborough, but the final events of his life, political and domestic, brought them together with the amiable pleasure delineated in Pope's letters to the Duchess. The portrait of Atossa does not accord with the character of the redoubtable Sarah, but it does fit the Duchess of Buckingham.

The Atossa portrait is not a scorpion sketch, like the picture Pope drew of "Sporus." It does not throb with hatred and cold indignation. Part of its seeming cruelty depends on the abstract weave of the qualities revealed. In it are to be found few of the sunny touches which kept Pope's satire good-humored and aspiring. The portrait of Atossa reveals a monster rather than a woman. Its impact is scarifying: here is the blood-congealing glitter Pope reserved for his worst enemies.

In spite of anything Pope said to the contrary, he grew to loathe Lady Mary, Lord Hervey, and perhaps Addison too. He must have had adequate reasons for those bitter dislikes. They will probably never be known to us in their completeness, but they would be inestimably more interesting than any so far adduced by his biographers, and would, in a sense, perhaps, justify Pope's intense dislike and the pictures he drew of his enemies. The cause of Pope's hatred for Katherine of Buckingham is more mysterious than that of his ultimate distaste for either Addison or Lady Mary.

The Duchess of Buckingham had once considered Pope the only worthy editor of her husband's papers. During this period, and even preceding it, Pope had been on cordial terms with this daughter of James II. He had observed her at close range over a considerable period of time with some degree of amity.

Was the casual forwarding of a hundred-pound note to him

through the Catholic lawyer Pigott the cause of his distaste for her, because in so doing she seemed to dismiss him like a servant? Did she talk of his relations with Atterbury, and, without meaning to do so, endanger Pope's safety? Or was the character of Atossa first jotted down in the period when Pope hated the Marlboroughs, and after being composed, found too good to throw away? In consequence, was it revamped to suit a woman Pope disliked, but did not actually hate? A factual answer to one or other of these questions would probably clear up many mysteries.

On the whole, the *Moral Epistles* are excellent. They fulfill the true function of valid satire, both in a clear-eyed discernment of evil, and in objectivity and detachment in exposing it. The portraits of the people used as illustrations are not really bitter. They abound in deft touches which make us see into the mystery of personality. Many fine qualities shine out from the dross of human character.

In the *Moral Epistles* and the *Imitations of Horace* Pope reached the height of his power as a *literary craftsman*. Of these two groups of poems, however, his sureness of manner shows to better advantage in the *Moral Epistles*, because they had a unity of one general consideration, empty magnificence or the ruling passion, which enabled the poet to arrange his portraits in shining order and bring his satires to the fullest flowering. The verse is firm, yet easy. The rhythms are varied to the casual music of good conversation, which is the *ne plus ultra* of English verse as distinguished from the grave march of the Roman or Greek metres, so beautifully at the mercy of duration. Pope's technique is more varied in the *Satires;* but they lack the force of generalization and the objectivity from which the *Moral Epistles* derive their immortality.

A sympathetic reading of the *Moral Epistles* today makes it possible to understand why Pope was loved and followed in his own time by the intelligent far more than he was hated by Grub Street and his enemies. Even old Jacob Tonson in his eighties, though he too had felt the flick of Pope's satirical whip, could write from the country to his nephew and successor in the publishing business something of the general opinion of his age:

> I wish you could let me know how I could in any way please Mr. Pope ne[v]our any onee in my opinion has so fine and just notions as him and I think his Prose excels all others as his verse—He has noe equal or any pen near his— My hand is lame, & yet I can neavour be weary in writing my sinceer thoughts about such a miracle of general knowledge.[3]

The smaller pieces which were included in the *Moral Epistles* do not properly belong there. Except for the epistle sent to Miss Blount with the poems of Voiture, there is little or no trace of satire in the epistles to Oxford, Craggs, Addison, and Jervas. They are a series of brilliant and complicated compliments, which may have been included in the *Moral Epistles* at the insistence of Warburton. Only the epistle dedicated to Lord Oxford has genuine significance. It is a superb tribute to a friend who has been for a time in the Tower. Although he was no longer in power or place, Pope's wholehearted admiration followed Oxford into retirement. The epistle's closing lines are an exquisite example of Pope's constancy and lack of fear:

> In vain to deserts thy retreat is made;
> The Muse attends thee to thy silent shade;
> 'Tis hers the brave man's latest steps to trace,
> Rejudge his acts, and dignify disgrace.
> When int'rest calls off all her sneaking train,
> And all th' obliged desert, and all the vain,
> She waits, or to the scaffold or the cell,
> When the last ling'ring friend has bid farewell.

Ev'n now she shades thy evening walk with bays
(No hireling she, no prostitute of praise);
Ev'n now, observant of the parting ray,
Eyes the calm sunset of thy various day,
Thro' fortune's cloud one truly great can see,
Nor fears to tell, that Mortimer is he.

The poems dedicated to Martha Blount at the close of the *Moral Epistles* are, for the most part, compliments in Pope's best manner. They are excellent examples of his early drift toward satire. Pope's declaration of his detached point of view ("In every scene some moral let it teach") and his good-natured outlook on life ("Let mine an innocent gay farce appear") are significant and truthful expressions. The poet fulfilled them in the whole thrust and atmosphere of his satires —with the exception of the portraits of "Sporus" and "Atossa." The graceful compliments to Martha Blount also display the secret of Pope's best word painting. Pamela and her Flanders Mares, and the pictures of country life to which the young woman returns after the coronation are warm instances of Pope's ability to suggest with amusing atmosphere an exact slice of his time:

She went from Opera, Park, Assembly, Play,
To morning walks and prayers three times a day;
To part her time 'twixt reading and bohea,
To muse and spill her solitary tea,
Or o'er her coffee trifle with the spoon,
Count the slow clock, and dine exact at noon;
Divert her eyes with pictures in the fire,
Hum half a tune, tell stories to the squire;
Up to her godly garret after seven,
There starve and pray, for that's the way to Heaven.

There are other touches of the same felicity in the two poems. From the evidence found there, in the *Rape of the*

[273]

Lock, and in the satire on Settle, we have magnificent proof of Pope's early inclination toward satire. It tears to tatters the picture of Pope settling down into middle age a disgruntled poet with a hatred of everyone. His intuitions very early told him the direction in which his talents lay. The hardening of his method and the impact of his lines came from the long use of the heroic couplet, and an understanding of those greasy interiors which lay behind the façade of the age. By holding the mirror up to nature with increasing realism through the passing years, by picturing the times as they were, Pope verified his constancy to the principles in the *Essay on Criticism* and confirmed his growth in artistry and knowledge.

The *Universal Prayer,* which is sometimes placed at the end of the *Moral Epistles* or the *Essay on Man,* has often been abused by critics who have lacked both sense and sense of fair play. It is usual to call it a weakling retreat from deism, or it is ticketed with arch comments in the following strain: "Pope had as little mind for dogma as most poets; but these verses represent what in view of the instructions of Bolingbroke, corrected by Warburton, he now believed himself to believe." Such statements mark the nadir of literary criticism.

In truth the ideas in the *Universal Prayer* are founded on the prayer of Francis Xavier, which Pope himself had translated, and knew also in Dryden's fine translation. This prayer was often sung at Mass in Pope's time, and still is. To these childhood certainties of Xavier, Pope added touches from the Lord's Prayer, Pascal and the Psalms. The *Universal Prayer* expresses Pope's religion perfectly. Why should it not seem mysterious to those who knew neither Xavier nor the significant details and circumstances of Pope's youth?

In the *Imitations of Horace* Pope extended and furthered the work of his *Moral Epistles.* According to Pope's own story, it was Bolingbroke who first suggested his series of satires. In

1732, the death of John Gay depressed Pope and plunged him into a protracted illness. During his convalescence, Bolingbroke called on him one morning. Noting a volume of Horace on Pope's table, Bolingbroke opened it at the first satire of the second book, which he remarked exactly "hit" Pope's case. When Bolingbroke had departed, Pope read Horace's satire with eager attention. In two mornings he had imitated it. His friends found it delightful, and Pope sent the poem to press within a week.

This story, which Pope told Spence, may well be true. It gives us a probable and personal account of the immediate cause of the first Horatian epistle. Pope, however, was not so dull that he was unable to see, or needed to have Bolingbroke point out to him, the similarities between his own situation and that of Horace. Though Pope had the oligarchy, instead of Maecenas, to screen him from the wrath of a King, he had become, without ever being appointed, the laureate of the ruling group. Pope could not have failed to see the likeness between himself and Horace, or between the eighteenth century and the period of Augustus. The raw nobility, the insane love of money, the jobbing, bribing, and immorality were all there. There was one tremendous difference: the contrast between Augustus and George, which Pope exploited to the full in the *Epistle to Augustus* and revived from time to time with telling effect.

Pope had been interested in politics for many years, but there was a difference between his early participation under the influence of Swift and Harley, and the Bolingbroke phase. Pope could hope for more than personal gain in the triumph of Swift and Harley. The fate of the Stuarts was involved in that success, and this in turn further involved the fate of Catholics. The poet had everything to gain and little to lose by participation in the struggle. The same hopes were out of

[275]

the question in the political events of Pope's later years. George would follow George in much the same way that "dunce the second followed dunce the first." The effort to unseat Walpole could only lead to the appointment—disappointment—of Pulteney.

It is easy enough to be led astray in this matter because it provides a convenient frame for the Horatian epistles to fancy that they indicate Pope's complete identification with Bolingbroke and the opposition to Walpole. This is not true. Pope was much more concerned to show his identification with Horace. In consequence, a large part of his couplets were devoted to his own biography and the defense and praise of his friends.

His strictures on the court and the court circle ought not to be confused with the political situation. It is more or less a distortion to do so.

Pope had come a long way since he wrote his *Dunciad*. That work had been concerned with Grub Street and the hacks. In the interval Pope may well have read and pondered Milton's words: "For a satyr as it was born out of a tragedy, so ought to resemble his parentage, to strike high, and adventure dangerously at the most eminent persons, and not to creep into every blind taphouse that fears a constable more than a satyr." In hitting at the Court and its gilded flies Pope was being true to Horace, himself, and the shrewd wisdom of Milton.

Pope was always fond of his friends and willing to fight for them in his verse. That he found Bolingbroke and Lyttelton delightful and said so, or that he praised them for their patriotism, is quite natural. And so, too, is his praise of Walpole. That great man had done Pope no personal harm. Pope had asked at least one great favor which had been granted. Walpole couldn't very well approve of Pope in public but there is every indication that he did so in private.

In any event the poet was careful to distinguish between the person of Walpole and the official devil the opposition had conjured up. Pope knew far too well "how like Whig ministers to Tory." Politics under the Georges, he saw, was more or less a game, not the vital struggle it had been under Anne.

In a large sense, then, the Horation satires concentrated on the state of the nation and the state of Pope in it. They were, in the main, objective satires which spared no noble knave and ignored no gilded knavery.

The *Imitations of Horace* contain some of the finest examples of Pope's style. It glitters, it burns, it etches, with the most casual elegance. Here, again, Pope insured his legal safety by pretending to translate Horace. Had he been accused of anything at law, he could have posed as a wronged but free translator of sentiments cooled by some eighteen hundred years.

The first Horation satire was dedicated to Fortescue, Pope's friend and legal adviser. In the Twickenham edition of Pope's poems, Professor Butt retailed some interesting speculations on the background of the poem.[4] He believed it was more than the general apology for all satire it appears to be, at least on the surface. Pope may indeed have designed the poem to be a "rear guard" for the moral epistles dedicated to Burlington and Bathurst. The poem is a clever defense of himself and his pen. That Pope had all his wits about him is indicated in his deft compliments to the King, the bishops, the lords, and above all to Sir Robert Walpole:

> *Libels* and *Satires!* lawless Things indeed!
> But grave *Epistles,* bringing Vice to light,
> Such as a *King* might read, a *Bishop* write,
> Such as Sir *Robert* would approve—F. Indeed!
> The Case is alter'd—you may then proceed.

> In such a Cause the Plaintive will be hiss'd
> My Lords the Judges laugh, and you're dismiss'd.

Pope further consolidated his position by means of the artful but demure character which he wrote for himself:

> *Envy* must own, I live among the Great,
> No Pimp of Pleasure, and no Spy of State,
> With Eyes that pry not, Tongue that ne'er repeats,
> Fond to spread Friendships, but to cover Heats,
> To help who want, to forward who excel;
> This, all who know me, know; who love me, tell;
> And who unknown defame me, let them be
> Scriblers or peers, alike are *Mob* to me.

Pope's next important imitation of Horace immortalized Hugh Bethel's sermon on simplicity. It contains among other excellent things an interesting summary on Pope's situation as a proscribed papist:

> Fortune not much of humbling me can boast;
> Tho' double-tax'd,* how little have I lost?
> My Life's amusements have been just the same,
> Before and after Standing Armies came.†
> My lands are sold, my Father's house is gone;‡
> I'll hire another's; is not that my own,
> And yours, my friends? thro' whose free-opening gate
> None comes too early, none departs too late. . . .

The satire dedicated to Arbuthnot contains Pope's great apologia for his life and works. His picture of the manner in which he was harried to death by rhymsters, or blamed for every mischance, private or public, is related with wit and the accuracy of genius. The satire contains the immortal portraits

---

* Pope refers to his fines for recusancy.
† They were thought necessary to maintain the succession.
‡ These were effects of the penal laws.

of Addison and Sporus; it concludes with Pope's defense of his father and mother. The poem is more subjective than the *Moral Essays*, but on the whole, is diverting and amiable and of unmistakable power.

In the epistle dedicated to Lord Cobham's friend, Colonel Cotterell, it is possible, Pope added further facts to his biography. He also made a general survey of his time: the mad thirst for honors, titles, and gold. The conclusion of the poem has a touch of droll humor:

> Learn to live well, or fairly make your Will;
> You've play'd, and lov'd, and eat, and drank your fill:
> Walk sober off; before a sprightlier Age
> Comes titt'ring on, and shoves you from the stage:
> Leave such to trifle with more grace and ease,
> Whom Folly pleases, and whose Follies please.

The *Epistle to Cotterell* may have been a trial balloon to test the weather for the *Epistle to Augustus*.

In this great satire, directed to Augustus and the Court, Pope reached the peak of daring, smooth effrontery. Considering his situation in regard to the laws, he was very brave. He treated the King with subtle irony, and the Court and the degeneration of public policy as well. The past glories of Britain and her present decadence rise before us in shimmering couplets. The darkness of the stage, the decline of poetry and wit, the inconsistency of the populace, come in for satirical comments arch and playful, yet ironical and casual, comments which are marvels of detached reporting.

In reading the satires today, one has more than a superficial respect for Pope's stark candor. He was on the verge of being in the extremest danger because of the *Epistle to Augustus*, as we know from Alderman Barber's letter to Swift, published in Swift's correspondence. The passage which had given the most offense was the following:

[279]

Let Ireland tell, how Wit upheld her cause,
Her Trade supported, and supply'd her Laws;
And leave on SWIFT this grateful verse engrav'd,
The rights a Court attack'd, a Poet sav'd.

It was, of course, outright criticism of the King and court, a privilege Pope did not often allow himself. His ironic references to the King and his court were usually capable of double interpretation. In the *Epistle to Augustus* Pope threw caution to the winds.

Alderman Barber's letter to Swift is probably correct in stating:

> Our friend Mr. Pope is very hearty and well, and has obliged the town lately with several things in his way; among the rest a translation of Horace's Odes; in one of which you are mentioned 'as saving our nation:' which gave great offence; and, I am assured was under debate in the council, whether he should not be taken up for it; but it happening to be done in the late king's time, they passed it by.[5]

The imitations of Horace dedicated to Murray and Bolingbroke broke the chain of apology and biography. Pope set up in these satires his somewhat confused principles of charity and virtue as guides for men, but failed to show their complete validity against the folly and inconsistency of the time.

Some of the other satires have more of a political tinge than the earlier ones. The two satires in imitation of Swift, the graceful compliment to Murray, and the second and fourth satires of Donne are all concerned with the work of shooting at the follies of the age. Donne's satires were versified by Pope many years before they appeared in print, but they contain many references to the times in which they were printed. They were, in fact, as new in satirical material as the latest post. In the two poems now known as the *Epilogue to the Satires*, but originally called *Seventeen Hundred and Thirty-Eight*, Pope blazed out once more and proved himself the first moral philosopher and premier poet of the day.

In these two dialogues Pope plumed himself on his objective stand and dispassionate utterance. He maintained his love of honesty and virtue and his praise of both. He showed himself proud of his eminence too:

> Yes, I am proud; I must be proud to see
> Men, not afraid of God; afraid of me:
> Safe from the Bar, the Pulpit, and the Throne
> Yet touch'd and sham'd by *Ridicule* alone.

The thought of his task and his achievement fired Pope to a new strain in praise of himself, Truth, and his defense of her:

> Yes, the last Pen for Freedom let me draw,
> When Truth stands trembling on the edge of Law:
> Here, last of *Britons!* let your Names be read;
> Are none, none living? let me praise the Dead,
> And for that Cause which made your Father's shine,
> Fall, by the votes of their degen'rate line.

Pope had solid reasons to be proud of what he had achieved in his *Moral Essays* and Horatian satires. There was no face of deceit or trickery in public life which he had not named or shamed. He had put his finger on the sore spots of his day, and if some people were pained or had had their withers wrung, the majority found themselves helped and enriched.

If, in shooting his arrows at wickedness in high places and envy that walks the night and hates the face of all things fair, Pope paused to defend himself and his family, who can blame him, or say that his own defense detracted from the crushing force of the lines he spun? He went beyond defense of himself to that of his friends, like Swift, who were maligned and slandered in the hot, coarse struggles of the era. And he often defended his religion against the unjust laws, the monuments and swaggering lies which forced Catholicism to function in secrecy or in the dark.

Pope's satires, it is suggested by some critics, are much like Hogarth's satirical pictures—a kind of "Rake's Progress" in verse. Any honest comparison of the satirical work of the two artists will disclose the complete lack of likeness between them. Hogarth was a caricaturist; he accentuated the evil aspects of the period without suggesting its magnificence and beauty. Pope's work is not like Hogarth's, but it may justly be compared with Goya's.

There are many similarities in the lives of Pope and Goya. Both artists lived at ease with governors and governments they found personally distasteful; both began as religious men; both paid compliments to kings, nobility, fools, and even to favorites like Godoy and Walpole. The two artists depended for survival upon their luck and cunning. They were insatiable observers; insatiable cataloguers:—stratify, codify, put the times away in honey, vinegar, or amber, but hold them for posterity at all hazards!

In swiftness of execution Pope and Goya are also worthy of comparison. They had that consummate dexterity of long-practiced genius which etched the "Caprichos" in a year, or produced one of the imitations of Horace in two mornings. Here is none of that tortured nineteenth-century agony which seems forever reaching for the word not there but to be found somewhere in the distant galaxies of the far-reaching imagination. With Pope and Goya, to conceive was to achieve.

Pope, like Goya, "penned a pasquinade upon the social, political and ecclesiastical conditions of his age; he fought against foppery and wantonness, against servile courtiers and venal functionaries, against the hypocrisy of the state religion and the stupidity of the people."

To the discerning minds of the time, whether those of

aristocrats or commoners, Pope, like Goya, seemed to be doing a good work. Those who could see further than their noses were no more than amused and laudatory if the satire touched or seemed to touch themselves at times—well, they were human after all.

"Poetry, like painting, selects what it wants from the universe for its own ends; these are necessarily objective." Pope, in the identical accents of Goya, "might well have protested against the use of any portrait of his as personal satire, for this would be to mistake the object of art and the means art has placed in the hands of artists."

In the portrait of Sporus, for example, Pope was demonstrating the evil of any lord who has the ear of the court and uses it for character assassination and smutted innuendo. Let the courtiers fancy such a lord innocuous as a curd of asses' milk—shatter that fancy with bone and gristle and emboweled lewdness!

It was the misfortune of Pope and Goya to have much read into their work. Nineteenth-century critics called them this or that—rogue, Casanova, unbeliever—their ponderous monographs were valueless, like the program notes which once accompanied nineteenth-century symphonies.

In their creations, Pope and Goya drew the conditions and facts of life without prejudice or pessimism. There were skeins of mingled light and shadow in all they produced.

Those who would attempt to judge Goya by the "Caprichos," "Proverbios," and "Disasters of War," or by his Swiftian fancies painted on the walls of his house, must remain always in the basement of their Prado. The marvelous children, the nobles and royal personages who blaze in sunshine, in inflamed pigment, and in joyous verve of line (always joyous verve of line) in the upper gallery, must be left to the inquisition of the light alone.

Of Pope the same must be said. To concentrate on the gloomy aspects of the *Dunciad*, the "screaming fury" of Sporus or Atossa, leaves to the "silver bookworms" that endless shining series of portraits in which joyous verve of line works its immortal magic.

Except for the portraits of Sporus and Atossa, Pope's satires move in an ambience of wit and high good humor. From the Duchess and her Flanders mares of the early epistle to Martha Blount, to the pun implying, "All but truth drops dead-born from the press, like the last Gazette, or the last address," of the *Epilogue to the Satires*, there is a vast amount of sunny amiability. Pope wrote as one who observed things with his eyes, not with his imagination and his ink. He had no need to imagine. At Binfield, London, Mawson's Buildings, and in particular at Twickenham, the whole intense civilization of his time swirled about the crooked island of Pope's person. Vain lords, magnificent in plum and silver velvet, or in rustling silk shot through with gold or silver, pointed their aristocratic noses at his ceilings, like beagles looking out through the dark underbrush of the periwig or silvered fringe of powdered hair. Deans, bishops, the minor clergy in gown and bands, intoned their theories of life and letters in the grotto or along the reaches of the casual lawns. The clatter of wheels—it was new chariots arriving! A bevy of ladies-in-waiting returning from court, heavy with musk. The arch serenity of memorable faces . . . the moving music of fans. . . . They streamed through the "great parlour," lighting up the fine eyes of the little man with their grace and insolent provocativeness. Whether in London, giddy Bath, or in the quiet of country homes not his own, Pope was forever at the center and heart of things.

Since Pope was both participator and moralist, his satires have balance and warm, human, humorous background. He may have condemned individuals or groups for their malign minds or grasping, selfish, and inconsistent acts, but he knew in his own mind and felt with his heart that men are dear and human at base. His feeling kept him from making his portraits a total condemnation. The early portrait of Dennis, in the *Essay on Criticism*, shows that the idea in it flows from Pope's quick sense of the ridiculous in men and not from any dislike of humanity. Belinda and her Sylphs follow the same pattern. By holding the mirror up to nature, human nature particularly, Pope let the characters reveal themselves. Their grimaces and oddities required no master of ceremonies. We see them as they were, and know them in action—with the same incisive magnificence which characterizes the paintings and etchings of Goya.

Perhaps Pope's balanced sense of the ridiculous made his enemies hate him more than they would have done had he condemned them completely. To see exposed the flaws and mannerisms your own glass has revealed to you in moments of self-honesty is more infuriating than to be caricatured. Those strictures, retailed with a chuckle, are more humbling to pride than the squeak of the infuriated voice which indicates to a wise man that you are at his mercy.

In looking upon life as a comedy which leaves the last act to be resolved in judgments and justice not of human but of eternal and Christian value, Pope fulfilled the true function of a moral philosopher of which Robert Greene, after a roistering life of wine and wassail, after sludging the depths of his wit and pawning sword and cloak, wrote from the abyss of his misery in the shoemaker's house near the river, his body covered with sores, his bones wracked with the pox, as death waited to remove the mask from the eternal grin: "Sweete boy might I advise thee, be advised, and get not many enemies by bitter words; inveigh against vaine men, for thou canst do it, no man better, no man so well."

[285]

13

The Actor and the Final Curtain

Play out the little scene before the night;
Play out the scene, but see you end it right.

THE *Satires*, for the most part, were written in the midst of throbbing life. Pope was busied with many things. His friends were legion. Allen of Prior Park offered both his purse and great home as a refuge from want and care. Bolingbroke philosophized and acted in the Little Trianons at Dawley and Twickenham. The Prince of Wales droned of literature, unlike the wine which sparkled in the decanter on the cherrywood table. The truculent Warburton strode in and out of the house; the ubiquitous Spence waited with a poised pencil to jot down the answers to his interminable questions. Often Bathurst would arrive with his aura of blithe animal spirits: there would be jests and more wine, and the bright blue eyes of Martha meeting the poet's whenever he glanced up for approval of his witticisms and comments. There were visits to Marble Hill and Mrs. Howard, to Burlington House and London, to Blenheim and Stowe, Oxford and Bath. Rhyming, punning, talking, drinking, life ran away in a soft-footed dance.

Then there was the question of fame and fresh editions of the completed works . . . printed proofs to be corrected,

[286]

pompous notes to be meditated, the choice of paper, type, and bindings, the ornaments and pictures to be used. Pope's sense of responsibility had always been sensitive in these items. His books were made opulent by a personal supervision of their production and the constant exercise of taste, balance, and discrimination. His correspondence was enormous: it touched all varieties of people and continued to flow out in a rich stream until shortly before the poet's death.

There was also the absorbing question of politics. Pulteney, Bolingbroke, Marchmont, and Cobham gathered all the dissident elements for a struggle to unseat Walpole. Time was frittered away in speeches and plots, in criticism and pamphlets. The secluded grotto echoed to burning sentences and ardent plans.

Yet when Pope rose early enough to watch the naïve dawn sprinkling the Thames with arabesques of fire, and looked into the rosy mirror on his wall, he was more conscious of another who walked with still more muffled footsteps than Time. The mirror told him his hair was nearly gone, the long oval of the face slashed with lines of concentration and pain, with a fan-work of fine lines spreading from the corners of his eyes to the flat temples. His skin was gray and flaccid. Under the arch above the eyes a waxy whiteness showed. There were pearly shadows on the corded lines of his neck—an added hint by which nature warns men that time is even shorter than they think. His breath too gave warning. It was shallow, rasping at times. At frequent intervals paroxysms of coughing shook his frail frame, and more frightening still was the pain which sometimes seemed to compress his heart and sent its sharp, long needles into the muscles of his arms and shoulders.

Some days he stayed abed, dreaming of the past, and only half awake while he watched the bright light of the fire flickering over the ceiling, followed always by little sylphs of

[287]

shadow. . . . In the evening he would dress painfully with the help of his two servants. Muffled in a bright dressing gown the poet would go down to meet some favored friends in the drawing room or about the dinner table. His hand was almost transparent about the ivory knob of his Malacca stick; his face was gnomelike under the heavy velvet of the nightcap he wore to protect his bald skull from the drafty halls. The wine still had its old sparkle in the luster glasses, the daffodils of fire threw out their remembered fragrance of warmth from the hearth, the lampreys, served sizzling hot in the silver saucepan, tantalized the taste buds and communicated a momentary sense of warmth and false good health.

The old itch for poetry persisted. He had been so long composing couplets. A part of him seemed forever engaged in making new ones: they seemed to well up out of his unconscious mind with the effortless ease of the frost silvering the grasses along the river.

At the insistence of his new friend William Warburton, it may be, Pope completed a fourth section to his *Dunciad* in 1742. Though many thought it shattered the tight unity of that production, it has an abounding life of its own. In the classic march of its lines, it enlarges upon the final vision of dullness, first exposed in the third book of the original production. In the fourth book England itself is surveyed with meticulous care. The methods of teaching, the universities, scholarship, music, wit, learning, science, statesmanship and politics, the court, the nobility, all earn the *denobling* approval of the Goddess.

Some scholars have a tendency to give Warburton too large a share in the production of the fourth book of the *Dunciad*, and because of this initial mistake they have in a cavalier manner dismissed the excellent things to be found in the work.

Since 1736,[1] Pope had been toying with many of the ideas

which appeared in *The New Dunciad*. They were designed
to enlarge the doctrines of the *Essay on Man*. Parts of this
completed material may have found their way into the new
work.[2]

Perhaps some of Pope's evocations are too long and
serious. These may show the heavy shadow of Warburton, but
there are passages in this Fourth Epistle which equal or out-
rank anything the poet ever wrote. The new *Dunciad* was
published in 1742. It is Pope's last work and the best possible
proof that he retained his poetic brilliance to the very end.

In the poet's picture of the young spark of the times, dully
lectured and dully tutored, making a dull "grand tour" about
a dull Europe, we have some of the finest lines in the poem:

> Intrepid then, o'er land and seas he flew:
> Europe he saw, and Europe saw him too.
> There all the gifts and graces we display,
> Thou, only thou, directing all our way!
> To where the Seine, obsequious as she runs,
> Pours at great Burbon's feet her silken sons;
> Or Tyber, now no longer Roman, rolls,
> Vain of Italian Arts, Italian Souls:
> To happy Convents, bosom'd deep in vines,
> Where slumber Abbots, purple as their wines:
> To Isles of fragrance, lilly-silvered vales
> Diffusing languor in the panting gales:
> To lands of singing or of dancing slaves,
> Love-whisp'ring woods, or lute resounding waves.
> But chief her shrine where naked Venus Keeps,
> And Cupids ride the Lion of the Deeps;
> Where eas'd of Fleets the Adriatic main
> Wafts the smooth Eunuch and enamour'd swain.

In these couplets the vulgar Goya touch is much in evidence.
The piece has that verve of line which signifies Pope's best:
a kind of animal intoxication with life and its sunny aspects.

[289]

The description of the finished product of aristocratic young manhood who had, in making the "grand tour"—

> Dropt the dull lumber of the Latin store,
> Spoil'd his own language, and acquir'd no more;
> All Classic learning lost on Classic ground;
> And last turn'd *Air*, the Echo of a Sound!
> See now, half-cur'd, and perfectly well-bred,
> With nothing but a Solo in his head. . . .

—is in Pope's best vein of elegant humor: a quality usually denied him by the dull, or those who remain indifferent to his genius.

Pope's unclouded brilliance flails out of his insight into the inevitable progress from unbelief to inhumanism. The poet, with infallible instinct, touched the sore spot which has become the cancer of our time. It is a remarkable instance of poetic seership:

> O would the Sons of Men once think their Eyes
> And Reason giv'n them but to study *Flies!*
> See Nature in some partial narrow shape,
> And let the Author of the Whole escape:
> Learn but to trifle; or who most observe,
> To wonder at their Maker, not to serve!

The danger was obvious to Pope, and close enough to his interest for frequent exclamation points to signify the importance of the subject, and the lover's *O* to indicate how near to his heart the subject was. With clairvoyant vision Pope beheld the inevitable denouement so clear to us now on our own doorsteps in the atom bomb, the hydrogen bomb, and chemical warfare. These are the children of rationalism and materialism: a world in which all things are Caesar's.

> Be that my task (replies a gloomy Clerk,
> Sworn foe to Myst'ry yet divinely dark;

Whose pious hope aspires to see the day
When Moral Evidence shall quite decay,
And damns implicit faith, and holy lies,
Prompt to impose, and fond to dogmatize:)
Let others creep by timid steps, and slow,
On plain Experience lay foundations low,
By common-sense to common knowledge bred,
And last to Nature's Cause thro' Nature led.
All-seeing in thy mists, we want no guide,
Mother of Arrogance, and Source of Pride!
We nobly take the high Priori Road
And reason downward, till we doubt of God;
Make Nature still encroach upon his plan;
And shove him off as far as e'er we can:
Thrust some Mechanic Cause into his place;
Or bind in Matter, or diffuse in Space.
Or, at one bound o'er-leaping all his laws,
Make God Man's Image, Man the final Cause,
Find Virtue local, all relations scorn,
See all in *Self*, and but for self be born:
Of nought so certain as our *Reason* still,
Of nought so doubtful as of *Soul* and *Will*.
Or hide the God still more! and make us see
Such as Lucretius drew, a God like Thee:
Wrapt up in Self, a God without a Thought,
Regardless of our merit or default.
Or that bright Image to our fancy draw,
Which Theocles in raptur'd vision saw,
While through Poetic scenes the Genius roves,
Or wanders wild in Academic Groves;
That NATURE our Society adores,
Where Tindal dictates, and Silenus snores.

This penetrating analysis of the progress of unbelief from its causes to its conclusions, and of its effect on man and learning, is one of the finest ever made.

With the conclusion of Pope's creative work, his final years became a pattern of visits, various ineffectual doctors, and the last editing of his collected works with the aid of his champion, the Reverend William Warburton.

In 1742, the fourth book of the *Dunciad* was combined with the original three and reissued. The whole poem had been thoroughly revised. In the process of revision, Pope deposed Theobald from the throne of Dullness and put Colley Cibber in his place. Courthope and others make a great mystery of this. There is nothing mysterious about it.

The great "Coll" had enjoyed his clown's role for many years. It went with his pert nature. He was an amusing fool and not without considerable talent in the theater. His efforts as Poet Laureate, however, were ludicrous, and the wits of the age had already given him considerable attention. It remained for the lordly Pope to put a crown on both the game and the culprit.[3]

To Pope there were still better reasons for putting Cibber in the place of Tibbald. Cibber's *Non Juror*, which ridiculed Pope's religion and good men like himself, had been the source of disproportionate rewards. In addition to the success of the play itself, Cibber was given the lucrative control of the theater in England and the Laureateship as well. The first may have been deserved; the second was fantastic.

The *Grub-Street Journal* with casual wit expressed something of the polite scorn of the gentry:

> What Cibber Laureate made! O heaven forebear
> All ye non-jurors, if you can, to swear.

It was a political triumph for Cibber, not a literary one. Pope had every right to protest it in his own name and in all those of his fellow Catholics, Quakers, and nonconformists who had refused the oaths for moral reasons.

"As Dunce the second followed Dunce the first," King Colley followed Tibbald. In demonstrating Cibber's worthiness to occupy the throne, Pope was defending genuine artists and literature, particularly poetry, which by this act of authority had been relegated to a mere province of politics.

In bringing out his new edition of the *Dunciad*, Pope may have been too ill to write the notes himself. He let Warburton do most of the editing, and Warburton trying to be arch and playful was like an elephant on a tightrope.

It cannot be doubted that Warburton had once disliked the Catholic poet: long before Pope met him he had been active with Concanen and Theobald in Pope's dispraise. The publication of the strictures of Crousaz on the *Essay on Man*, for some unexplained reason, brought Warburton to Pope's defense in a series of five letters published in 1738.

Pope was always grateful to those who aided or defended him. In the same fashion in which he had acquainted himself with Spence, Pope sought out Warburton, made him his friend, and gradually employed him as his chief defender and literary confidant. He did more, for in introducing Warburton to Ralph Allen, he paved the way for Warburton's marriage to Allen's favorite niece and heir, and for his ultimate and most lucrative translation as Bishop of Gloucester.

Warburton, like most men, had a strange mixture of qualities. In his quarrels he seemed a bully and a beast: he talked loudest when his logic or facts were most wanting. His great work, *The Divine Legation of Moses*, is a forest of ponderous lumber, of the very kind Pope loved to satirize. Warburton, in spite of his pride of scholarship, was something of a genuine scholar. He had suggested some of Theobald's best emendations of Shakespeare, and if his knowledge of the classics was biased and one-sided, it was accurate, and even imaginative in a pompous way.

That Warburton had facets in his character other than his bullying tendencies may be observed in the ease with which he attained Allen's confidence and that of his niece. Something of his amiability is apparent also in the easy manner with which he continued to retain Pope's interest and good will.

Toward the end of his life Pope may have learned to dislike Warburton. The postscript in his letter to Martha Blount, which calls Warburton "a sneaking parson," is some indication of this. It may have been the reaction of a moment of excitement and general bad feeling. Whether or not a strain of dislike had grown up, Pope left Warburton the copyright of his works and the task of all further notes and editions. Pope had found Warburton a valuable ally in his quarrels: he was useful in that he was able to deliver upon demand a full broadside from his tongue or pen.

Bolingbroke had a horror of Warburton, and the future Bishop had as little taste for the noble lord. Pope did his best to bring them together, but sickness prevented him from exercising his charm in the circumstances of their first meeting. They met without him, and parted from each other confirmed in their dislike. Bolingbroke despised Warburton's pushing ways and metaphysical certainties; he had an eighteenth-century gentleman's contempt for parsons who came after the wine and left before the pudding, as Thackeray suggests in *Henry Esmond*. Warburton, it is possible, detected the cloven hoof of Bolingbroke's deism and cringed at or envied his theatrical pose and slashing brilliance of conversation. Pope had long been Bolingbroke's sole concern, and perhaps in Warburton's intrusion Bolingbroke fancied he detected a gradual turning of Pope's interest from my lord's opinions to those of the Establishment.

Both men had one dislike in common: they cordially detested Martha Blount. During Pope's last years, it annoyed them to see her always at Twickenham, and to know that she followed Pope about in his journeys to Marble Hill, Blenheim, Bath, and the most intimate shrines of the oligarchy. Pope was happiest with her; more rested, easy, and smiling. It must have been obvious to the two men that Martha had Pope's complete confidence, while they had merely his mind or his attention. Worst of all, Mrs. Blount was a devoted Catholic. She was assiduous in going to Mass. Bolingbroke and Warburton suspected the "Scarlet Woman," a phrase which expresses their suspicions of the Roman Church with picturesque mildness.

Pope tried to keep peace between these warring factions, but in this, and in every other matter, he had less and less energy to draw upon, with the progress of his asthma and dropsy. Yet his temper was sanguine, as it had always been. He spent time and energy on his grounds at Twickenham: the placing of various obelisks and multiplying shrines which ornamented and focused attention on his little lawns. Friends still sent ores and stones for the "camera obscura." Almost every day visitors trouped out from London to see the grotto, hoping no doubt to catch a glimpse of the "Sage of Twickenham."

Pope also pursued good works: he helped Savage with a yearly pension until 1743, aided his Catholic confrères with advice, assisted his sister with her investments, found a place for his nephew, and used his good offices in behalf of Samuel Johnson.

Johnson's *London* and Pope's satire, *Seventeen Hundred and Thirty-Eight*, had been published the same day. Pope had read Johnson's work and liked it. Hearing that Johnson was ill and poor, Pope wrote to Lord Gower and asked that something be done for the young poet. Pope's appeal failed to move Gower to action, but the good intention remained to

Pope's credit. Years later Johnson remembered to set down his appreciation of Pope's kindness, when he observed to Boswell in his blunt way, "Who would not be proud to have such a man as Pope so solicitous in enquiring about him?"

While Dr. Arbuthnot lived, he had been both friend and physician to the poet. Upon his death, Pope transferred his bodily welfare to Cheselden, the famous surgeon of Chelsea hospital. As 1744 dawned, however, none of Cheselden's prescriptions seemed to be bringing Pope the remotest alleviation from the pain and discomfort of his various diseases. In February, Bolingbroke wrote to Lord Marchmount asking that Ward, who had been frequently ridiculed in Pope's satires and in the pages of the *Grub-Street Journal*, be called in to prescribe for Pope. His remedies were of no avail, and Pope kept to his room the whole of March. He still looked forward to a visit to London, which he had always found stimulating in the past.

As a last resource, in April, Pope put himself in the hands of a quack named Thompson. He had been recommended by Hugh Bethel. Dr. Thompson drew from Pope "a great quantity of pure water," which, though it brought temporary relief, was of no lasting aid.

The poet himself seems to have known the end was not to be long deferred with any remedies short of miracles. He commented to Lyttleton, who had come to call, "I am dying from a hundred good symptoms."

In the previous December, Pope had made his will. It excited comment because his chief heir was Martha Blount. Pope left her £1,000, to be paid to her immediately after his death; his furniture, plate, and household goods; and the movable ornaments of his grounds. During her lifetime Martha was to have the interest on his total estate, bonds, and money.

Pope's half-sister Magdalen showed a disposition to contest

the will, which she considered unjust to her, but after initiating a *caveat* against the document, she dropped the action. We may suppose Pope's sister was loud in dispraise of Martha Blount. Her complaints may be one of the chief sources of the gossiping bad fame which dogged Martha's reputation and which attained its final crystalization in Horace Walpole's picture of "Patty" Blount, Pope's mistress, fat and red, picking her way along the rain-drenched street with lifted petticoat, as she went to visit "blameless Bethel."

Pope left to Bolingbroke his set of Erasmus and the care and sorting of his papers, and to Warburton the copyright and editing of all further editions of his work. These two bequests paved the way for confusion and trouble.

Among other interesting things, Bolingbroke found in Pope's papers fifteen hundred copies of his *Patriot King*, which Pope had secretly printed, altering a few words and phrases in the process. Doubtless this discovery was one of the surprises which changed Bolingbroke into Pope's bitterest enemy. In his first angry revulsion, Bolingbroke circulated the untrue and unjust story that the character of Atossa was intended to satirize the Duchess of Marlborough. According to Bolingbroke, Pope had received £1,000 from the Duchess to suppress the portrait.

There is nothing in the character of Atossa or the gossip about the supposed gift in relation to it which would serve to prove the truth of Bolingbroke's story. Yet the incident has long been used to indicate a suspicion of Pope's double-dealing. Bolingbroke did more than suggest the story; he broadcast it among his friends. Their various accounts of it were later brought forward as corroborating evidence of Bolingbroke's original suspicions.

Either because he hesitated to do the deed himself, or because he feared Warburton's tongue or the comments of

Pope's noble friends, Bolingbroke hired Mallet to blast Pope's character. As an assistance to the act, Bolingbroke may have revised his *Minutes of Essays* with the purpose of giving them a closer likeness to the *Essay on Man*. In any event, Mallet became the editor of Bolingbroke's literary papers, including the *Minutes*.

Pope's memory had more to contend with than the active animus of Bolingbroke. Warburton's edition of Pope's work was of genuine disservice to the poet. It added Warburton's guesses and glosses to a life and works already heavily fogged with mystery. Warburton's belligerence also kept Pope's quarrels warm long after his death. With loud surety Warburton needled the poet's enemies into doing their utmost to increase the wild growth of accusations against Pope, which of themselves might have died a natural death with Pope's demise. All these vexations were far away in May, 1744. Pope lay dying at Twickenham. He could no longer be in doubt of the final outcome of his illness. His mind wandered at times and was unable to focus properly. Horace Walpole reported an instance in which Pope at Chiswick with the Burlingtons startled Lady Burlington with the sudden statement, "Look at our Saviour there! How ill they have crucified him."[4] The poet had returned in mind and heart to his youth. At times he was back in London in the midst of the conversational brightness at Will's . . . old memories of "lobster nights" . . . Windsor Forest where the nightingales were singing. . . . Realities of time and memory fused and became indistinguishable. . . . His eyes at times saw everything in false perspective and colors: a veil seemed to hang between him and reality. Spence noticed him a few days before his death gazing off into the corner of the room. "What's that?" Pope asked the Oxford don, pointing into the heavy shadows. He turned his great eyes once more upon Spence and smiled, saying in a soft voice, " 'Twas a vision."

Sometimes traces of his old activity and energy returned. One morning at four o'clock he was discovered in his library writing on the immortality of the soul. He insisted on receiving his close circle of friends with the ashes of the old warmth, and when the sparkling eyes of Martha Blount met his gaze, he smiled and seemed illuminated with a fresh flame of life.

He suffered intensely, gasping for breath, agonizing with the pain of his laboring heart. Watching him, Bolingbroke broke into audible sobs, saying again and again, "O great God what is man?"

On May 27, Pope felt well enough to be carried downstairs where his friends were at dinner. His appearance was frightening. Looking at him, Anne Arbuthnot exclaimed, not without that touch of humor which the century appreciated, "Lord have mercy upon us! This is quite an Egyptian feast." We have no record that the skeleton laughed. Two days later, Pope was driven out in Bushley Park to pay his last farewell to woods and skies and the subtle light. The hawthorn was in bloom, pink and white along the river.

When Pope returned from his drive, Nathaniel Hooke, the historian, approached the poet and asked if he might send for a priest. According to Spence, Pope replied, "I do not suppose that is essential, but it will look right and I heartily thank you for putting me in mind of it."

That there is some discrepancy between Spence's cautious statement and Pope's real feelings is shown by what ensued. A messenger, probably Hooke himself, was hurriedly dispatched to the nearest Catholic priest. He soon returned with the priest, who carried the holy oils for the last anointing and the Blessed Sacrament for *viaticum*.

[299]

When the priest came into the freshened room where the crippled man lay, Pope rose painfully from the bed and attempted to throw himself on the floor in veneration of the Sacramental Presence of his Lord. His friends and the priest restrained him. Then the poet made his last confession and was anointed according to the age-old ritual. The soft phrases of Latin were at once a plea for the poet's health and a preparation for his departure. The Host was placed on his thick tongue while the little man struck his breast and said, "O Lord I am not worthy that Thou should'st enter under my roof! Say only but the word and my soul shall be healed!"

He lay silent then. The candles on the bedside altar were quenched. Little wreaths of smoke rose from them in the chilly evening air. The priest departed. Pope relaxed on his pillows. He had returned to the bright cloud of his childhood purity.

Hooke told Warburton that the priest whom he had provided to do the last office to the dying man came out from him, penetrated to the last degree with the state of mind in which he had found his penitent, resigned and wrapt in the love of God and man. "The priest had scarce departed" (says Warburton) "when Bolingbroke, coming over from Battersea, flew into a great fit of passion and indignation on the occasion" of his being called in.[5]

The following evening Pope, with a faint smile, looked up at his friends about the bed. They bent to catch his words: "I am so certain of the soul's being immortal I feel it within me as by intuition." It was the last brightness—in a few moments the great man was dead.

Literary history has nothing to say about the Catholic aspects of Pope's burial, but Mrs. Blount, who mourned him and was his heir, must surely have seen to it that all the pieties were observed in spite of the law. Spence, if he knew these details, maintained a discreet silence in keeping with his own sweet nature and abounding charity.

When the Catholic rites were over, Pope, like his mother, was carried to Twickenham Church by six poor men in new gray suits. The slow bell clamored again in the tower. They laid the poet's quiet body by the ashes of his mother. A new line was added to the monument which had long proclaimed his love:

Obiit anno MDCCXLIV, aetatis LVI.

Bibliographical Notes

I

1. W. Maziere Brady, *Annals of the Catholic Hierarchy* (London: 1877), pp. 83–84.
2. W. Maziere Brady, *op. cit.*
3. W. Maziere Brady, *op. cit.*
4. W. Maziere Brady, *op.cit.*, Section II.
5. Norman Ault, *New Light on Pope* (London: Methuen, 1949), pp. 1–26.

II

1. Spence, Anecdotes, edited by Singer (London, 1820), pp. 25–26.
2. Elwin Courthope *Letters,* VI, 208. Letter 32, To Caryll, May 1, 1714. [This edition is well known: it requires nothing further than I have given. In future notes, nothing more will be put down than E.C., Vol. and Page.]
3. *Twickenham Edition of Pope's Works* (London, Methuen, 1940), II, 315–316.
4. *Ibid.,* II, 325.
5. First printed by Charles Wentworth Dilke, *Papers of a Critic* (London: John Murray, 1875), I, 120.

III

1. E.C., V, 70.
2. E.C., VI, 141–143.
3. E.C., VI, 147–148.
4. E.C., VI, 155.
5. E.C., VI, 163.
6. *Twickenham Edition,* II, 88–102.

BIBLIOGRAPHICAL NOTES

IV

1. R. H. Griffith, *Alexander Pope, A Bibliography* (Austin, Texas: University of Texas, 1927), Vol. I, Part II, Introduction, IV–VIII.
2. Spence, 196.
3. Norman Ault, *New Light on Pope* (London: Methuen, 1949), p. 223.
4. R. H. Griffith, Part I, Vol. 1, 41.

V

1. E.C., VI, 241.
2. E.C., VI, 238–240.
3. Ayre, *Life of Pope*, I, 76.
4. *Twickenham Edition of Pope's Works*, II, 331, note 2.
5. *Ibid.*, II, 331, note 3.
6. *Twickenham Edition of Pope's Works*, IV: Introduction XVI.
7. E.C., IX, 110–111.
8. *Twickenham Edition of Pope's Works*, IV, Introduction, XV–XX.
9. E.C., IX, 332–333.
10. E.C., IX, 333–335.
11. *Loc. cit.*
12. E.C., IX, 337–338.

VI

1. E.C., VIII, 325–326.
2. *Ibid.*, V, 182.
3. E.C., IX, 9.
4. E.C., IX, 10–12. Letter 4, To Atterbury, November 20, 1717.
5. E.C., IX, 462–463.
6. *Ibid.*, IX, 463–464.
7. E.C., IX, 464.
8. E.C., VI, 280.
9. E.C., X, 199.
10. Spence, I, 156.
11. George Sherburn, *The Early Life of Alexander Pope* (Oxford: Oxford Press, 1934), pp. 245–246.
12. Lewis Theobald, *Shakespeare Restored* (London, 1726), pp. II–III.

13. Samuel Johnson, *Lives of the Poets* (London, 1781), IV, 74.
14. *The Odyssey of Homer* (London: Printed by Bernard Lintot, 1726), V, 285–286.
15. *Ibid.*, 286–288.

VII

1. E.C., VII, 57.
2. *Ibid.*, p. 64.
3. *Ibid.*, pp. 65–66.
4. *The Dunciad, with Notes Variorum, and the* Prolegomena of Scriblerus (London, 1729), Prolegomena, p. 179 n.(a).
5. E.C., VII, 104.
6. *Ibid.*, VII, 113.
7. *Ibid.*, VII, 116.
8. E.C., VII, 123.
9. *Gulliveriana or a Fourth Volume of the Miscellanies, being a sequel of the Three Volumes, published by Pope and Swift. To which is added Alexanderiana* (London, 1728).
10. R. H. Griffith, in *Philological Quarterly*, XXIV, 2 (April, 1945), 154–155.
11. R. H. Griffith, in *Philological Quarterly* (April, 1945), pp. 155–156.

VIII

1. See James T. Hillhouse, *The Grub-Street Journal* (Durham, N.C.: Duke University Press, 1928), pp. 3–46.
2. George Sherburn, *Early Career of Alexander Pope* (Oxford: Clarendon Press, 1934), pp. 153–154.
3. E.C., II, 276.
4. Spence, 272.
5. Mark Pattison, *Essays* (Oxford: Clarendon Press, 1889), II, 381.
6. E. Audra, *L'Influence Française dans l'Oeuvre de Pope* (Paris, 1931), p. 482.
7. J. P. Crousaz, *An Examination of Mr. Pope's Essay on Man* (London, 1739), pp. 74, 100, 104, 106, 110, 140.
8. E.C., II, 285.
9. *Index Librorum Prohibitorum* (Rome, 1911): La Fontaine,

p. 176; Addison, p. 39; Burnet, p. 74; Locke, p. 195; Hugo, p. 160.
10. E.C., II, 275–286.
11. *Ibid.*, V, 328.
12. *Ibid.*, III, 450.
13. E.C., V, 359.
14. Spence, *Anecdotes*, Singer, 1820, pp. 272, 321–322.
15. Bolingbroke, *Works* (London, 1754), V, 351–356.
16. *Ibid.*, II, 276–279.
17. *Ibid.*, V, 329–338.
18. *Ibid.*, V, 346–347.
19. E.C., V, 345.
20. Bolingbroke, *Works*, V; I, 3–31.
21. E.C., VI, 141–164.
22. Spence, *Anecdotes*, pp. 192–193.
23. Mark Pattison, *Essay on Man* (Oxford, 1869), p. 75.
24. Bolingbroke, *Works*, III, 317–318.
25. Spence, p. 144.
26. Spence, 355.
27. Mark Pattison, *Essay on Man*, pp. 1–2.
28. E.C., V, 345.
29. Pattison, *Essay on Man*, p. 5.
30. Bolingbroke, *Works*, V, 2.
31. Leslie Stephen, *English Thought in the 18th Century* (London, 1902), I, 177–184.
32. *Ibid.*, p. 177.
33. E.C., II, 343.
34. Leslie Stephen, *op. cit.*, I, 177–181.
35. E.C., II, 279.
36. Leslie Stephen, *English Thought in the 18th Century*, I, 183.
37. Bolingbroke, *Works*, V, 311 (and 63).
38. E.C., II, 279.
39. Bolingbroke, *Works*, V, 2.
40. E.C., II, 280.
41. *Ibid.*, II, *Essay on Man*, Epistle I, lines 205–206, p. 363.
42. Ibid., II, 354; Ep. I, lines 87–88.
43. E.C., II, 413, line 159.
44. *Ibid.*, II, p. 418. Ep. III, lines 225–226.
45. E.C., 418–420, lines 225–240.

IX

1. Cudworth, *Intellectual System of the Universe* (London, 1678), pp. 414, 415; and Contents (c3).
2. *Ibid.*, p. 874.
3. *Ibid.*, 881.
4. *Dictionary of National Biography* (London, 1887), pp. 130–131.
5. E.C., V, 358.
6. Cudworth, p. 303, 304.
7. *Ibid.*, 305.
8. *Ibid.*, 341.
9. *Ibid.*, 530.
10. William King, *Origin of Evil* (London, 1731), Preface, X.
11. *Ibid.*, 81–84.
12. Facsimile of a letter addressed by Pope to Louis Racine, preserved in the National Library, Paris. Frontispiece to Audra's thesis, *"L'Influence Française dans l'Oeuvre de Pope* (Paris, 1931).
13. Blaise Pascal (trans. Thomas Walker), *Thoughts* (London, 1688), p. 216.
14. *Ibid.*, 142.
15. *Ibid.*, 146–147.
16. *Ibid.*, 147.
17. *Ibid.*, 147–148.
18. *Ibid.*, 214.
19. *Ibid.*, 144.
20. *Ibid.*, p. 50.
21. E.C., II, 393–394, lines 221–230.
22. Pascal, 157.
23. E.C., II, 397–398, lines 283–294.
24. Pascal, 156–157.
25. Fénelon, *A Demonstration of the Existence of God* (London, 1713), Advertisement.
26. Pascal, 142–216.
27. Fénelon, 52–53.
28. *Ibid.*, 17–43.
29. *Ibid.*, 224–225.
30. *Ibid.*, 219–221.
31. *Ibid.*, 226.

32. *Ibid.*, 137–138.
33. *Ibid.*, 46–49, 56–59.
34. *Ibid.*, 21.
35. *Ibid.*, 46–51.
36. *Ibid.*, 167.
37. E.C., II, 272.
38. R. H. Griffith, *Pope Editing Pope* (Austin, Tex.: University of Texas), "An Essay on Man," II, 50.

X

1. E.C., VII, 430–431.
2. *Ibid.*, VIII, 244.
3. E.C., IX, 127.
4. E.C., IX, 314.
5. E.C., IX, 504–505.

XI

1. Charles Wentworth Dilke, *Papers of a Critic* (London, John Murray, 1875), Vol. I, pp. 96–106.
2. R. H. Griffith, *Alexander Pope*, A Bibliography, Vol. I, Part II, 267–268.
3. *Preface to Pope's Letters*, London, 1737.
4. Ault, Norman, *New Light on Pope*, p. 17.
5. Sherburn, George, *E.L.H., A Journal of English Literary History*, Vol. 7, No. 3.
6. *Preface to Letters*, London, 1737.
7. Ault, Norman, *New Light on Pope*, p. 18.
8. *Preface to Letters*, London, 1737.
9. Norman Ault, *New Light on Pope*, pp. 10–19.

XII

1. *Epistle of False Taste*, lines 99–112.
2. *Moral Essays*, Epistle III, to Allen, Lord Bathurst (*"Of the Use of Riches"*), lines 177–196.
3. From a letter in the Rare Book Collections, University of Texas.
4. *Twickenham Edition*, IV. Introduction, xiii–xv.
5. *The Works of Jonathan Swift, Epistolary Correspondence of Jonathan Swift* (London: Roscoe, 1841), II, 794.

XIII

1. *Twickenham Edition*, V, xxx–xxxii.
2. *Ibid.*, xxx–xxxi.
3. *Ibid.*, V, xxxv.
4. Horace Walpole, *Correspondence* (London: Richard Bentley, 1840), I, 345.
5. Joseph Warton, *Genius and Writings of Pope* (London, 1782), II, 202, n.

Index

INDEX

Marlborough, Duke of, 92, 139, 271

Messiah, The, 44, 59, 66–7

Michelangelo, 166

Milton, 46, 57, 167, 276

Miscellanies, 160–1, 163–4

Mist's Journal, 148

Montagu, Lady Mary Wortley, 90, 100, 104, 107–15, 117, 123, 179, 223, 255, 270

Montagu, Viscount, 13

Moore, 169, 175, 178

Moral Essays, 67–8, 221, 224, 279, 281

Moral Epistles, 262, 269, 271–4

More, Thomas, 10

Narrative of Dr. Robert Norris, 76, 81, 179

Newton, 87

Ode to St. Cecelia, 44, 66

Ode to Solitude, 54

Odyssey, Translation of, 138, 140, 144, 148–53, 155

Oldmixon, 101, 102, 163, 172, 218

On the Use of Riches, 263, 267

On Two Lovers Struck Dead by Lightning, 110

Origen, 201–2

Ovid, 67

Oxford, Lord, 75, 84, 165, 167, 227, 236, 238, 248, 272

Panzani, 14–20, 63

Parnell, 39, 83–5, 179, 199, 227

Pascal, 4, 57, 182, 196, 200, 204, 208–16, 219–20, 274

Pastorals, 54, 56, 80–1

Patriot King, 297

Penal Laws, 5–25, 97, 131, 143, 161, 278

Petre, Lord, 69

Philips, Ambrose, 54–6, 59, 65, 79–80, 82–3, 156–7, 170, 172, 218, 227

Plato, 181, 200

Plotinus, 200–3

Pope, Alexander, Birth, 27; Early Education, 28–33; His Father, 27, 33–5, 50, 64–5, 97, 116, 131–2, 135, 228–30, 232, 236, 279; His Mother, 27, 64–5, 104, 106–7, 116, 124, 135, 158, 180, 228, 230–7, 259, 279, 301; Physical Description, 36; Religious Attitudes, 39–49; Death, 298–301; *Works,* index by title.

Prayer of Francis Xavier, The, 259, 274

Prologue to Cato, 66, 75, 79

Rabelais, 38, 162

Racine, Louis, the younger, 208, 210

Rackett, Magdalen (Pope's half-sister), 27, 28, 296

Rape of the Lock, 34, 59, 68, 80, 82, 86, 108, 156, 173, 258–9, 273

Reynolds, Joshua, 103, 256

Richardson, 180–1, 227, 230, 234, 252, 257, 259

St. Thomas, 220

Sappho and Phaon, 59

Satires, 271, 280, 284, 286

Scriblerus Club, 84, 129, 156, 177, 179, 252

Settle, Elkanah, 54, 60, 92–3, 171, 218, 227, 274

Seventeen Hundred and Thirty-Eight, 280, 295

Shaftesbury, Lord, 204

Shakespeare, 41, 104, 105, 107, 138, 140, 144–8, 155, 172, 174, 215, 221, 258, 293

Sheffield, John, 139–40

—*See* Buckingham, Duke of

Shelley, 219

Smith, Bishop, 13–4

Spence, 4, 28–32, 54, 74, 79, 90, 143, 181, 188–90, 199, 275, 287, 293, 298, 301

Spinoza, 182, 209

Steele, 55, 59, 66, 76, 87, 89, 246, 253, 255

Sterne, 38

Stuarts, the, 6, 109, 129–30, 260, 275

Swift, 32, 37, 41–2, 74, 84, 87, 95, 113, 117, 122, 129, 156–65, 172, 175, 177, 179, 181, 199, 218, 223–5, 227, 232, 238, 251–2, 254, 260, 262, 275, 279–81